COLLIER WORLD TRAVELER SERIES

Northern and Central Europe

Collier World Traveler Series

Greece and Yugoslavia

Mexico, Belize, Guatemala, and the French Antilles

Northern and Central Europe

**COLLIER
WORLD TRAVELER
SERIES**

Northern and Central Europe

Editors:
Philippe Gloaguen and Pierre Josse

Translated by
Richard Kaplan

COLLIER BOOKS
Macmillan Publishing Company
NEW YORK

Collier Macmillan Publishers
LONDON

English-language edition copyright © 1985 by Macmillan Publishing Company, a division of Macmillan, Inc.

Copyright © 1984 by Hachette
Translated from *Le Guide du Routard*, Director Philippe Gloaguen

All rights reserved. No part of this book may be reproduced or transmitted in any form or by any means, electronic or mechanical, including photocopying, recording or by any information storage and retrieval system, without permission in writing from the Publisher.

Macmillan Publishing Company
866 Third Avenue, New York, N.Y. 10022
Collier Macmillan Canada, Inc.

Library of Congress Cataloging in Publication Data

Gloaguen, Philippe.
Northern and central Europe.

Translation of: Europe du nord et du centre.
1. Europe, Northern—Description and travel—
1981– —Guide-books. 2. Central Europe—Description
and travel—1981– —Guide-books. I. Josse, Pierre.
II. Title.
D909.G56313 1985   914.3′04   84-23268
ISBN 0-02-097030-7

Macmillan books are available at special discounts for bulk purchases for sales promotions, premiums, fund-raising, or educational use. Special editions or book excerpts can also be created to specification. For details, contact:

Special Sales Director
Macmillan Publishing Company
866 Third Avenue
New York, New York 10022

10 9 8 7 6 5 4 3 2 1

Printed in the United States of America

CONTENTS

Appetizer *xi*
How to Get There *xii*

HOLLAND 1

Useful Addresses in New York *1*
Entry Formalities *1*
Money *1*
Dutch Vocabulary *1*
Some Distances *3*
How to Get There *3*
To Go by Bus *3*
By Train *3*
Transportation in Holland *3*
Train *3*
Bicycle and Moped *4*
Car *4*
Holidays *4*
Country of Flowers *6*
Food *6*
Some Culinary Specialties *6*
Drinks *7*
Shopping *7*
Amsterdam *7*
Hoge Veluwe *22*
Haarlem *22*
Alkmaar *23*
The Hague *24*
Delft *24*
Zeeland Islands *24*
Keukenhof Gardens *25*
Northern Islands *25*
Groningen *25*

FEDERAL REPUBLIC OF GERMANY 26

Useful Addresses in New York *26*
U.S. Consulates in Germany *26*
Train *26*
Hitchhiking *26*
Highway Network *28*
Museums *28*
Carnivals *28*
Beer *29*
Bistros *30*
Money Exchange *30*
Mensa *30*
Other Suggestions *31*
Youth Hostels *31*

Work in Germany *31*
German Vocabulary *31*
Munich *33*
Hamburg *38*

SCANDINAVIA 42

Climate *42*
Where to Sleep *42*
Food *43*
Languages *44*
Bits of Advice *45*
By Car *45*
By Train *45*
Swimming *46*
The Sauna *46*
Useful Addresses in New York *46*
Entry Formalities *46*
Distances Between Some Cities *46*

DENMARK 47

The Country *47*
The Great Danes *47*
Useful Addresses in New York *47*
Where to Sleep *48*
Things That Are Good to Know *48*
Meals *48*
What to Eat and Drink in Denmark *49*
Movies *49*
Purchases *49*
How to Travel in Denmark *49*
An Itinerary *52*
Copenhagen *52*
North Zealand *65*
Louisiania Museum of Modern Art *65*
Helsingør (Elsinore) *65*
Fredensborg *66*
Tisvildeleje *66*
Frederiksborg *67*
Roskilde *67*
Køge *69*
Island of Møn *70*
Falster Island *71*
Lolland Island *72*
Nysted *72*
Maribo *72*
Fyn Islands *73*
Langeland *73*
Tåsinge *74*
Aero Island *74*
Fyn *75*
Svendborg *75*
Egeskov Castle *76*

Odense 77
Kolding 78
Billund 78
Århus 79
Mols Region 81
Ebeltoft 82
Grenå 83
Randers 84
Hobro 84
Mariager 85
Himmerland 86
Rebild National Park 86
Alborg 86
Nørresunby 89
Dronninglund 89
Saeby 89
Frederikshavn 90
Skagen 90
Tvind 91

SWEDEN 92

Useful Addresses in New York 92
Currency 92
Where to Sleep 92
Business Hours 93
Gas 93
Hitchhiking 93
Driving Rules 94
Distances Between Swedish Cities 94
Railways 94
By Plane 94
Food 95
Drinks 95
So . . . Swedish Women? 95
Vocabulary 96
Malmö 97
Lund 97
Ystad 99
Helsingborg 100
Mörrum 100
Ronneby 100
Karlskrona 100
Kalmar 101
Jönköping 101
Vadstena 102
Linköping 102
Stockholm 103
Toward Swedish Lapland 115
Uppsala 115
Gåvle 116
Sundsvall 117
Kiruna 117
Kebnekasje 119
Abisko National Park 120

Southern Lapland *121*
Aland Islands *121*
Toward Oslo *121*
Göteborg *121*
Toward the North *126*
Lysekil *126*

NORWAY 127

Useful Addresses in New York *127*
By Train *127*
By Boat *127*
By Car *128*
Road Maps *128*
Lodgings *128*
Distances Between Norwegian Cities *129*
Food *129*
Akvavit *130*
Temporary Jobs *130*
Wooden Churches *130*
Fjords *130*
Store Hours *130*
This and That *131*
How to Get to Norway from Denmark *131*
For Going Farther *131*
Special Inter-Rail Itinerary *131*
Norwegian Vocabulary *134*
Fredrikstad *135*
Moss *135*
Oslo *135*
Telemark *143*
From Oslo to Stavanger *144*
Kristiansand *144*
Mandal *144*
Flekkefjord *144*
Stavanger *145*
From Stavanger to Bergen *146*
Bergen *146*
Myrdal-Flåm Railway Line *150*
From Bergen to Balestrand *151*
From Balestrand to Åndalsnes *151*
Florø *152*
Ålesund *152*
Åndalsnes *153*
Molde *153*
Røros *154*
Sunndalsöra *154*
Trondheim *154*
Grong *159*
Mo i Rana *159*
Bodø *159*
Narvik *160*
Lofoten and Vesteralen Islands *161*
Tromsø *163*
Norwegian Lapland *163*

Finmark *163*
Alta *163*
Hammerfest *164*

FINLAND   **165**

Useful Addresses in New York *165*
Language *165*
How to Get There *166*
Food and Drink *166*
Interior Transportation *167*
Campgrounds *168*
Finnchecks *168*
Cottages along the Water *168*
Geography *168*
A Little History *168*
The People *169*
Hours *169*
Medical Care *169*
Post Office and *Post Restante* *169*
Midnight Sun and Polar Night *169*
Nightlife *169*
Turku *170*
Salo *171*
Helsinki *171*
Tampere *173*
Jämsä *174*
Lake Saimaa *175*
Savonlinna *175*
Imatra *175*
Kuopio *175*
Lieksa *176*
Vuonislathi *176*

FINNISH LAPLAND   **177**

Generalities *177*
Rovaniemi *177*
Kemijärvi *178*
Södankyla *179*
Vuotso *179*
Tankavaara *179*
Ivalo *179*
Inari *180*
Karigasniemi *180*
Enontekio *180*
Palojoensuu *181*
Karesuando *181*
Kilpisjärvi *181*
Kuusamo *181*

NORTH CAPE   **182**

Via Norway *182*
Via Sweden and Finnish Lapland *183*
Via Finland *183*

ICELAND

Useful Addresses in New York 184
Climate 184
Be Truly Ecologically Conscious 184
Equipment 184
Topographical Maps 184
Lodging 185
Means of Transportation 185
State of the Roads 186
Interior Boat Line 186
Food 186
Beverages 186
Cigarettes 187
Film 187
Purchases 187
Store Hours 187
Commercial Holidays 187
Employment 187
Know-How in One Easy Lesson 187
Reykjavik 190
Krisuvik 191
Vestman Islands 192
Laugarvatn 192
Geysir 192
Gullfoss 192
Selfoss 193
Thórsmörk 193
Skogar 193
Vik 193
Hveragerdi 194
Kirkjubaerjarklaustur 194
Skaftafell 194
Jökulsárlón 195
Höfn 195
Egilsstadir 195
Seydisfjördur 196
Egillsstadin–Grimsstadir 196
Njardvik 196
Dettifoss 196
Asbyrgi 196
Húsavík 196
Reykjahlid (Lake Myvatn) 196
Godafoss 197
Akureyri 197
Grimsey 198
The Northwest 198
Isafjördur 198
Husafell 198
Akranes 199
Midsandur 199
Thingvellir 199
Faerøe Islands 199

APPETIZERS

The Collier World Traveler Guide to *Northern and Central Europe,* unlike a good wine, ages badly. We don't want to appear to be pushing the book, but you should avoid using an old edition. From one year to the next, changes can be made in as much as, if not more than, 40 percent of the previous edition.

How should you visit a big city when you're in a rush? Number on the guide the monuments, places, and restaurants that you want to see. Next, write these numbers on the map. Then trace your itinerary. It's simple.

HOW TO GET THERE

The quickest, cheapest, and most convenient way to travel to the Netherlands is by air. CIEE and APEX are two very well known and reputable charter flight organizations that offer flights to various parts of the Netherlands. Your best bet is to check the Sunday Travel section of *The New York Times* (or your local newspaper) for charters and rates for flights to your city of choice (or takeoff point). A solid relationship with a travel agent you trust can be immeasurably helpful, as well.

COLLIER WORLD TRAVELER SERIES

Northern and Central Europe

HOLLAND

*God created the world,
except for Holland, which was created by the Dutch.*

Land and water, originally commingling, finally found their own levels and seem to stay there. Formerly, their relations were tumultuous, and it is certainly because of these very difficulties that the Dutch people, perpetually on guard, have acquired their obstinancy, their methodical spirit, and their taste for reflection and liberty.

Holland is one of the rare countries where democracy is not a hollow word but something that is lived every day. Amsterdam is not merely beautiful blonds or sex shops but an atmosphere of tolerance, with everyone brushing elbows with everyone else: rich diamond merchants, puritans, Hare Krishnas, freaks, and others. The right to be different is probably the right to which the Dutch are most attached.

Useful Addresses in New York

—*Netherlands National Tourist Office:* 576 Fifth Avenue, New York, NY 10036. Telephone (212) 245-5320 or 223-8141.

—*Dutch Consulate General:* 1 Rockefeller Plaza, New York, NY 10020. Telephone (212) 246-1429.

—*United States Student Travel Service (USSTS),* 801 Second Avenue, New York, NY 10017. Telephone (212) 867-8770.

Entry Formalities

A valid passport is required.

Money

One florin (gulden = 100 cents). You can change your money at the border. Each time that you change money in a bank, present your international student card, if applicable. Sometimes they offer a better rate to students.

The exchange offices in the central train station and airport of Amsterdam are open every day of the week until 10 P.M.. Banks are closed on Saturday, but there are exchange services in the main post offices in the large cities that are open Saturdays.

Dutch Vocabulary

yes	*ja*
no	*nee*
today	*vandaag*
tomorrow	*morgen*

where?	waar?
how much?	hoeveel?
to the right	rechts
to the left	links
enough	genoeg
too expensive	te duur
what time is it?	hoe laat is het?
tourist office	toeristen informatie (V.V.V.)
train station	station
post office	post
police	politie
bank	bank
hello (good day)	dag (goede dag)
good night	goede nacht
how are you?	hoe gaat het?
goodbye	tot ziens
please	als 'tu blieft
thank you	dank u
pardon (excuse me)	excuseer (verontschuldig me)
I don't understand	ik begrijp het miet
youth hostel	jeugdherberg
hotel	hotel
restaurant	restaurant
to drink	drinken
to eat	eten
to sleep	slapen
water	water
coffee with milk	koffie met melk
beer	bier
milk	melk
bread	brood
roll or loaf	broodje
cold	koud
hot	warm
good	goed
bad	slecht
toilet	toilet
one	een
two	twee
three	drie
four	vier
five	vijf
six	zes
seven	zeven
eight	acht
nine	negen
ten	tien
twenty	twintig
thirty	dertig
forty	veertig
fifty	vijfig
sixty	zestig
seventy	zeventig
eighty	tachtig
ninety	negentig

hundred .... *honderd*
thousand .... *duizend*

Some Distances

—Amsterdam–Paris . . . 325 miles (520 km)
—Amsterdam–Rotterdam . . . 46 miles (73 km)
—Amsterdam–The Hague . . . 36 miles (55 km)

How to Get There

If you're hitchhiking from Paris during the summer, you can have 20 or 30 hitchhikers ahead of you leaving Paris. We suggest the following itineraries:

—Lille (by highway or the National Route), Tournai, Courtrai, Gand, Anvers, Rotterdam, the Hague, Amsterdam.

—Lille, Halluin, Bruges, Sluis, Bresken (a bus every half hour), Vissingen, Rotterdam, the Hague, Amsterdam.

• *To Go by Bus*

—*Saint-Michel Voyages:* 99 Boulevard St.-Michel, 75005 Paris. Telephone 634-17-40. At least one bus per week for Amsterdam. Very punctual and not expensive. There is a very interesting "weekend" plan in which you leave Friday evening and arrive Saturday morning.

—*L'Autobus:* 4 bis rue St.-Sauveur, 75002 Paris. Telephone 233-86-72. Métro Réaumur. A bus group created for meeting and partying.

—*International Pullman* (formerly Magic Bus): 16 rue de Rivoli, 75004 Paris. Telephone: 271-23-33. A bus and weekend pioneer.

—*Tours 33:* 85 Boulevard St.-Michel, 75005 Paris. Telephone: 329-69-50. A wide range of buses, planes, and tours.

—*O.T.U.:* 137 Boulevard St.-Michel, 75005 Paris. Telephone: 329-12-88. Specializes in student travel.

—*Club Alliance:* 92 Boulevard Raspail, 75006 Paris. Telephone: 548-89-53. Métro St.-Placide. Weekends and tours in Northern Europe.

• *By Train*

Wasteels and Transalpino are two agencies that sell BIGE tickets for Amsterdam at attractive prices for youths under 26 years of age.

—*Wasteels, J. S. F.:* 7 rue de la Banque 75002 Paris. Telephone: 261-53-21.

—*Transalpino:* 16 rue Lafayette, 75009 Paris. Telephone: 247-12-40.

Transportation in Holland

• *Train*

Distances in Holland are minimized: Trains are frequent and roll rapidly. You can cross the country from east to west (Enschede to the Hague) in less than 3 hours and also go from Groningue, in the north, to Amsterdam in less than 3 hours.

—One-way and round trip tickets are valid only on the day they're issued. There are also evening return trips (valid on trains that leave after 6 P.M.), weekend round trips (leave on Saturday, return on Sunday), 8-day passes, and daily passes.

—*Tiener Toer* card: With this card those under 20 can travel during June, July, and August for 8 consecutive days, zigzagging across Holland on all the railways in second class. In addition, you can benefit from a 50 percent reduction on interurban bus routes.

—General 8-day pass allows travel throughout Holland for 8 days. You can buy it in all stations. No age limit. There are first-class and second-class passes. Its price becomes advantageous after 375 miles (600 km). Children under 10 ride for half fare. You must show a photo identity card or a passport number when using the ticket. This pass gives a half-price fare on nearly all the interurban bus lines.

—The daily pass allows you to travel at will on any line for one day; it can be extended for 5 days by paying a supplement. For these passes, an identity card from the Netherlands Railways is required (with a photo I.D.). You can get these free at the stations.

From May to September the Netherlands Railways organize one-day trips throughout Holland at set prices; similar offers are available for 2 to 3 days in the autumn and winter.

The one-day fare is higher for distances above 100 miles (160 km) and the fare per mile is barely raised.

International tickets, used on set routes in Holland, are valid for only 2 months.

•*Bicycle and Moped*

Holland is riddled with good rideable routes that are not too tiring because the terrain is very flat.

Mopeds, like bicycles, must use the cycle routes. You can ride them on main roads designated by a square blue sign inscribed with white letters: *Rijwielen met hulpmotor toegestaan* (bicycles with auxiliary motors allowed), and also on roads not marked as cycle routes.

Mopeds are forbidden on highways. With the motor disengaged they are permitted on cycle routes designated by a square black sign, with a dark blue sign below it inscribed with white letters: *Rijwielen met hulpmotor toegestaan*.

•*Car*

Holland's network of roads is one of the best in Europe, with an excellent highway system without tolls that enables rapid connections in spite of the population density.

Never forget to apply the emergency brake when parking, for the plunging of cars into the canals is so frequent that a fee for hauling by the firemen had to be instituted!

Holidays

February
—West Frisian Flora flower show
—Carnivals especially in the provinces of northern Brabant and Limburg (7 weeks before Easter, from Saturday to Ash Wednesday)

March
—Spring fair in Utrecht
—Performance of the "Passion According to St. Matthew" in the large church of Naarden (16 miles—25 km—east of Amsterdam), on Holy Thursday, Good Friday, and Easter Sunday

April
—Large Keukenhof flower gardens in Lisse, from the end of March to mid-May
—Parades of flowers on floats in the region of the flower fields (the last Saturday of April)
—Queen's Birthday celebrated throughout the country on April 30

May
—Traditional cheese market at Alkmaar (Friday mornings from the beginning of May to the end of September)
—Cheese market at Gouda (Thursday mornings from the beginning of May to the end of September)
—Sea fishing day at Scheveningen (the second Saturday in May)

June
—Festival of Holland (concerts, ballets, theater, and opera) at Amsterdam, the Hague, Rotterdam and in other cities (from June 15 to July 8)
—Antiques fair at Delft
—Folklore market at Hoorn (on Wednesdays from June 15 to August 31)
—International motorcycle races (the Grand Prix of Holland) at Assen (last Saturday of June)
—Automobile races (the Grand Prix of Holland) at Zandvoort (June–July)

July
—Exhibition of lilies at Akersloot, near Alkmaar (5 days at the beginning of July)
—International exhibition of roses at the Hague (Scheveningen, Westbroek Park)
—Folklore markets at Meppel and Schagen (Thursdays from the beginning of July to mid-August)
—Regattas of old transport sailing ships (Skûtsjesilen) at Sneek and other places in Frise (July–August)

August
—Historic parade of Delft (end of August to the beginning of September)
—Festival of fruits and flowers at Naaldwijk
—International horse show at Rotterdam (end of August to beginning of September)

September
—Frans Hals Day, September 1, at Haarlem
—Flower parades at Aalsmeer (the first Saturday) and at Zundert (the first Sunday)
—Festival of fruits and flowers at Tiel (the second Saturday) and at Goes (the third Saturday)
—Fall festival at Utrecht (beginning of September)

October
—Celebration of the raising of the siege of Leude (October 3)
—Flowerings of autumn at the Singer Museum in Laren

Country of Flowers

The best period for tulips is from April 15 to May 15, for narcissus April 1–15, and for hyacinths April 15–30. To seduce you, Holland transforms itself into bouquets. The most subtle and delicate nuances are found in the immense carpets of tulips transformed by the whims and caprices of a springtime sky. Numerous lovers of beauty congregate in the fields of flowering tulips between Leiden and Haarlem. Around the cities of Rijnsburg, Warmond, Katwijk, Nordwijk Binnen, and Sassenheim, an immense floral army mounts a pacific guard.

In the area of Lisse, there are 60 acres of flowering parks, among them the Keukenhof, Hillegom, De Zilk, Vogelenzang, and Bennebroek. Vast fields of flowers stretch to the coast, where Den Helder is the center of the largest flower region; crocus, narcissus, hyacinths, tulips—all for you to create your own bouquet! In the Netherlands, the cultivation of flower bulbs is so important that they have dedicated a museum to them; it's at Limmen.

If you love islands, if you love flowers, go to Texel where you find both. This island, situated 20 minutes from Den Helder, has a magnificent beach, shady forests, and a picturesque village.

In the new polders of South Flevoland, from mid-May on, there are fields of colza whose unbearably golden yellow brilliance will amaze you. A road intersects them and leads you to Lelystad. In this city of modern architecture, there's a terrific information center on the polders. The polders! Their existence is the most fantastic victory of man over the sea: Forests, lakes, fauna, and flora have replaced the waves.

Food

The passing tourist hardly has the chance to adapt to Dutch eating habits (except in family inns or boardinghouses), except for breakfast, an astonishingly lavish spread of various breads, plain or flavored, cheese, ham or cold meats, all washed down with coffee or tea. Generally, your lunch will consist of a cold meal with an occasional small hot dish and a salad. That's called the *koffietafel*. Between 1 and 5 o'clock in the afternoon it is customary to have tea, sometimes accompanied by small cakes and cookies. Dinner, the principal meal, is generally eaten between 6 and 8 o'clock in the evening, composed of soup, a meat dish with potatoes and green vegetables, and dessert.

Some Culinary Specialties

Salted herring, eaten raw, is known throughout the world. For the true connoisseur, its best flavor is at the beginning of the fishing season—in May. It is sold under the name *groene* or *nieuwe haring* (new herring). The Dutch prefer to eat their herring in the street, by a little stand; you can also order it in a restaurant.

Outside of Indonesia, only in the Netherlands can you be served a good *rijsttafel*. This famous rice dish is a must for those who love spicy dishes. It is generally accompanied by a glass of beer.

All sorts of chocolates and candies are presented in attractive packages. Unique are the chocolate granules *(hagelslag)* that the children (and we, too) adore on toast. The most famous of all sweets in the Netherlands is the *Haagse Hopje.*

Also available is a vast array of sweet and spicy breads, such as those from Groningen, Deventer, and Frise, not to mention all the gingerbreads. *Viaai,* a regional pastry of Limburg, is a light leavened bread garnished with fruits or stewed fruit.

Drinks

Beer and gin are the two best-known beverages in the Netherlands. Gin enthusiasts recommend the lemon and currant gins. In addition, there is a great selection of good liqueurs, such as *advocaat.* The most requested aperitif is 38 percent gin, to which is added occasionally a little angostura (and called *borreltje*) or another elixir (and called *bittertje*). Instead of asking for a "new" gin you can also ask for "aged" gin, which has a slightly sweeter taste.

Shopping

You will be especially tempted to purchase some Delft, which is tinted not only the traditional blue but also red or multicolored. It is still made by two manufacturers, but numerous small workshops make more or less successful imitations. We cannot keep silent about the rustic pottery (mainly green and rust-colored) that are copies of those which had formerly decorated the kitchens of Holland. It generally comes from small locations in Makkum and Workum. Painted furniture is made at Hindeloopen. From the swamps and polders grow the reeds that are used in the manufacture of countless basket works, which can't be found anywhere else, and which one finds particularly in Zeeland.

Onions and bulb flowers must be inspected by the agricultural department. It is easier to have them sent home by Dutch florists who know the legal regulations and are accustomed to filling orders throughout the world.

Among the food specialties of Holland let us mention: chocolates (especially the bitter, called *puur*), the famous Edam and Gouda cheeses, smoked eels *(gerookte paling);* gins, curaçao, and various liqueurs. We should also mention cigars and various tobaccos.

Note that the stores are always closed on Monday morning and are not necessarily open that afternoon.

AMSTERDAM

The Dutch are used to having their city compared to Venice. Amsterdam offers itself easily to the visitor. It is an open, transparent city. There are neither shutters nor bars on the windows of the houses. Nothing is hidden.

A Word on Drugs

Certain day trippers are interested in drugs. But the sale of drugs is not at all as "cool" as the press might have you believe. In fact, the dealers are mostly guys who use heroin and therefore need a lot of money, so they rip off youngsters who want to pay for a joint or two.

In short, get it into your heads that to buy here *is dangerous!* Finally, certain travelers ignore the fact that using drugs is forbidden in Holland. A group of these cats, now in the clink, can confirm this for you.

Useful Addresses

—*Tourist Information Office* (V.V.V.): Postbus 3901, 10 Stationplein. Open from 9 A.M. to 10 P.M.. Many brochures and maps of the city. Hotel reservations. Ask for the brochure "Amsterdam This Week." Exchange office (useful when the banks are closed).

—*Exchange Office:* The one in the Centraal Station is open every day from 6:45 A.M. to 10:45 P.M.

—*Headquarters of the VISA card:* 617-629 Keizersgracht. Telephone (20) 21-46-21.

—*American Express:* 66 Damrak.

—*NBBS* (charters and student flights): 17 Dam. Telephone 23-76-86.

—*Transalpino:* 44 Rokin. Telephone 23-99-22. Train tickets at reduced fares for those under 26.

—*Central Post Office:* 182 Nieuwe Zijds Voorburgwal (near the Dam). Open Monday through Friday from 8:30 A.M. to 6 P.M. and on Saturday from 9 A.M. to 12:30 P.M. Closed on Sunday.

—*Central Telephone Office:* 182 Nieuwe Zijds Voorburgwal.

—*Hospital* (day and night): Wilhemina Gasthuis, 104 Eerste Helmersstraat. Telephone 578-91-11. Tram #1. It's free. You pay only for medicine.

—*Viking Sauna:* 18 Martelaarsgracht. Upon leaving the station, go to the right and walk for 5 minutes. They have these super bathtubs with bubbling water.

—*American Consulate:* 19 Museumplein. Telephone: 79-03-21.

For Orientation

It's fascinating to find a civilized city where it's possible to get lost. In this concentric city not one street is straight. The center of Amsterdam *(centrum)* is bounded on the north by Centraal Station, from where most of the buses and trams depart; on the south by the Dam (Commodities Market) and the Centraal Post Office; in the east, Walletjes, the red light district, extends to Rembrandtsplein and Muntplein in the south; in the southeast, Leidsestraat, the most likeable section of the city, enclosed between Spui in the north and the museum area in the south (Van Gogh Museum, Stedelijk Museum, Rijksmuseum, and Concert Hall).

Urban Transportation

You can travel easily by public transportation: train, subway (small), bus, and tramway. The system is dense, well marked, and practical.

There are several ways to purchase tickets:

—*Book:* More advantageous than individual tickets. Buy them from the driver.

—*Unit:* 1 zone (the whole center) or 2 zones, valid for 1 hour; three zones valid for 2 hours.

—*"All-day":* contract allows for 1 or 3 days. On sale at the G.V.B. ticket windows in front of the Centraal Station.

Trams take you everywhere in the city. Almost all of them leave from Centraal Station.

—#1, Nieuwe Zijds Voorburgwal, Leidsestraat, crosses Leidseplein and meets the Overtoom.

—#2 follows the same route until Leidseplein, then goes to the corner of Rijksmuseum.

—#16, #24, #25 pass Damrak, Rokin, and Muntplein. From there, #16 goes to the KLM terminal in Museumplein, then to the Hilton; #24 goes down Beethovenstraat to Stationweg; #25 goes to Churchill Laan.

—#4 and #9 go from the station to Muntplein; #4 reaches Frederiksplein via Utrechsestraat; #9 goes toward Artis Zoo.

—#7 goes to Amstel Station.

If after all this you get lost . . .

Bicycle Rentals

The bike is the best way to visit this city in which the distances are so short. It's less expensive to rent by the week. Besides the flea market, where you can purchase a used bike for 100 Fl., there are stores where you can find the same thing at the same price. Hardly worth renting them. Only after 20 days is it worth it; besides, you can always resell an old bike. No problem in crossing the border.

—*Rent-a-Bike:* 6 Stationplein (Centraal Station). It costs 5.50 Fl. per day; 200 Fl. deposit.

—*Koenders:* 33 Stationplein, next to the Centraal Station. Telephone 25-38-45. Open from 6:30 A.M. to 6:30 P.M. Closed Saturday and Sunday except in the summer. Daily or weekly bike rentals; 200 Fl. deposit. They suggest a very interesting itinerary for a one-day trek.

—*Heja:* 39 Bestevaarstraat. Telephone 12-92-11. Tram #13 or bus #33. Also has motor scooter rentals.

Boat Excursions

Visit the canals and the port of Amsterdam. Commentaries in French and English. Reduced rate for those under 14. Not great. Lasts 1 hour. The ride through the modern harbor installations lasts ½ hour. Bergman's is truly a tourist industry (enclosed boats and unbearable heat). It is impossible to take photos. The completely open boats of the competitors are much better.

Where to Sleep

Having seen the number of stone-broke hitchhikers in quest of cheap beds, it's advisable to arrive early in Amsterdam in order to start the search in the morning. It isn't easy to find reasonable lodgings in the summer or on long spring weekends. The simplest solution is to go to the Tourist Information Bureau (V.V.V.) across from the Centraal Station. They make hotel reservations.

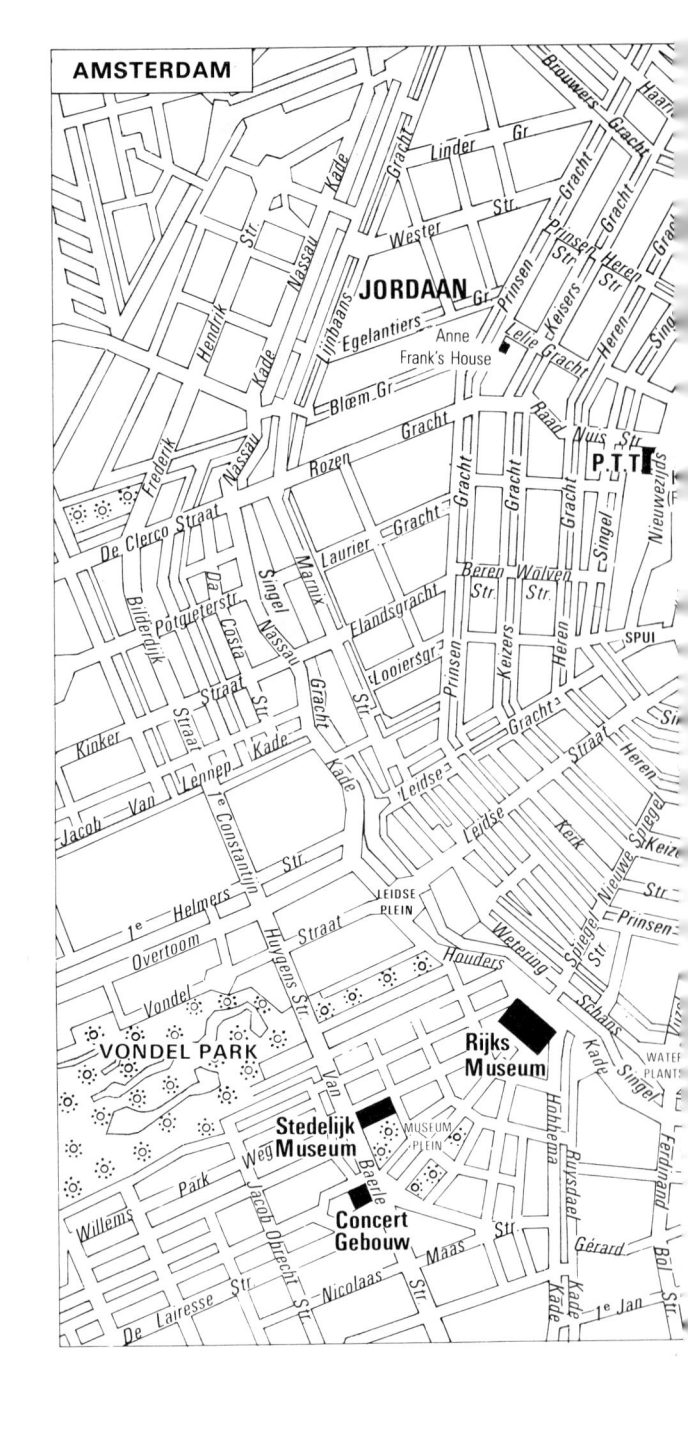

AMSTERDAM

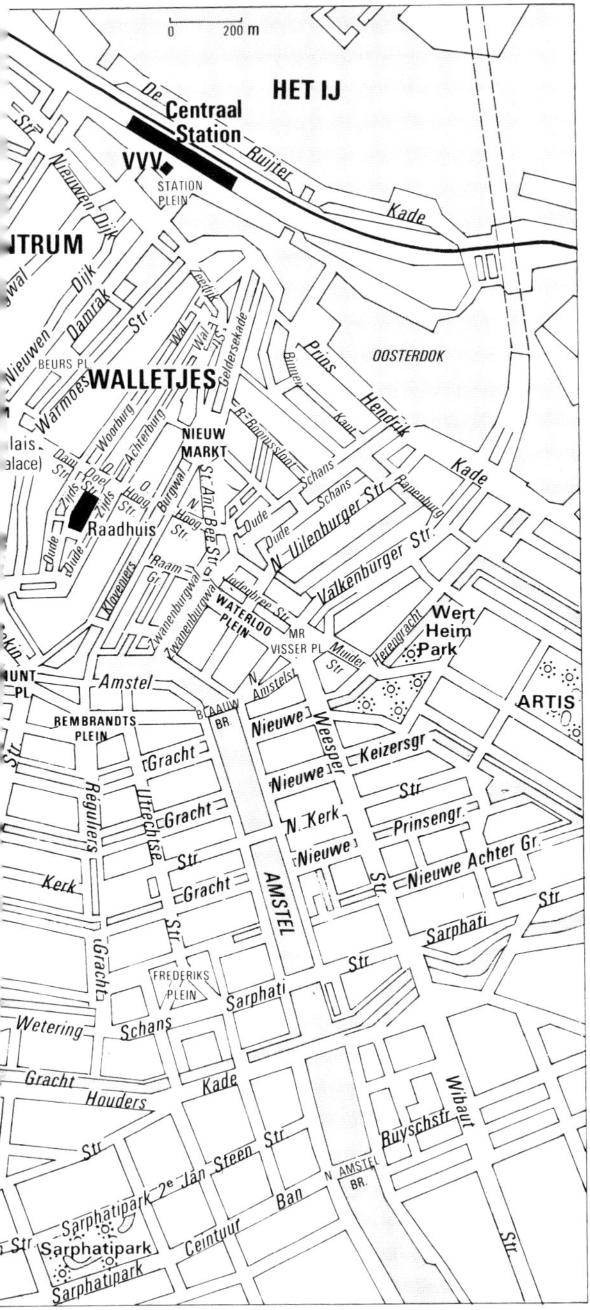
0
200 m
HET IJ
De
Centraal
Station
Ruijter
Kade
VVV
STATION
PLEIN
Nieuwen
Dijk
TRUM
Dijk
Damrak
Str.
Nieuwen
BEURS PL
Warmoes
WALLETJES
Zeedijk
Wal
Geldersekade
OOSTERDOK
Prins
Binnen
Kant
Hendrik
Kade
Voorburg
Achterburg
NIEUW
MARKT
R. Boomssloot
Schans
Oude
Schans
lais
alace)
Dam
Str.
Doel
Str.
Zijds
Zijds
O.
Hoog
Str.
Burgwal
St. Ant. Bree
Str.
N.
Hoog
Str.
Oude
Oude
N. Uilenburger Str.
Rapenburg
Valkenburger Str.
Raadhuis
Raam
Gr.
Kloveniers
Zwanenburgwal
Jodenbree
Str.
WATERLOO
PLEIN
MR
VISSER PL
Muider
Str.
Herengracht
Wert
Heim
Park
ARTIS
Amstel
N.
Amstelst
BLAAUW
BR.
REMBRANDTS
PLEIN
Nieuwe
Weesper
Keizersgr
Gracht
Nieuwe
Str.
Gracht
N. Kerk
Prinsengr.
Reguliers
Utrechtse
Str.
Nieuwe
Kerk
Gracht
Str.
Nieuwe Achter Gr.
AMSTEL
Str.
Sarphati
Str.
Gracht
FREDERIKS
PLEIN
Sarphati
Wetering
Schans
Gracht
Kade
Houders
Wibaut
Buyschstr
Str.
Jan Steen
Str.
2e
N. AMSTEL
BR.
Sarphatipark
Ban
Str.
Sarphatipark
Ceintuur
Sarphatipark
Str.

• In the Joordan Quarter
Southwest of the station. The bohemian neighborhood of Amsterdam where the canals are the prettiest and the streets the calmest. People live on barges here. In short, our favorite spot.

—*Youth and Student Hostel:* 15 Keizersgracht. Telephone 25-13-64. Truly lovely along the canal. Buses #18 and #22. Night bus #72. Not necessary to have a student card nor to be a student. A gigantic dormitory is placed at your disposal. (Watch out, it's the open door policy to all vices! Girls and boys are mixed. Yes!) Cold fish may take refuge in the bedrooms with one, four, or six beds. There, the boys are with the boys, the girls with the girls. But it's more expensive. Avoid the breakfast. Rather expensive for not much at all. Hot showers, but nothing to write home about.

—*H 88:* 88 Herengracht. Telephone 14-44-46. Trams #13 and 17. For 13 Fl. you can have a bed with breakfast. Open from June to mid-September. 120 beds. Graffiti is really everywhere. Situated along the canal.

—*Eben Haëzer:* 179 Bloemstraat. Telephone 24-47-17. Tram #10, buses #171 and #172. Night bus #74. Very clean, on a particularly quiet little street. Owned by a Catholic organization. A small supplement if you don't have a sleeping bag or sheets. Interior garden with a lovely arbor and small pond. A very reasonable cafeteria. Evening meal at 6 P.M.

—*Sleep-in:* 168 Rozengracht. These vast dormitories where you can sleep for the best price in town are part of the grand period of Amsterdam. In this former warehouse, 550 beds have been installed. The place is squalid. The cleaning women don't come often. But it's not too bad, for generally you laugh the most here. You can get out without having paid too much. Note: It's open only in the summer. Check the opening date with the Tourist Office near the station. Generally closed from noon to 4 P.M.

—*Private Youth Hostel, the Happy Hours:* 8 Binnen Wieringer Straat. Rooms with 4 beds. Coffee, tea, and cake in the morning included. You pay for the hot showers. A safe is available for valuables.

—*Groenendael:* 15 Nieuwendijk. Very good. 46 Fl. for a double with shower; 25 Fl. for a single. No breakfast.

• Near the Station
—*Bob's Youth Hostel:* 92 Nieuwe Zijds Voorburgwal. Telephone 23-00-63. Very central—5 minutes from the station. Trams #1, #2, #17, #13. Night bus #74. Dormitories with clean sheets and towels at 16 Fl. per person, breakfast included.

—*The Boat:* A barge in front of 145 Prins Hendrikkade. Telephone 27-14-35. Make a left on leaving the station, cross the second bridge, and it's on your immediate left. 10 Fl. per night. Closes at 1 A.M. and during the day from 11 A.M. to 4 P.M.

—*The Last Waterhole:* 12 Armsteeg. Telephone 24-48-14. Very central—behind the Tourist Information Office. 10 Fl. per night.

• In the Red Light District
On leaving the station, go to the left and take Zeedjik Street.

—*Christian Youth Hostel, "The Shelter":* 21 Barndesteeg. Bus #56 and night bus #76. Telephone 25-32-30. Youth card not required. They have guts, these priests, to plant themselves in the middle of the red light district. It's said that the young people in charge are very nice and keep the hotel in impeccable order. It is 9.75 Fl. if you have a sleeping bag, 10 Fl. without a bag. Note: The door closes sharply at midnight. The cafeteria overlooks a very tranquil garden complete with a little fountain. Breakfast is 3.25 Fl.

—*Stadsdoelen:* 97 Kloveniersburgwal. Telephone 24-68-32. Bus #56 and night bus #76. A real youth hostel (card is mandatory). Along the canal, near Muntplein. There are even two benches along the water. Wake up with music (classical!). The cheapest cold food in the city, and pop music all day long. The attendants are very pleasant. They prepare a bed and a breakfast almost voluntarily. Bicycle garage in the basement. The reception desk is closed from 6 P.M. to 7 P.M. Decent sanitary conditions.

—*Parima:* 91 Warmoedsstraat. Telephone 24-14-06. Rooms with several beds. Behind, the hotel looks out on a pretty church. Hot showers. Restaurant and bar on the ground floor.

—*Kabul Young Budget:* 38 Warmoedsstraat. Trams #16 and #25. Night bus #75. Telephone 23-71-58. Near *Parima*. More expensive but much better. It's the first-class hotel for hitchhikers. Rooms or dormitories. Some rooms look out on the canal. An impeccable self-service eatery nearly level with the water. They exchange money (only in emergency, for their rates are not very good).

—*Fat City:* 157 Oudezijds Voorbugwal. Telephone 22-67-05. Along the canal. Not very nice, but a good bargain. Bar on the ground floor. Quite noisy.

• Southeast of the Station

This area is located between Waterlooplein and Rhijnspoorplein, on each of the banks of the Amstel River.

—*Adam en Eva Hotel:* 105 Sarphatistraat. Trams #6 and #10. Subway. Night bus #76. Telephone 24-62-06. A large building along a grand avenue. 108 beds in dormitories. The ambiance is very touristy. A copious breakfast in a marvelous room in the basement. TV and Ping-Pong. Reduced price from the second night on (breakfast included). Bring a padlock for locking your closet; otherwise you'll have to rent one.

—*Adolesce:* 26 Nieuwe Keizersgracht. Trams #9 and #14. Night bus #76. Telephone 26-39-59. Along the canal. Very clean. 120 beds. Double rooms for lovers.

—*Hans Brinker:* 136 Kerkstraat. Telephone 22-06-87. Trams #16, #24, and #25. Night bus #74. On a very nice small street which resembles those of Greenwich Village. 256 beds. Restaurant. Very well kept but a little expensive otherwise. 5 minutes from Leidseplein. Restaurant with a small interior garden.

—*Sleep-in:* 28 Mauritskade. Telephone 94-74-44. Subway stop at Weesperplein. Trams #10 and 9. Bus #56 and night bus #76. Near the Artis Zoo. Very big, therefore there is often room. Open from June 24 to September 6. 9 Fl. per night.

• Near Vondelpark

In the southwest of the city. A very residential area, full of trees and greenery. An inconvenience; it is far from the center of town, though very well serviced by trams.

—*Vondelpark Youth Hostel:* 5 Zandpad. Telephone 83-17-44. Youth card required. A very substantial, enormous building that looks directly onto the park. Lodgings in the dormitory with breakfast (more expensive if you don't have a sleeping bag or sheets). Very nice.

—*Hotel Metro:* 19 Van Eeghanlaan. Telephone 79-61-64. A small, very quiet street that runs along Vondelpark. Tram #2 or #16. Kept by a very nice old lady. Double rooms only. Paupers will go elsewhere. Garage for motorcycles (1 Fl).

—*Cok:* 34 Koninginneweg. Telephone 64-61-11. Tram #2 from Centraal Station. Night bus #74. Stop on Willemsparkweg. *Cok* is at the end of the street, 2 steps from Vondelpark and a pretty lake. Very residential area. Dormitories or double rooms, breakfast included. Very clean. Money exchange (only in emergency, for the rate is rather prohibitive). Self-service restaurant.

Campgrounds

Impeccable, with showers and a small grocery store.

—*Vliegenbos:* 138 Meeuwenlaan, North Amsterdam. Telephone 36-88-55. Bus #39 from the station during the day and night bus #77 after midnight. Very cosmopolitan. This camp really jumps. There are often campfires and kids who pluck at their guitars. Truly super, and what's more, you can rent bicycles. At the entrance they give you a newspaper with all the good addresses in the city.

—*Camping AYC:* 45 Ijd Gampad. You can get there by trams #6, #16 and #26 from Centraal Station. On leaving terminal head toward Olympisch Station; 100 yards down, turn right. It's marked. Good camping.

—*Camping Zeeburg:* 34A Zuider Ijdik. Telephone 94-66-88. In the direction of Schellingwoudelberg, situated on a small island that separates North Amsterdam from South Amsterdam. Trams #3 and #10. Buses #36 and #38. Night bus #76. Very convenient and pleasant.

—*Amsterdam Bos:* 1 Kleine Noorddijk, Ailsmer-Bovenkerk. Telephone 41-68-68. Very pretty forest. Yellow bus #171 or #172 from the station.

Where to Eat

—Brookjeswinkels are a kind of snack bar where they serve sandwiches. There are also many ambulatory carts that sell french fries.

—The ancestors of the Dutch liked to travel to Indonesia in search of spices. In the balancing out of things, many Indonesians have immigrated to Holland. Be sure to go to Indonesian restaurants. Their cuisine is a clever mix of Chinese sophistication and Malaysian quality. In short, good places to investigate.

—*The Egg Cream:* 19 Sint Jacobstraat. A small street 3 minutes by foot from the station. Telephone 23-05-75. A tiny restaurant with wainscotting covering the walls. Vegetarian cuisine: soups, salads, omelettes, homemade cake. Very pleasant. Be aware: It closes at 7:30 in the evening.

—*Keuken van 1870:* 4 Spuistraat. On leaving the station, take a right and walk for 5 minutes. Open from noon to 7 P.M. The clientele is a bit elderly. If formica doesn't bother you too much, you can eat here cheaply. From the station, tram #1, and get off at the second stop. Closed on weekends.

—*The Pancake Bakery:* 191 Prinsengracht. On the edge of a stunning canal, in the bohemian section of Amsterdam. From the first ray of sun, the owner places the tables outside, and you eat by the water. Great selection of crepes.

—*Hema Department Store:* 174 Nieuwendijk (a pedestrian street leading to the Dam). On the first floor of this department store is the least expensive self-service eatery in Amsterdam. No charm but very clean. You will be in the company of mothers in the middle of their shopping. Be aware: It closes at 6 P.M.

—*Mensa Academia:* 3 Damstraat, right next to the Dam. The design is not very new, the air is often smoky, but it's the meeting place of travelers. Reasonably priced food, and the menu changes daily. Be aware: The restaurant is open only from 5 to 7 P.M. On the ground floor, a very freaky bar with pop music. Closed Sunday.

—*Tijbulan:* 35 Zeedijk. A good Indonesian restaurant in the heart of the red light district. Fairly reasonable. No liquor license. Open from 4 P.M. to 2 A.M.

—*Fong Won:* 85 Narmoes Straat. A very nice and inexpensive Indonesian restaurant.

—*Cantharel:* 377 Kerkstraat, right near Utrechstraat. A small, charming restaurant with American tablecloths on the tables. Central European cuisine. Open from 5 to 9:30 P.M. Closed Sunday.

Where to Get Breakfast

—*Grand Hotel Krasnapolsky:* On the Dam. What's the matter with the authors of this guide recommending such luxury hotels? In fact, the place is truly not in a hitchhiker's budget. Certain readers, impressed by the sumptuous facade, will refrain from entering. Nevertheless, we recommend this as special, something you won't forget for a long time; an exceptional breakfast (you serve yourself as much as you want!) in a gigantic glass-framed room decorated with luxurious plants. Go there at least once; you won't be disappointed (proper dress required). Breakfast is served until 10:30. And avoid leaving without paying. There are eyes on you!

—*Bloom Bakery:* 119 Nieuwendijk, not very far from the station. A stunning boutique where they serve excellent breakfasts.

Stores for Grub

—*Het Karbeel:* 58 Warmoedsstraat. An incredible choice of cold delicacies, each better than the next. Owned by young people. Pleasant decor. In the back, some tables for eating what you've just purchased. From noon to 2 P.M. they serve cheeses and meats, with wine to wash it all down. Be aware: It closes at 6 P.M.

—*Avonderkoop:* At the intersection of Zeedijk and Stormasteeg. A minuscule shop with a fantastic array of chocolates. And when the Dutch apply themselves to making chocolate, they really do it well. We've tasted almost all of them (tough job!). Consider buying some lollipops shaped like tulips... the way to cast spells on your little cousins.

The Brown Cafés (Bruine Kroeg)

They call them "browns" because they religiously conserve the color of the walls derived from the smoke of generations of pipes and cigars. These cafés resemble English pubs, at least in respect to the coffee and the closing time. The atmosphere differs each time depending upon the mood of the managers, their personalities or those of the regulars. The Brown Café is evidently a special watering hole, given its obvious function. But with a little intuition, you are more or less able after a while to choose the faces that you like or, if you prefer, to begin to chat with a little old lady.

You need extensive practice and some discrimination to hit upon the most colorful and lively of the cafés, but it is personal preference. Something is happening all the time. Sometimes it's a game of cards or dominos, which are pulled out from under the table to where the stakes will return; sometimes it's a story told with facial mimicry and brusque expressions that provoke fantastically lively comments. Then, suddenly, a strange silence will settle, as if everybody was a mere passersby. There are several special customs in the cafés in general. The tobacco jar is often on the bar, and we don't see why you shouldn't serve yourself. If you plan to stay some time and consume several beers, tell the waiter your name; he will keep the tab and you can pay upon leaving. Generally, there's a bell suspended above the bar: You rarely hear it, but it signals when someone buys a round for the house. In some cafés it seldom rings any more—only when someone leaves a tip. You should know that a *coca-bier* is only a beer in a cola glass. If long hours of hitchhiking have frozen you, ask for hot milk with anise. Wonderful! Closing time at certain cafés (yes, there is one) is announced sometimes in a strange, full scream, as in a noisy school or at an auction. Some Brown Cafés that we adore:

—*Amsterdam Litterair Café:* 59 Kloveniersburgwal, toward Muntplein. At the end of the canal. In the back of the room, a player piano; in the cellar, a bookstore. Somewhat intellectual. The patrons talk a lot.

—*Karpershoek:* 2 Martelaarsgracht. Across from the station. The proprietors insist that it's the oldest Brown Café in the city. In any case, it is one of the most typical. Low ceiling, Delft on the walls, and sawdust on the floor.

—*De Schutter:* 13 Voetboogstraat. Students and artists make up for the culinary blunders with bursts of music and laughter. Pizza.

—*Volledije:* 2 Prinsengracht. Has Delft tiles on the walls and a typical old stove.

—*Amstel Taverne:* At the corner of Amstel and Halve Maan Steeg, near Muntplein. An impressive collection of beer mugs on the ceiling.

Other Places

—*The Ark* (houseboat coffee bar): 14 Steiger (wharf 14). Behind the station. A barge where you can drink delicious tea while chatting amiably. Open from 8 to 11 P.M. except Friday and Sunday.

What to See in the Heart of the City

—*Canals:* A stroll along the main canals is mandatory. They were dug according to a plan resembling a spider's web. Because of the unstable nature of the soil, the buildings are supported on wooden piles. These decaying piles give a slightly sloping aspect to many houses. The canals traverse a few dozen miles within the city. You can enjoy the prettiest while saving wear and tear on your feet. Starting with the *Singel Canal,* you will find at #7 the narrowest house in the city. Across from that, at #40, a moored barge has become the domain of 150 cats who have lived there for years (you see cats only on boats). The most sumptuous townhouses were erected along *Herengracht,* the canal for lords, and less grand along *Keizersgracht* (the Emperor's Canal) for shipowners, bankers, doctors, lawyers, master glass blowers, carpenters, jewelers, and sheriffs. They were not satisfied to have houses just for themselves but built them for their entire families; many of the mansions were built by the same owner. They are high, narrow residences with small, square windows; for the most part their facades are decorated in baroque, rococo, or neoclassical styles. Observe the jutting beams on the outside; they serve and still serve to hoist furniture into these homes whose stairways are very narrow. Along Herengracht you will now find consulates and the headquarters of flourishing businesses. Only one building remains a residence. Those who have money can take a tour boat (which leaves from the top of Damrak, across from the station).

Along the wharves to *Osterdoch,* you must see the barges transformed into homes. Many young people live there. You can see the people gardening in the middle of paved wharves, and even some chicken coops.

—*Begijnhof* (The Convent): 134 Kalverstraat, but the entrance is on the Spui. Superb, typically Flemish houses surrounding a peaceful square. Truly charming. The convent was previously a residence for religious women who dedicated themselves to prayer, needlework, and visiting the sick. At #34 stands the oldest wooden house in Amsterdam (1475).

—*Madame Tussaud:* 156 Kalverstraat, next to *Begijnhof.* Open every day from 10 A.M. to 10 P.M. Trams #1, #2, and #16 from Centraal Station. England's wax museum has opened this branch. Rembrandt, Jerome Bosch, the royal family, and the great personalities found in all wax museums. Oddly, Van Gogh has both his ears. Some beautiful scenes. Fairly high admission price.

—*House of Craftsmen:* Kalverstraat, where you can admire the work of shoemakers, cheese makers, and printers.

—*Cinema Tuschinsky:* 26 Reguliers Breestrad, near Muntplein. Regardless of the film (there are 5 theaters, so you have a decent chance of finding something good), the astonishing decor alone—"art deco"—is worth the trip. Everything is from the period, from the glowing carpets to the chandeliers, the wood, subtle lighting, parlors, and deep armchairs. A great architectural delight.

—*Zeedijk:* 50 yards from the station. On leaving the station, bear to the left. Along the canal, the famous "women in the windows" who have given this area its worldwide fame. The soberness and serenity of the day, where moderation reigns, is transformed at night into frenzy and folly. Entertaining, especially after 10 P.M. But most fascinating are the shining eyes of desire, the patrons' drooling mouths of lust in this place of luxury, debauchery, and fornication. But nothing is more tedious than an overdose of pornography. For the followers of "direct" and "applied" transcendental meditation. Several "live show" clubs stretch the length of the canal. A little more expensive and much less erotic than one would suppose. Besides, you can find the same thing in New York or Paris, more or less.

—*Rembrandthuis* (Rembrandt's House): 4 Jodenbreedstraat.

Open from 10 A.M. to 5 P.M. Tram #9 or the subway to Waterlooplein. Rembrandt lived here when he moved permanently to Amsterdam, and it's here that he met his future wife. His passions as a collector cost him dearly, and his house was never paid for (ahhh, artists!). The interior is a little too restored for our taste, but you can discover the graphic work of the master: etchings, drawings, self-portraits, and manuscripts.

—*Anne Frank's House:* 263 Prinsengracht. Trams #13 and #17. Red bus #21 and #33. Open from 9 A.M. to 5 P.M.; open on Sundays and holidays, from 10 A.M. to 5 P.M. No discounts. 5 minutes by foot from the Dam. A young Jewish girl of 14 lived hidden here with her family during the German occupation, and wrote a journal that has today become a literary classic. She died in a concentration camp. The newspapers hung at the exit show that fascism is not dead. The Anne Frank Foundation supports the fight against all racism.

—*Diamond Works:* Don't bother looking for *Van Moppes,* which is a veritable factory. Ask the Tourist Information Office instead for the address of a small craftsman. Here are some addresses:

Amstone Diamond Center, 129 James Wattstraat

Holshuysen Stoeltie, 13–15 Wagenstraat

Generally, you must make an appointment to visit the workshops. The visit is free. Open from 9 A.M. to 5 P.M.

What to See in the South of the City

—*Brasserie Heineken:* 30 Van der Helstraat (10 minutes by foot from the Rijksmuseum). From the station, tram #25. Closed Saturday and Sunday. The entrance for visitors is on Stadthouderskade.

Visits begin at 9 and 11 A.M. (at 10 A.M. only in the off-season). Completely packed in the summer. But the beer is excellent . . . and it's free. We suggest you arrive half an hour earlier if you want a chance to get in. You receive a Delft mug if you visit on their anniversary. Give our regards to Freddy.

—*Rijksmuseum:* 42 Stadthouderskade. Open from 10 A.M. to 5 P.M. from 1 to 5 P.M. on Sunday. Trams #1, #2, and #16 from Centraal Station. No student discounts. Free checkroom. One of the most popular museums in the world and deservedly so. In any case, it contains the best displays of Dutch cultural life since the Middle Ages. It is the best place to find the two Dutch painters Frans Hals and Rembrandt. Don't miss the small art room in the basement. Instructive and interesting. You can buy a card *(jeugdmuseumkart)* that allows you free use of all museums for one year. But you must expressly ask for it, for there is no sign about it (for those under 21 only).

Room 221 of the museum houses its most famous painting, *The Syndics of the Cloth Guild.* This painting is the symbol of liberty and religious tolerance. *Night Watch,* in room 22, is the portrait of 15 officers, wealthy, well-known men who formed the honor guard of the Queen of France, Marie de Médicis. It was highly criticized for not having considered either precedence or social rank.

Rembrandt was born on July 15, 1606, at Leiden. Though not belonging to high society, his family was well off, and the young boy first attended a Latin school, then the university. Abandoning higher studies, he entered the studio of a painter. The Lievens family, with whom he was close, helped him discover art and an extremely erudite milieu. If his family life was not very intellectual, it did include daily readings from the Bible and sacred texts; his mother, in particular, was imbued with these tendencies, and Rembrandt was very close to her. After spending 3 years in the studio of Swanenburgh, Rembrandt went to Van Schooten's studio and learned the art of earning money by flattering and embellishing his models. Rembrandt stayed with him only a few months. After these years of apprenticeship, Rembrandt moved to Amsterdam and went to the studio of Pieter Lastman (1623), who was influenced by Italian painting and particularly by Caravaggio, under whose spell Rembrandt never fell. He always said, "I will always have enough to do in my life to paint what I see around me," and he never understood Italy's attraction.

After spending several months in Amsterdam—the months of the plague, by the way—Rembrandt returned to Leiden. He shared a studio with Jans Lievens; they co-signed works. He worked zealously. He studied beggars, the destitute, and the crippled. He ceaselessly drew and painted the faces of those around him, his mother and sister in particular. In 1631 he attended an anatomy lesson given by Dr. Tulp, which made him decide to return to Amsterdam. His first studio was at Bloemengracht. Fame came quickly enough, and Rembrandt then resided at the home of a well-known art dealer at 4 Jodenbreestraat (wide street of the Jews). He married and lived a life of opulence, receiving orders from affluent, important people. The governor, among others, ordered a series of compositions illustrating passion, and Rembrandt received 600 Fl. for each canvas. During this time Rembrandt satisfied his passion for collecting: marble statues, paintings, sumptuous jewelry from the Orient, and expensive furniture. After several more years of living among his compatriots as a renowned artist, the number of orders declined, for many were shocked by his nonconformism and his conversion to Mennonism. In 1656, one of his creditors demanded a vast sum from him. Rembrandt had to part with some treasures and, unfortunately, like a good many of his fellow citizens, he had speculated and speculated badly. His finances were so bad that he had to leave his lovely abode and move into a modest apartment in Rozengracht with his son, Titus, and Hendrickje Stoffels. The painter kept his students and continued to receive orders from faithful friends, but what he created was not understood. The public did not feel that there was anything mysteriously fascinating in his sumptuous and secret art. Rembrandt continued to produce masterpieces, but he suffered from misunderstanding and solitude even more than from poverty.

After the death of all his friends, he died on October 4, 1669, and was buried in Westerkerk.

—*Van Gogh Museum:* 9 Paulus Potterstraat, behind the Rijksmuseum. Open daily from 10 A.M. to 5 P.M.; open on Sunday from 1 to 5 P.M. Tram #2, #3, and #16 from Centraal Station. Free checkroom. No student discounts. The most important paintings are *Self-Portrait with Straw Hat, Vincent's Room in Arles, Three Olive Trees,* and *Cornfield with Rooks.*

Vincent Van Gogh was born March 30, 1853, in the parsonage of Groot Zundert, to a family in which if one wasn't a pastor or a sailor, one was an art dealer. His father was a pastor, three of his uncles were art dealers, and a fourth was an admiral. In 1869, in the Hague, Van Gogh made his debut in the Goupil Art Galleries. He lived very isolated, enclosed in such a ferocious timidity that his slightly fanatical knowledge of the Bible frightened the friends he did have. Dismissed by Goupil because of his eccentricity, he became a successful schoolteacher in England and then a bookstore salesman in Dordrecht. He began studying theology in order to become a pastor, but his outrageousness complicated his relations with the clergy and the people. He lived as a volunteer evangelist in the mining town of Borinage, but his generosity and his brotherly ties with the miners, whose poverty shocked him, caused difficulties with the authorities. He started studying painting with financial aid from his brother Theo. In 1886 he returned to Paris where he made the acquaintance of artists such as Toulouse-Lautrec, who painted a beautiful portrait of him that can be seen in the Stedelijk Museum in Amsterdam. In Paris he discovered the enchantment of light colors—from imported Japanese prints. But after his initial enthusiasm, Van Gogh was horrified by Paris and decided to move to Arles in 1888. During the spring he became so intoxicated with sun and light that he thought everything had been arranged for him. Gauguin joined him in the summer, but his presence, however desirable, did not help at all. The state of Van Gogh's mental health was so poor that he had to go to the mental hospital at Saint Remy, once at his own request and another time at the request of his neighbors. Judging himself well in 1890, he returned to Paris to see his brother who had just married. Pissarro advised him to move to Auvers-sur-Oise near Dr. Grachet, who would perhaps know how to cure him. But his state deteriorated. His conscience bothered him because he was living off his brother, and he was convinced he would be a failure no matter what he did. He committed suicide on July 27, 1890. His brother died January 21 the following year. Both of them are buried at Auvers.

Vincent Van Gogh completed more than 800 paintings during a 10-year period. His work is a public confession made with color so that one could, from his paintings, retrace the steps of his brief existence. "Color by itself expresses something," he said. What became the fundamental principle of Fauvism was already evident in his works. Color corresponded to a state of spirit. When he painted stars and suns—and even sunflowers—the yellow, the very visible yellow, for him was the symbol of faith, hope, and love. If he wanted to express "the terrible human passions," he used greens and reds. The dark strokes are not there to mark figures but translate into "a little bit of anxiety." He started to use browns and blacks because he could not otherwise translate the hard daily labor of the miserable people of Borinage. Others before him throughout the centuries had painted the ordinary people but had never achieved this barely suppressed violence and passion. In Paris, mingling with impressionists, his colors became very light, his painting seemed to be liberated, but it was not until Arles that he "painted with all the lucidity and blindness of a lover," giving birth to his great works. Beginning in 1889 his colors exploded and his large brush strokes showed the disorder of his mind which foundered in its madness, as cruel as it was intermittent. The cypresses, olive trees, sunflowers, and people, all tense and twisted, were only the expression of everything in him that smoldered with suffering, passion, and the search for excellence. All this burst into drama at Auvers-sur-Oise.

—*Stedelijk Museum:* 13 Paulus Potterstraat. Next to the Van Gogh Museum. This is the principal museum. Open daily from 9:30 A.M. to 5 P.M.; on Sunday from 1 to 5 P.M.; closed on Monday. Trams

#2 and #16 from Centraal Station. Reasonable admission price. Lovely terrace that looks out on the water.

Don't miss the works of Manet, Cezanne, Léger, Picasso, Braque, Chagall, Mondrian, Kandinski and, from a more recent period, Dubuffet, American Action Painting, English Pop Art, Op Art, and the New Realism.

—*Vondelpark:* This superb park is planted with beautiful trees and endowed with a green English lawn, and sometimes cows (yes!) pass close by. Lakes are strewn with tiny islands full of little secret spots. In the summer, every Thursday at noon, there is a jazz or folk concert, and every Sunday at 4 P.M. a pop concert. Some evenings you can also go to free concerts of "experimental" theater plays. The superb ambiance in the park at night has disappeared. Besides, at 10 P.M. it's a desert. In any event, you must visit this truly magnificent park—one of the most beautiful we've seen.

—*Hortus Botanicus* (Botanical Gardens): Some greenhouses shelter a remarkable collection of tropical plants, notably the *Queen Victoria* which lives in South American waters and can grow to a height of more than 6 feet. Open from 9 A.M. to 5 P.M.

The Markets

—*The flea market at Valkenburgestraat:* Open from Monday to Saturday from 10 A.M. to 4 P.M. Tram #9, bus #56, or the subway. A little more lively on the weekend. Used clothes, textiles, and so forth. Not as extraordinary as you might think. It's not for those who like antiques. You can, however, find old jazz records.

—*Stamp Market:* Nieuwe Zijds Voorburgwal. Across from the telegraph office and #280. Open Wednesday and Saturday afternoons from 1 P.M. to 4 P.M. Trams #1 and #2.

—*Flower Market:* On the Singel Canal, on the barges near Muntplein. Open from 9 A.M. to 5 P.M. The barges are lighted in the evening. The market is famous for its dried flowers.

Discothèques and Bars with Music

The musical reputation of Amsterdam started with the Provocative Movement, which gave birth to *Paradiso,* followed closely by *Fantasio,* which became *Kosmos,* and finally the last of the group, the most turbulent, *Melkweg,* which occupies the site of a former dairy.

—*Melkweg:* 234a Lijbaansgracht, just behind Leidseplein. This is our favorite club (anyway, it's better than *Paradiso* which unfortunately changed managers and does not seem smitten with pop music). Well, *Melkweg* is more than a simple disco; there's a movie house that frequently shows films not shown elsewhere, dance studios, theater, paintings . . . . From time to time you will really get to hear a jam session. Bookstore and restaurant. Membership card required, plus admission fee. Open Wednesday through Sunday from 6 P.M.

—*Paradiso:* 6 Weteringshans (near Leidseplein). One of Amsterdam's many famous clubs. Membership card required. Movie house, TV, cafeteria, and jam session. It has greatly aged. The temple of the counterculture has moved into a secularized church. Another time, another religion. Open (in principle) Wednesday thru Saturday after 8 P.M.

—*Kosmos:* 142 Prins Hendrikskade. A freaky place for meeting freaks. Numerous interesting activities: yoga, meditation courses, pottery and ceramic workshops, sauna, music. A visit is almost a must! Open from 6 P.M. to midnight on Monday, Wednesday, Thursday and Friday. Closed in July. At Kosmos music isn't the core of communication but meditation, metaphysics, as you will discover.

Hitchhiking out of Amsterdam

—Toward Paris: Take tram #25 until the last stop.
—Toward Haarlem and the sea: Bus #22, tram #3 until Zandvoort.
—Toward Rotterdam. Tram #16 or #24 to the last stop.
—Toward the north: Bus #22 until Zeeburgerdijk.

Finally, for the lazy, an organization for hitchhiking without thumbs: *Diemen,* Postbus #133. Telephone 93-38-02. We're not sure that it still exists.

Near Amsterdam

—About 9 miles (15 km) from Amsterdam is the island of *Marken,* with its green-painted houses and traditionally costumed inhabitants. A little farther is the small port of *Volendam,* with its charming glazed and brick houses, symbol of a sweet and peaceful way of life.

—About 16 miles (25 km) from Amsterdam is Zandvoort, a seaside resort with a long beach.

HOGE VELUWE NATIONAL PARK

This park is near Arnhem. Admission charge. On this large, sandy, and slightly valleyed landscape stands a very beautiful museum with paintings from all periods along with contemporary Dutch sculptures (from the Kröller-Muller Foundation). You can ride through the park on a bicycle; there are at least 37 miles (60 km) of cyclable routes. You can rent bikes or bring your own. There are small kiosks for eating. You can also camp (don't mess up the place, please). Finally, you can hike for one or several days in nature! The cost is about $2 per person.

HAARLEM

Full of tulips and more tulips, in the tulip season, of course (April–May).

—*Tourist Information Office* (V.V.V.): 1 Stationplein.
—*Youth Hostel:* 3 Jam Gijsen-Haarlem North.

There's also a camping site far enough from the city; reasonable enough, but not very comfortable.

ALKMAAR

Northwest of Amsterdam. Very pretty city where you should go on a Friday for the cheese market (only in the summer, from 10 A.M. to noon). If you want to see something, arrive an hour before the opening, set for 10 A.M. This is the most important one in Holland. The famous red cheeses are tasted by specialists and transported on these curious "planks" by porters (men belonging to a very ancient guild) clothed in white and wearing hats that resemble those of Venetian gondoliers.

A vigorous handclasp officially binds the sale. Then the cheese porters enter the scene. The guild is comprised of 4 groups distinguished by their colors: green, blue, red, and yellow. Each team consists of 6 men and a "head man" (the one who weighs). Each barrow can hold 352 pounds (160 kg) of cheese.

From Amsterdam, take bus #100 to Purmerend, then bus #107 to Alkmaar. You have time to see the countryside on a bus.

Where to Sleep

—*Camping:* Bus #117, #118, or #119. 500 yards from the train station. Very well equipped.

—*Sleep-in:* 12 Verdronkenoord. Telephone 072-11-01-36. Count on 5 Fl. for the night. Very clean. Around 40 beds, therefore very cozy. Reasonably priced vegetarian food for dinner. You can rent bikes. (Bike rentals also available near the station.) The countryside around Alkmaar is magnificent.

Where to eat

—*Roode Leew:* 93 Samrak Place. Good Dutch cuisine and not expensive.

—*Snack-bar Rische:* 13 Ritsevoort. A small restaurant that serves Dutch cuisine. Good daily specials and good prices.

Where to Knock Back a Great Beer

—*13 Balken Bar:* 11 Zivenhuizen, near the post office. Jazz on Wednesdays. The group plays behind the bar, between the counter and the hot plates that heat the sausages! Good atmosphere. Free admission.

—*Café Bruintje Beer:* Ritsevoort, not far from the windmill. Mostly folk music on Tuesdays. Free admission, and the beer is no more expensive than usual. The show starts at 9:30 P.M.

—*T'Hartje:* Near the cheese market. Decor like the Brown Cafés. Music and atmosphere to your heart's content.

—*Café Stapper:* Near the cheese and fish markets. In this bistro, you realize they know how to bend the elbow here. The dives of the city are not very far.

—*Pizzeria Taormina:* Facing Saint Jean Church. We recommend to gourmets Dama Bianca, a famous ice cream. The waiters are attentive, nice, and very Italian . . .

THE HAGUE (DEN HAAG)

Administrative capital of the kingdom.
—*Tourist Information Services* (V.V.V.): Station HS and Gevers Deijnootplein Scheveningen.

Where to Sleep

—*Youth hostel at Monsterseweg:* A gigantic factory administered by a manager who is very strict about the rules and hours.
—*Campground:* Duinrell, Wasseraar. Open all year but not inexpensive and very large.
—*Ockenburg Campground:* Bus #26 from Centraal Station. Nice but expensive.

To See

—*Mauritshuis Museum:* 8 Korte Vijverweg. Closed for 5 years for restoration. Several Rembrandts.
—*Costumes Museum:* 14 Vijverweg.
—*Madurodam:* 175 Haringkade (Scheveningen). A miniature model of the most famous buildings in Holland. Illuminated in the evening. Open only in the summer. Accessible by tram #9 or bus #22.
—*Flea Market:* At Hobbemaplein. A little less interesting than Amsterdam's, but it's worth a glance anyway.

Dives

—*Paard van Troye:* 12-14 Prinsengracht. Trams #10 and #6. Not too hard to find in the center of the city. Excellent groups.
—*Haagse Jazz Club:* 32 Papestraat. An excellent jazz club. Speaking of which, on the second weekend in July, the famous North Sea Jazz Festival takes place in the city.

DELFT

Famous for its Delft blue ceramics. Also has other attractions, such as canals and small narrow streets in the style of Bruges or Amsterdam.
—*Student Houses Krakelhof Oudraadweg:* Jacoba van Beierenlaan. Telephone 015-135-953. Open from noon to 1 P.M. and 5 P.M. to 6 P.M. Student rooms rented to tourists during school vacations (from the end of May to the end of August). You can cook here. Showers. A 5-minute walk from the station. Security deposit required.

ZEELAND ISLANDS

A paradise of small villages and ports on islands joined by ferries or bridges that span several miles. Note: At holiday time heading south on the Breskens ferry there's a 1 hour wait on line after 3 P.M.!

Many beaches, surely, but brrrr! . . . From on top of the dikes you can see the sea a little higher than the polders. A small, particularly marvelous port is *Veere*. You can bring your own sailboat! There's a nautical club and everything. Also an interesting crafts boutique, but what prices . . . go to look.

KEUKENHOF GARDENS

In the middle of the tulip region, an enormous park full of all kinds of flowers, of all colors, where it's great to walk but crowded on holidays. Obviously, the prettiest time is still tulip season (April–May).

NORTHERN ISLANDS

Interesting as much for its ornithology as for the trip, with its sea birds in the dikes and lowlands. We strongly advise you to rent a bike here. The islands that we know are Texel and Schiermonnikoog (pronounced s-chimonikor).

You must go to Vlieland, a truly superb island. It has one small village, with one main street bordered by sweet Dutch houses. The remainder, 13 miles (20 km) long, is nothing but dunes, moors, and forests where you can pitch tent without being bothered by anyone. Rent a bike or a tandem in the village for three times nothing. To get there, take a train or hitchhike to Leeuwarden, then a train to Harlingen and, from there, the ferry (2½ hours).

GRONINGEN

—V.V.V.: Grote Markt.

Where to Sleep

—*Sleep-in:* Slaaphuis Druif, 2 Munnikeholm. Telephone 050-12-71-21. 100–200 beds. Situated in the center of town. Nice atmosphere. Open from 7 P.M. Jam-packed in September because students looking for apartments live here in the meantime.

FEDERAL REPUBLIC OF GERMANY

You will be struck by these Teutons, great fans of good beer, good cheer, and the good life. A country where people still know how to live well.

Useful Addresses in New York

—*Consulate General of the Federal Republic of Germany:* 460 Park Avenue, New York, NY 10022. Telephone (212) 940-9200.

—*West German Tourist Office:* 747 Third Avenue, New York, NY 10017. Telephone (212) 308-3300.

We advise you to take as many brochures as you can from home —hotel lists, city maps—because in Germany the tiniest sheet of paper costs.

U. S. Consulates in Germany

—5 Koeniginstrasse, 8000 Munchen 22 (Munich).
—170 Clayallee, 1000 Berlin 33.
—7 Urdanstrasse, 7000 Stuttgart.
—21 Siesmayer Strasse, 6000 Frankfurt.
—U.S. Embassy: 5300 Mehlemer Ave., Bonn 2.

Train

Ach! The Germans do things well, and their trains are among the most comfortable in Europe. Second-class cars have compartments for 6 people. All you have to do is to pull the seats facing each other to make a sleeper with built-in pillows.

The Inter-Rail trains, which have the insignia I.C., are direct trains for an additional fare of 5 DM. It's better to have a little extra change before taking one or risk hassles with the conductors. You will save about an hour and travel more comfortably.

On long runs, it's better to make reservations, even for one night, for the cars are full, corridors and toilets included. In fact, there are no more cars on a German train than in any other. Since the traffic on the main lines is greater than those of the rest of Europe and the cars hold fewer people—squeeze on, pals!

There is a monthly pass called *Tramper Monats Ticket* that costs about $90. These are sold on the Inter-City trains.

Hitchhiking

West Germany is an excellent country for hitchhiking. A tip for all hitchhikers: Hang an American flag on your backpack. Never hitchhike on the autobahn itself; drivers won't stop, and you risk a fine. If you are picked up, pretend you don't speak a word of German; when they see your American passport, the generally fun-loving cops will tell you to get lost. Truckers generally don't pick up, for if they're found with a hitchhiker, they can lose their license.

The highway is really great for hitching. You have to ask the driver to stop at the nearest rest stop or parking area, but absolutely not in the city. With a little luck you can easily do several hundred miles a day.

If you want to go quickly, don't leave the autobahn. At the very first service station, ask for a map of the highways with the rest stops and gas stations indicated. Always position yourself near service stations, at the side of highways or at the *"rastplatz"*—used frequently. You will find roadside restaurants, gas stations, and toilets well lit at night. Don't hesitate to ask people for a lift.

For hitching, a destination sign is strongly recommended. To write the letters for the target city: A for Augsburg, B for Berlin, BN for Bonn, D for Düsseldorf, DO for Dortmund, DU for Duisburg, E for Essen, F for Frankfurt, H for Hanover, HB-Hansastadt Bremen, HD-Heidelberg, HH for Hansastadt Hamburg, M-München (Munich), N-Nuremberg, R-Regensburg, S-Stuttgart . . .

Highway Network

The highways are free, and the network is very extensive. Something worth remembering: Gas stations are relatively rare on the highways—nearly every 30 miles (50 km).

We advise you to pay attention to the highway exits: For the cities, *mittel* means *middle* (often between north and south or east and west). *Ost*—East; *West*—West.

Otherwise, the highways were made to service only the biggest cities. There are sometimes fairly long stretches between two cities, so don't miss the exit!

Also pay attention to the highway intersections. There's one every 30 to 60 miles (50–100 km). It is to your advantage not to make a mistake; a map with all the highways is truly a necessity!

Museums

Don't forget your student card. It will get you into museums, galleries, castles at half price or free.

If you want to go by car, avoid parking in the museum parking lots, for a watchdog, armed with his book of tickets, will make you pay.

Carnivals

It's a general meeting of the population; the most famous are those of Mainz, Munich, and Cologne. Obviously, the dates change each year according to the religious holidays. For once in your life you must:

—dance like a fool all night while drinking beer with congenial Germans;

—eat bratwurst (grilled sausage), sometimes with vanilla ice cream, bought in a kiosk during the wee hours;

—go to get bratwurst, pretzels, candies, and so forth, issued by the village mayor's office.

The best is to do all this at once—and still other things, too. . . . and to have gone to a Swabian carnival.

We particularly know the one in Cologne, with its grand parades, floats, dancing in the evening at cafés, sausages, and beer. All the big cities in Germany have carnivals like these; the best known are in the center. There are others in France and, especially, Belgium.

The true German carnival still occurs in the southern part of the country, below the Stuttgart-Munich line, and gets in full swing on Swabian turf, near Bodensee (Lake Constance). In fact, during Lent it goes down toward Bodensee and ends in Switzerland. In the small Swabian villages, everyone participates. The children are costumed, and wear masks, mostly carved from a block of wood. It's a very important event for these people, so many don't hesitate to spend $400–500 for a costume (the mask is very expensive).

Viewing the different displays, which are not limited to parades for tourists, you rediscover the true meaning of a carnival. To show that everyone can participate, even those habitually excluded from society, they start with the taking of power by the madmen *(Narrenrechtabholung)* at the town hall. The mayor wears a straw hat, and the madmen proclaim their governmental program (which reviews the public's discontent of the past year, in a satiric form). The municipal council really gets its square in the jaw, but you have to understand German. From this moment on, you can say anything to anybody since it's the reign of madness (this lasts about a week). Since they are masked, some villagers take the opportunity in the evening to settle their accounts with others—verbally, of course. The carnival is also the supreme social event where the whole village unleashes its rancor accumulated over the year, and since they are enjoying themselves and drinking a lot, it doesn't do any harm to take it in stride for one round.

The Swabian carnival has existed for more than 400 years—older than most of our readers. Formerly, it lasted until Easter and symbolized the victory of spring over winter. Today, the dates vary depending upon the cities; it lasts an average of one week in February or March and ends with the burning of a big wooden tower on the Swiss side of the Bodensee. The fire celebrates the beginning of spring.

Beer

Generalities

If you have the instincts (we don't doubt it), you'll find the cellars where the patrons have their favorite brands of beer just as others have their favorite brands of cigars. Some solitary figure will slowly sniff his beer before raising it to an invisible god and then toss it down the hatch. See for yourself. And as a guide, you should have a small dictionary to help you if you fall into these good little joints:

Hell—clear, therefore light ale.

Dunkel—dark, therefore brown.

Bock—stoneware jug (also called *krug*); we advise you to say *krug*. A *bock* is also a goat; an *alter bock* doesn't mean "a glass of old beer" but "an old goat"!

Flaschenbier—bottled beer.

Fassbier (or *Bier vom Fass*)—a keg of beer (on tap).

Bier anzapfen—to tap a keg. For those who are very thirsty as well as courageous.

A Little Advice from Someone Who Has Escaped

The alcohol content can be very high; therefore, be careful. On the average, 2 glasses of beer are stronger than a small carafe of wine and almost as much as a half bottle of wine. The average German drinks 150 liters (264 pints) of beer a year. Since many Germans don't drink, our advanced intelligence pushes us to calculate that those who do drink, drink well, which you can readily verify. Remember, a happy man does not drink alone and gladly buys a round. Keep an eye on the happy loners. . . .

Different Types of Beer

Those found everywhere include: *Helles Bier*, with variations, *Pils*, *Normales* (most often barley-based), and *Weize* (wheat-based). Note that *Malzbier* (malt-based) is basically kids' stuff.

Dunkles Bier, brown, is rarer. The designation *Pils* is replaced by *Bock* and *Doppelbock* (double bock, therefore thicker).

Regionally you will find *Kölner Bier*, *Dortmunder*, *Münchner*, and so forth, each with the name of the city that produces it.

The Bavarian and Swabian light ales are very much alike, but the

Bavarian browns are stronger than the Swabian ones. If you find *Andeckser Doppelbock,* don't deny yourself a taste; it's the ultimate. Even rarer, in the Augsburg region, look for *Kulmbach.* We don't know if we should mention this beer, for it could kill you or make you go mad, but we survived (go find out why). In short, you will never forget *Dunlen Walzen Doppelbock.* Those who have tried *Eisbock* or *Kulminater* can try . . . We won't say anything more.

Weizbier is a beer made with wheat and yeast. The yeast remains at the bottom of the bottle. For the few who like its rather special taste, you will quickly become fans. A little tip to make you look like a connoisseur: After pouring most of the bottle into a glass, shake the rest, roll the bottle on the table, and then shake again. The yeast will separate from the glass and you can pour the rest. The taste is extraordinary, and people will think you're a real Bavarian. Don't forget that every smooth talker (or almost everyone) has his own preference and that the beer that is best is the one being drunk where it is brewed.

Bistros

We drink beer in cellars *(Bierkeller)* or in bistros (the real ones where you drink only beer called *Bierstube*—are more and more rare, alas!). They sometimes serve it in tearooms. Between 3 and 5 in the afternoon you can see many German women sitting over a glass brimming with foam, playing cards or recounting the latest neighborhood gossip. Their femininity sometimes pushes them to sport a coquettish little feather on their felt hats. From fifteen yards you could take them for hunters without guns.

Note: Before reaching this state, German women pass through a state of being delightful young girls. You might say that the same goes for German men.

Money Exchange

Banks are closed on Wednesday afternoons. To change money, avoid Sparkasse. It is better to go to *Deutsche Bank;* it's less of a rip-off.

Mensa

Each university has its own student co-op; you should know where the universities are located in each city, and then go to the nearest for its *Gasthaus* (restaurant). The international student card is sufficient in most cases. If not, find a sympathetic German who will pass you one of his duplicate student cards. There's no photo, so it works.

Note: Verify this information for areas other than Bavaria, Baden-Würtemburg, and Schwarzwald (the Black Forest). The Germans have varying rules according to the area, notably for the universities. Although we thought it was valid for the whole territory, we actually were unable to make a tour of all the university mess halls in the country!

To pay, first you take tokens or tickets, usually from an automatic machine. Then you join a short line. You can eat some very decent meals (minimum quality assured) in a nice enough setting. In addition to the good Mensa, which is respectable enough, there is a moderately priced cafeteria where you can get dessert (big slices of pie with whipped cream on top), coffee, and so forth.

Other Suggestions from the Same Barrel (of Beer)

Buy your food in grocery stores or butcher shops. (Those who think Germans don't know how to cook pork win a trip to a Muslim country. Cafeterias of large department stores are highly recommended; we discuss them in the following pages. Go there, but certainly not to have coffee! For that, go to the pizzerias where they really know what it is. However, if you prefer warm cat pee . . .

—We strongly advise against the panoramic restaurants, not because the view is ugly but because the bill is ugly and steep.

—What costs the least in Germany is eating and drinking American. Oh, yea!

Youth Hostels

You can obtain a list of youth hostels in the Tourist Offices as well as at *Deutsches Jugendherbergswerk*.

You must have a sleeping sack (not a sleeping bag, but sheets sewn into a sack) or have to pay a charge of 3 DM per sheet.

Work in Germany

—*Zentralstelle Für Arbeitsvermittlung:* 6000 Frankfurt am Main, 42 Feuerbachstrasse. This organization sends work requests to the German employers, for temporary (minimum of 2 months in the summer for youth) as well as long-term work. A female over 18 might consider work as an "au pair girl."

—*Zentralstelle Für Arbeitvermittlung* (Hotel und Gasttätengewerbe): 600 Frankfurt am Main, 2 Banhofstrasse. For those who would like to work in hotels.

It is also possible to write directly to employment agencies in large cities; in this case, the address is as follows: *An das Arbeitsamt* —followed by the name of the city.

We recommended that you converse in German to make a favorable impression. When writing, correct mistakes with the assistance of the high school's German teacher or your little brother or sister.

German Vocabulary

yes	*ja*
no	*nein*
today	*Heute*
tomorrow	*Morgen*
where?	*wo?*
how much? / how many?	*wieviel?*
to the right	*rechts*
to the left	*links*
enough	*genug*
too expensive	*zu teuer*
what time is it?	*wieviel Uhr ist es?*

good day	*guten Morgen*
good afternoon	*guten Tag*
good evening	*guten Abend*
how are you?	*wie geht's?*
goodbye	*auf Wiedersehen* or *servous*
please	*bitte*
I don't understand	*ich verstehe nicht*
tourist office	*Turistburo*
station	*Bahnhof*
post office	*Post*
police	*Polizei*
bank	*Bank*
youth hostel	*Jugendherberge*
hotel	*Hotel*
restaurant	*Gasthof*
to drink	*trinken*
to eat	*essen*
to sleep	*schlafen*
water	*Wasser*
coffee with milk	*Kaffee mit Sahne* or *mit Rahn*
beer	*Bier*
milk	*Milch*
bread	*Brot*
roll	*Brotchen*
cold	*kalt*
hot	*warm*
good	*gut*
bad	*schlecht*
toilet	*Toilette*
one	*eins*
two	*zwei*
three	*drei*
four	*vier*
five	*fünf*
six	*sechs*
seven	*sieben*
eight	*acht*
nine	*neun*
ten	*zehn*
twenty	*zwanzig*
thirty	*dreissig*
forty	*vierzig*
fifty	*fünfzig*
sixty	*sechzig*
seventy	*siebzig*
eighty	*achtzig*
ninety	*neunzig*
hundred	*hundert*
thousand	*tausend*

MUNICH
Useful Addresses

—*Tourist Office:* Fremdenverkehrsamt. Located in the same building as the Central Station, on the left facing the main entrance. Note: Information is free, but you must pay for all printed matter.

—*Mitfahr Gmbh:* Fina Parkhaus, 4 Lammerstrasse. Behind the Central Station. Telephone 59-45-61. Hitchhiking organization located a few minutes' walk from the Central Station. Good for the hitchhikers as well as the drivers. In fact, for hitching, the fee is two times less than the train. Everybody wins. In any event, it's good to enroll 3 or 4 days in advance. Closed Saturday afternoon and Sunday.

—*Post Office* (where letters can be left until called for—*Poste Restante*): 7 Bahnhofplatz (near the station).

—*American Express:* 1 Admiraplatz (3 Promenadenplatz).

—*Police Emergency:* Telephone 22-26-66.

Station (Bahnhof)

Right in the middle of the city. An exchange office is open there every day from 6 A.M. to 11:30 P.M. If your traveler's checks are in marks, change them at the station; they don't take a commission, but make it up on other currencies. You can buy foreign newspapers and possibly even reserve them. The station's cafeteria is reasonably cheap.

Upon arriving at the station in Munich (*Hauptbahnhof*) at night, you can take train #21 on Dachaver Strasse to Botanischer Garten, a youth hostel (Kapuzinerholtz), where you can sleep (see below).

Transportation

Public transportation (bus and subway—*U-Bahn*) is very expensive. You should buy a 24-hour student ticket that costs a few marks and allows you to use public transportation for 24 hours. If not, there's a book of 8 tickets that isn't too expensive either. It's good to know that at the back of the bus there are ticket sellers. Stations are announced over the microphone. Subway: Directions are well marked.

Where to Sleep

—*St. Paul's Kolleg:* 18 Paul-Heyse-Strasse. For male students only.

—*Haus International* (International Hotel for Youth): 87 Elisabethstrasse. Telephone 18-50-81. 420 beds. Really good but a little expensive. You can use the pool in the hotel.

—*Pension Isaria:* 95 Bayerstrasse. 500 yards from the station. Single rooms with breakfast for 35 DM. Right next to *Jederman Hotel*. 44 DM with a very full breakfast.

• *Youth Hostels (Jugendherberge)*

We must point out that they're often jammed in the summer.

20 Wendl-Dietrichstrasse. Telephone 13-11-56. 576 beds. Not far from the station. Take tram #4 or #21. Hostel card is required.

8023 Pullach, Brug Schwaneck. Telephone 7-93-23-81. 122 beds. Far from the center, but it's really worth the trip. Take S-Bahn 7 at the Central Station for ½ hour. The youth hostel is in a charming little village and occupies a castle. The atmosphere is friendly and the management is terrific. Lounge and rooms with 4 beds. You can eat here. It doesn't open until 5 P.M. Telephone ahead since it's often full.

Wohnheim des Bayrischen: 8 Lehrerverbands. 68 Cimberstrasse. Telephone 74-66-12. 40 beds. No restaurant, but you can cook.

One of the cheapest places in Munich: Jugendlader am Kapuzinerhöhzl. Telephone 14-14-300. Tram #21 across from the Central Station. Stop at Botanischer Garten. Go 200 yards and take Franz Schrank street, then a left. They furnish blankets and a sheet free of charge. Open from 5 P.M. to 9 A.M. Free tea, a canteen, toilets, and pop music. You sleep in a very big tent, a great atmosphere. Alas! You can't stay more than three days in a row.

• *Campgrounds*

München-Tchalkirchen: 39 Zentrallandstrasse. Telephone 73-17-07. 2½ miles (4 km) from the center, near the Hellabrunn zoo. To get there: subway (U-Bahn), then bus #57. Good, even if the airport isn't far away. Noisy, though.

München-Obermenzing.

Otherwise, you can always settle for *pensions* which abound in Munich. There are often apartments occupying 1 or 2 floors of a building.

Where to Eat

—*Mathäser Bierstadt:* 7 Bayerstrasse. A very cheap self-service eatery with Bavarian decor. Chickens, french fries, sausages, and beer. A few minutes' walk from the station. A bar. Excellent beer with slices of horseradish.

—*Two Indonesian restaurants* offer "student" menus at a very good price:
- *Euro-Asia:* 76 Schleissheimerstrasse (at the corner of Hesstrasse).
- *Java:* At the corner of Schwindstrasse and Schleissheimerstrasse.

—*Augustiner Grossgaststätten:* 16 Neuhauser Strasse. Not very expensive (the most reasonable dish is soup with bread). Particularly interesting for its typically Bavarian decor and ambiance. Watch out; the restaurant has 2 rooms; the one on the right is more expensive than the one on the left.

—*Olympia Gastätte:* 29 Kellerstrasse (corner of Steinstrasse). A small Greek restaurant that we discovered by chance. Very good and not expensive. There's no menu; the customers go to the kitchen themselves to choose their food. One minor inconvenience: it's a little far from the center of town.

—*Mövenpick:* Künstlerhaus, 8 Lenbachplatz. Here are 5 restaurants inside this former theater. Each restaurant has its specialities and style. The decor is simply wonderful. Must be seen (particularly the Venetian restaurant). The prices are not exactly meant for hitchhikers, but from time to time a small exception is a sterling idea. On the first floor, in the rustic restaurant, there is a buffet (you serve yourself at your pleasure).

—*Cafeterias* in department stores (Kaufhof, Hertie, et cetera) near the station. Very reasonable prices.

—*Isabella Hof:* At the corner of Isabella and Neurentherstrasse (across from the art cinema where they often show old foreign classics—not dubbed). A Yugoslavian restaurant where they serve dinner until midnight. Friendly atmosphere and young clientele. Best deal for a restaurant in Munich. Plentiful, but mediocre quality. Bus #12.

—*Haider's Pizza:* Siegesstrasse. Best pizza in Munich.

—*Windmühle:* 21 Johannisplatz. You'll eat well and "healthy."

—*University restaurant on Leopoldstrasse.* Subway: Giselastrasse. Open only for lunch in August. Worthwhile when you know the price of food in Germany; Or go to the one at 17 Arlisstrache, which is open from 11 A.M. to 2 P.M. Monday through Friday. Practical when you visit the old and new movie houses, a few steps away.

—*Café Holz:* Dachaustrasse. Expensive and delicious pastries and chocolates.

—*Venezia Eis:* Near the Wendl-Dietrichstrasse youth hostel. Famous for its ice cream.

—Almost everywhere in the city you'll find a McDonalds.

—*The Best . . .*

Coffee: *Tabu*, 37 Leopoldstrasse.

Ice Cream: *Ranft*, on Baldeplatz.

Beer: *Hofbrauhaus,* 9 Platzl. Unfortunately many tourists. But spend an evening in this colossal pub. They'll serve you a pint, half liter, or liter of H. B. beer (excellent!). Bavarian orchestra at night (when the musicians arrive to play, which isn't always the case). Note: Only the ground floor is truly interesting. Upstairs the atmosphere is more selective, and it's a shame.

Das Haus der 111 Biere: 3 Frantzstrasse. Not inexpensive, but the setting is nice. Subway: Münchner Freiheit.

Schneide Weisbeer: Near Marienplatz. Here you drink *Aventinus.* Watch out for this brew—It's really very strong. But it's so good.

For shopping, go to *Viktualienmarkt,* a fruit and vegetable market. The atmosphere is very lively. The women who hawk their produce are very amusing.

To See

—*Schwabing:* This area is to Munich what Greenwich Village is to New York. Located around Leopoldstrasse, which is a continuation of Ludwigstrasse. Very lively at night: discothèques, shops, nice restaurants (not cheap). The center of this section is *Wedekindplatz,* a charming square with a drugstore (1920s style). Next to the drugstore is *Papillon,* a bar and billiard parlor.

—*Neuhauser Strasse:* A street reserved for pedestrians in the heart of Munich. It starts at Karlsplatz and ends at the town hall square. Many department stores. At the slightest trace of sun, everybody sits on the terraces of the bars. Every day at 11 A.M., 5 P.M. and 9 P.M., on the town hall clock, figures turn at the chiming of the bells. (After a survey we decided that hip travelers don't give a damn; neither do we).

Don't miss a stroll in the evening on the pedestrian streets (closed to traffic) near the station. There's music everywhere, not only free concerts but also Americans playing guitars on porches and singing folk and pop songs.

—*Leopoldstrasse:* The Champs-Élysées of Munich. Restaurants and fashionable cafés. Artists sell their canvases on summer evenings near the intersection of Mariusstrasse. Generally their work is poor. The atmosphere is otherwise enjoyable.

—*Bavaria:* A gigantic statue that dominates Messegelände Park. A small staircase leads to the head of the statue. Student discount. A pretty view of the city. For connoisseurs of fantastic sensations, the statue trembles in the wind.

—*Beer Festival:* A great festival that brings together thousands of connoisseurs and the curious during the last week of September and the first week of October. Huge banners are decorated with the major beer labels in Messegelände Park. The Germans know how to drink, but they also know how to have a good time. It is strongly advised to use public transportation to this festival of beer. Tram #2 or #9 from Hauptbahnhof.

—*Nymphenburg Castle:* Take tram #21 (near the Central Station). Located west of the city, the castle is not terrific. Take a general admission (50 percent discount for students), and don't miss the museum of carriages. But the visit becomes truly interesting when you get inside the park. You must visit the botanical garden, one of the most beautiful in the world (we are not exaggerating). One greenhouse is filled with orchids; another contains all sorts of carnivorous plants. Then get a drink at the garden's cafeteria (and not at Palmenhaus). Avoid ordering tea or coffee, which are much more expensive than Coca-Cola, for example.

—*Asamkirche:* 63 Sendlingerstrasse. We don't mention this church just because the priest is a pal of ours but because the kitschy and rococo styles can't be beat. A true triple-layer cream cake. And the stonemason must have improvised, for the 2 styles combat each other head-on on the facade. But you ain't seen nothing yet: Look at the interior. We'll tell you only that!

—*Olympia Park:* A prestigious accomplishment due to the Olympic games. Those intrigued by original architecture will be blown away. Even more, it works. The pool is open to the public. From the top of the tower a beautiful panorama of the city and its environs. To get there, U-Bahn, line 3.

Museums

Most of the museums are open from 9 A.M. to 4 P.M. without interruption. Free admission for those who have an international student card, but you must leave coats and bags in the checkroom (which is not free).

—*Alte Pinakothek:* 27 Barer Strasse. Among the greatest and richest museums in the world. Chiefly collections of the great painters of the fifteenth to eighteenth centuries: Rembrandt, Rubens, El Greco, Velasquez, Giotto, Titian, and so forth. Closed Monday. Free on Sunday, but you should avoid eating in the cafeteria—the prices are doubled. Tram #15 or #25.

—*Staatsgalerie Moderner Kunst:* Prinzregentenstrasse. This gallery of modern art has masterpieces by Dali, Picasso, Klee, and Warhol.

—*Glyptothek:* On Königsplatz. For those who appreciate ancient objects and sculptures. Interesting in this museum is Louis II of Bavaria's collection of Greek and Roman vases. On the lower level, one room is devoted entirely to Etruscan gold jewelry.

—*B.M.W. Museum:* Near Olympia Park. This museum is in the shape of a gigantic champagne glass. All the cars and motorcycles of this famous German manufacturer are exhibited. Free admission. You can also visit the factory Monday through Friday. Tours begin at 9 A.M. and 2 P.M., and last 2 hours. Closed in July.

—*Deutsches Museum:* Ludwigsbrücke. Museum of natural sciences and technology, which will interest hip travelers and others. Boats, cars, musical instruments, and a great planetarium. They have all the modern technologies: electrical, mechanical . . . Superb.

—*Residenzmuseum:* 3 Schatzkarmer, Max-Joseph-Platz. Houses about 1,000 pieces of jewelry and insignias from the Carolingian to the Empire periods. Doubtlessly requires a very deep interest.

Discothèques and Jazz Clubs

For discothèques, you must be hip to the German system: the bar-café-pub is located on street level, while the club is generally located on the lower level. You get in by a stairway that is often difficult to find. But once you get in, they'll ask for your membership card . . . which, of course, you don't have! And these clubs are usually the best. *Crazy Alin* is one of the best for rock fans.

Discothèque lovers won't have any trouble finding happiness in the Schwabing. They are all over. On the other hand, good jazz clubs are more difficult to find. We suggest these few:

—*Allotria:* 33 Türkenstrasse. Certainly Munich's best Dixieland jazz club. The atmosphere is almost as good as in Preservation Hall in New Orleans. Come early enough if you want to take advantage of a small part of a chair. They serve good *Spaten* beer (one of the best German beers).

—*Domicile:* 19 Leopoldstrasse. Telephone 39-94-51. One of the best jazz clubs in Munich. Closed Sunday. Subway: Giselastrasse.

—*Memoland:* 19 Siegestrasse. In the heart of Schwabing. Live Dixieland.

—*La Cumbia:* 2 Taubenstrasse. Live South American music. Well known among local aficionados.

—*Drehlier:* 23 Balanstrasse. International folk music. On Mondays, amateurs join forces and try their luck.

—*Pop Club:* 51 Lilienstrasse. "Beat" music Wednesday and Saturday (typically German, it includes a little of everything, from the Beatles on). Rock 'n' roll Friday and Sunday. Rock, with an emphasis on hard rock, on Thursdays.

—*Disco-Land:* 6 Rosenstrasse. Not a bad club (though expensive) where you can easily cut a rug (so to speak).

—*Der Albe Burg:* On Bismarkstrasse. The exterior is worth a look.

—*La Tomate:* Werneck-Strasse. Nice and okay music.

—*Gaststätte Weinbauer* (Braverei Wifling): Corner of Fednstrasse and Knollerstrasse. It's good and not expensive.

—*Schwabinger Podium:* Corner of Siegestrasse and Wagnerstrasse. Super jazz band. The atmosphere is very N'Awlins!

To Leave Munich by Hitching

—*For Stuttgart and Frankfurt:* Tram #21 to Amalienburgstrasse, then bus #75 or #73 to Blutenburg (highway). Another way: take S-Bahn (a subway that goes to the station) to Pasing, then bus #73 or #76. Get off at the seventh stop, the beginning of the highway.

—*For Nuremberg and Berlin:* Bus #33 or #133 to Münchner-Freiheit, then U-6 to Nordfriedhof.

—*For Lindau via Landsberg:* Bus #33 to Basketballhalle.

—*For Salzburg and Vienna:* From the station take subway U-I or U-8 toward Neuperlach Sud. Get off at Karl-Preis-Platz. The beginning of the highway is 500 yards to the south.

HAMBURG

When it comes to the Reeperbahn, You won't see anything to write home about, especially in Hamburg where it rains so often that these "working girls" get all wet. It's a little sad. Hamburg is a large city (the biggest in Germany, besides Berlin), all modern (it had been bombed), but it's no longer so earth-shattering, we must say.

Useful Addresses

—*Tourist Information:* Bieberhaus, on Hachmannplatz, near the Central Station *(Hauptbahnhof)*. Open during the week from 7:30 A.M. to 6:00 P.M., Saturday from 7:30 A.M. to 1 P.M. Closed Sunday. They are very nice, knowledgeable. Avoid information desks for hotels *(Hotelnachweis)* in the station itself: these old biddies are unbearable; they have the audacity to ask you to pay for the brochures they distribute free at the Tourist Information.

—*Poste Restante* (where letters may be left until called for): In the Central Station, near Kirchen Strasse.

—*Mitfahrer Zentrale:* In Markthof, 4 Amsinckstratt. Open Monday to Friday from 8 A.M. to 7 P.M. Telephone 040-23-07-87. An organization that puts hitchhikers and drivers together. It is 500 yards south of the Central Station.

—*American Express:* 16 Bergstrasse (corner of Hermannstrasse).

Where to Sleep

• Youth Hostels

—*Auf dem Stinglang:* 5 Alfred Wegener Weg, HH 11. Telephone 31-34-88. 330 beds. Card required. Well located (right near St. Pauli —the dogs!). To get there, S-Bahn or U-Bahn to Landungsbrucken station. The breakfast is included but not very filling. The hostel's rules will shock the free-wheeling traveler. Closes at 1 A.M.

—*Horner Rennbahn:* 100 Rennbahnstrasse, HH 74. Telephone 651-16-71. 286 beds. Card required. Fairly far from the center of the city. To get there: U-Bahn to Horner Rennbahn station.

• Campgrounds

These sites are all grouped in the same area (that's practical). To get there, take S-Bahn #2 to E Delstedt station.

—*Campingplatz Buchohlz:* 374 Kielerstrasse. Telephone 540-45-

32. It's possible to rent campers here for up to 5 people. A good deal if you're 3 or more.

—*Camping Brüning:* 86 Kronspalsweg (Kielerstrasse). Telephone 54-55-36. The biggest of them all.

—*Ramckesplatz:* 620 Kielerstrasse. Telephone 570-94-19.

—*Camping Anders:* 650 Kielerstrasse. Telephone 570-44-98. The smallest of the 4.

• *Hotels*

They are obviously not affordable for budget travelers. We've hunted for the least expensive, but it's far from being a bargain:

—*Hotel Franck:* 76 Lange Reihe. Telephone 24-32-71. It's tiny.

Where to Eat

Throughout the city you find *Imbiss,* a type of cheap snack bar. You'll taste their famous hamburgers (ah yes, they come from there! At least we think so).

—*Skyline Turn:* Restaurant in the television tower. For one hour (3:30 to 4:30 P.M. and 4:45 to 5:45 P.M.) you can eat as many cakes and drink as much as you want. Don't throw yourself gluttonously upon these excellent pastries, for you'll be full in half an hour. That would be a shame. All for a few marks! We're hoping they won't abandon their brilliant idea.

—*Blave Blume:* Not far from Bahnhof Altona. They serve enormous salads amid very pleasant surroundings. In the summer, you can eat outside in the garden—and inexpensively.

—*HL MARKT:* A fairly priced supermarket in Barmeisterstrasse.

—*University cafeteria,* but it's not too good and not filling. To get there, S-Bahn to Dammtor station. The university is located on Edmund Siemers Strasse.

—The cheapest restaurants are the Chinese near the Reeperbahn.

—Many inexpensive restaurants (not great, though) on Reeperbahnstrasse. In certain pizzerias, good food and really not expensive if you stay at the counter.

—Hunger: After the stores close and on the weekends, who doesn't die of hunger? The readers of this guide know that you can hit the food machines at #45 Grindelberg, as well as Stresemannstrasse at the corner of Eifflerstrasse. And, obviously, at the station.

How to Get Around

There are 2 systems in Hamburg: A subway called U-Bahn (3 lines) and suburban trains that go through the center called S-Bahn (6 lines). A small reminder: *Bahn* means train. The Tourist Office gives out maps of the system.

There are also city buses. A funny aside: The central bus station near the train station has a strange sign: ZOB (slang for male sex in French) in enormous red neon letters. This is a guaranteed photo gag and a free 15 minutes of laughing.

It's in your interest to buy a tourist ticket, valid one day (from 9 A.M. to 4:30 P.M. the following day). It's not very expensive and allows you as many trips as you want on subway, bus, and boat on the Alster. This ticket is also available for several days, at a slightly higher price. Available at Tourist Information.

To See

—*Reeperbahnstrasse* (U-Bahn to St. Pauli): Obviously. It's the great spectacle of Hamburg. Among others, an Eros Center is at #170. Here is what the very official *Hamburg Guide* says of this hall of mirrors; "All these striptease and sex shows are money traps. . . . In the Eros Center, one rarely gets what one wants for the price settled on at the entrance. If you want to meet with a girl at St. Pauli, be careful—not all are "for sale," and you might not be able to afford those who are."

Just the same, these Germans are very honest. The sex shows on Grosse Freiheit, a small street leading to the Reeperbahn, are more decent. Have a good time checking this out.

The prostitutes in the windows are near Herbertstrasse. The corner is closed off to prevent minors from partaking prematurely. (When the time comes . . .)

—*Grossneumarkt* (S-Bahn to Stadthausbrücke): In the heart of things. A corner where you can drink and eat. Many young people meet here to play music. Good atmosphere.

—*Hamburger Kunsthalle:* 1 Glockengiesserwall. Right near the station. The principal museum of the city. Free on Wednesday. Closed Monday. Hours: 10 A.M. to 5 P.M.

—*Alster:* Leisurely Sunday cruises on the lake. Depart every half hour from Jungfernstieg (U-Bahn and S-Bahn with the same name). Considering the climate of Hamburg, it's really a first-class rip-off.

—*St. Jacob Church:* Steinstrasse (U-Bahn to Mückebergstrasse). This Catholic church was almost razed during the war. What you see dates from 1960. It houses a famous seventeenth century organ signed by Arp Schnitger. Bach played on it. Organists try to touch these celebrated register keys, shaped like human heads.

—*Opera* (Hamburische Staatsoper): 28 Dammtorstrasse (U-Bahn to Stephansplatz). One of the best in the world. Small hall for mini-operas, the *Opera Stabile.* Boldly modern repertoire. If you're a fan, try to attend a performance—it's worth it. There are also numerous concerts and many theaters. Schedules in *Hamburger Vorschau* monthly.

—Finally, there's the Salambo (formerly *Star Club*) for nostalgic rockers. On Grosse Freiheit. This is where the Beatles and Jerry Lee Lewis played memorable concerts.

Odds and Ends

—*Exhange office:* Open every day from 7:30 A.M. to 10 P.M. in the Central Station.

—*Swimming pool* (Alster Schwimmhalle): Sechslingspforte. U-Bahn to Lübeckstrasse. A fabulous, immense pool in the center, open from 6:30 A.M. to 9:30 P.M. Discounts on Tuesday. Warmer water on Friday (it's true—the temperature is raised to 82° F (21° C).

—You can get work at the fish market (U-Bahn to Braumwall) unloading boats. You must check into the local bars early in the morning. You will see what it's like to be an immigrant laborer.

—*Hamburg Führer:* Free magazine that lists shows and restaurants.

To Leave Hamburg by Hitching
—For those who are heading for Denmark, go in the direction of Lübeck-Putt garden. Take U-Bahn #3 and get off at Rauhes Haus. The beginning of highway E4 is here.

—If you want to go to Kiel and Oldenburg, take S-Bahn #21 and get off at Stellingen. There it is. Good luck!

SCANDINAVIA

The key words of the 4 countries that comprise Scandinavia are, as everyone knows, tolerance, porn, alcoholism, and model of economy and ecology. What we need to know is exactly where each of these takes place.

First, if you imagine that Scandinavia is a gigantic cat house, you risk being cruelly disappointed, especially if that's why you are going there. In Stockholm, for example, you will see very dignified old ladies wearing gray, bottle-green, and even red velvet hats (but these are certainly the eccentrics). It's these women who are the key to the mystery: careful about respectability, they are not any less tolerant. It's the same with the old men and many young people as well. To tolerate, which has never meant to liberate, has a certain condescending aspect: "Do what you want in your own corner, but we who have morals won't even think about it." Well, of course there are sex shops, but compared to other countries (no, we're not being chauvinistic), they may seem slightly old-fashioned because of their discretion.

Model of economy? Ask a Scandinavian what he thinks. If he doesn't snicker, it's because he's an immigrant worker or a political refugee. There are many of them. The Scandinavians now have aspirations other than material comforts. After poverty, which has practically disappeared, they are struggling to preserve their environment. A sign of the times.

But perhaps alcoholism, which ravages all four of these nations on set days—Friday and Saturday—is a response to a certain disenchantment. You won't have any trouble distinguishing these "dregs." They hit the streets at 10 sharp with their big American road hogs; the cops gather there as well, which creates joyous jams. A significant sign of the boredom of youth. And yet, in Scandinavia, they've got it good!

Climate

Impossible to predict: always variable and changes quickly. Temperature especially pleasant in the summer. The second half of June and the first half of July are the best times to sample the pleasures of the Scandinavian summer. The days are the longest, the weather is generally sunny, and nature is in full splendor. And it's never really cold at this time.

We don't want to worry you too much, but a raincoat is absolutely necessary. Perhaps you should borrow a folding umbrella. Very practical.

Where to Sleep

—*Denmark:* Wilderness camping is forbidden, but campgrounds are plentiful, well priced, and pleasant.

—*Sweden, Norway, Finland:* Go camping in the wilds! It's not space that is lacking. Official campgrounds are fairly expensive: The prices vary depending upon reputation, whether there's a sauna or not, lake fishing or not . . .

We strongly suggest camping for all of Scandinavia, given the price of hotels and even some youth hostels. In certain campgrounds, there are *hytters,* small wooden houses (2 or 4 beds) with electricity. Very cozy.

Avoid camping near lakes because of mosquitoes; it's better to go far from lakes, at least 500 yards. We don't want you to panic, but mosquitoes are the great specialty of these countries. Fortunately, they do sell mosquito repellent that effectively chases away the little buggers.

In summertime the nights are very short, and it's therefore very bright in a tent. A very useful accessory is a "slumber shade" (sometimes given out on airplanes).

Some campgrounds place small portable stoves at your disposal.

Especially in Sweden, Norway, and Finland, thanks to the vast stretches of land, you can find farms where you can ask the owner permission to sleep in his barn . . . There are always some near small cities.

Youth hostels are numerous. It is wise to telephone before arriving with your backpack at a youth hostel or other sleep-in, at least in the big cities. Avoid useless hardship. The youth hostel card is not always required, but without it you will pay a much higher price. We strongly advise you to buy this card at home (much more reasonable).

Youth hostels in Scandinavia are frequented by everybody, regardless of age. Some have rooms for families with children or for couples. If you do use them, you should remember that they usually close their doors from 10 P.M. to 4 A.M.. And you have to have a special sleep-sack. Sleeping bags are forbidden, and they are very strict about this.

Food

Very, very expensive in Scandinavia. If you are arriving by car, don't forget to carry the maximum of provisions, and combine them with fish that you can buy in the markets. It's the least expensive food, and there's a big choice. You'll find something called *Kaviarpaste,* a caviar pâté (it can't contain much, given the price) that has the taste of fish. Shrimp, cheese, and other pâtés are also available.

Milk products are sold in liter cartons. Check the date of freshness if you don't want curdled yogurt in your coffee. In Scandinavia, we strongly advise you to carry along some cooking utensils. And considering the cost of food, it's wise to bring some packaged soups, spaghetti, canned food . . .

It is sometimes difficult to find camping-gas (large refills) in Norway, Sweden, and Finland.

In some restaurants they serve wine and alcohol, in some only beer, and then in others alcoholic beverages are forbidden! *Skol,* globetrotters! Speaking of which, do you know the origin of the word *skol?* It's simple: They drank out of skulls held with both hands while looking into the other person's eyes. (*Skol* comes from the old German word that means "To see and partake," and not "skull" at all.) And yet one more legend bites the dust!

They dine early in Scandinavia. Dinner is around 7 P.M. This is good to know, particularly in small cities, unless you like to fast. To make up for it, though, you find supermarkets everywhere, they sell a little of everything, especially a variety of frozen dishes.

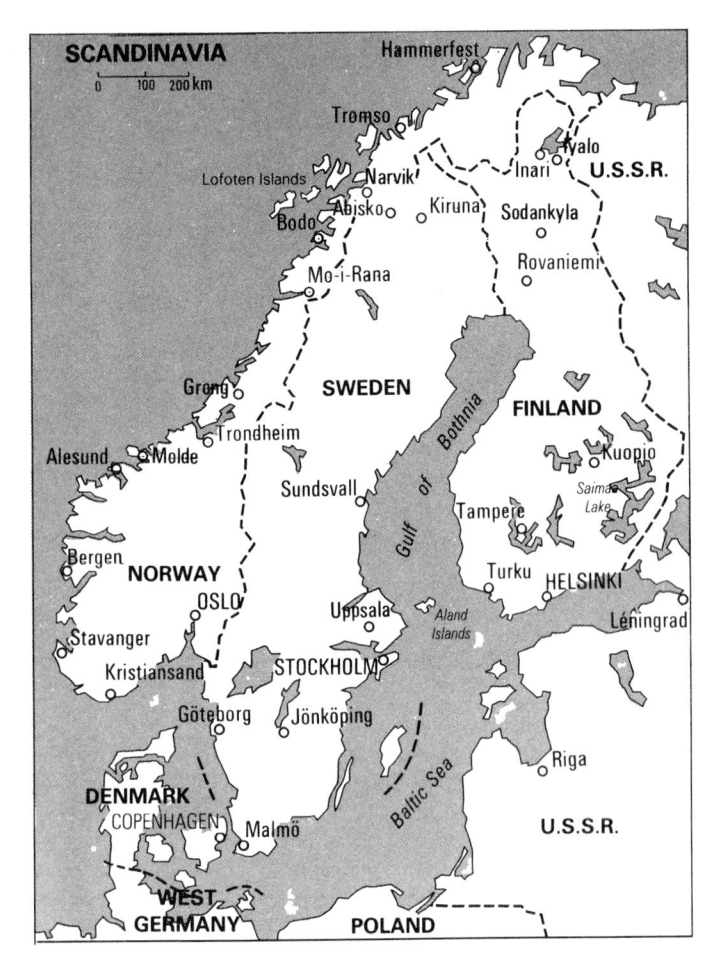

The *smörgasbord,* or cold Scandinavian buffet, is a royal treat for the eyes as well as the palate. You serve yourself and eat dishes in a traditional order: first fish and cold meats, then hot dishes. Everything is washed down with beer or mineral water.

You must taste the salmon *(lax)* (the best being *gravlax*), herring *(sills),* shrimp *(rakor),* smoked eels *(al),* and cold meat—especially dried reindeer. In restaurants, these dishes are sometimes served with potatoes or huckleberries.

Languages

English is often spoken, especially by the young—and with such facility that they will succeed in giving you a complex. You can always tell Mom and Dad that your trip to Scandinavia is to perfect your English. It's true. Hot dog vendors in the street speak with Oxford accents. German is also heard (the second language in schools).

Bits of Advice

—Amateur photographers will be pleased. Fans of black-and-white photography should nevertheless bring some color film if they don't want to regret it for the rest of their lives.

—Don't stay too long in the cities, which aren't of great interest, but instead inhale deeply the oxygen of nature and rediscover wilderness camping.

—Nicotine addicts should bring their own cigarettes because the tobacco prices are exorbitant. It's almost cheaper to smoke paper money. You'll notice that most young people roll their own cigarettes; this isn't snobbism, it's simply because it's half the price. Carry your own rolling papers (even that's expensive).

By Car

—In the north, always drive with your headlights on. You'll find out for yourself that when you have the sun in your eyes, you can't see anything but the headlights of the oncoming car. It's the law in Sweden.

—Be careful of the roads. If you're lucky enough to be on a blacktop road, watch out anyhow: Potholes are frequent enough in the Great North, and it would be a shame to break down a hundred miles from the nearest service station.

—Pay attention to your gas gauge! Distances are vast and gas pumps rare. Garages with attendants are closed on Sundays, but there are self-service pumps that work with 10 Kr notes. Keep your eyes open. The price of gas varies from one station to another, but there are large price signs.

—Drink or drive—you must choose (hic!). The alcohol test is rigorously enforced here. Even with a rate of alcohol of 0.5 grams per liter, you are still liable for prosecution. To cut your thirst: The minimum penalty is 3 weeks in prison plus a year's suspension of your license plus a 2,000 Kr fine. *Skol!*

—Buckle your seat belts. It's the law, and the ticket must be paid in cash.

By Train

There is a tourist train ticket *(Nordturist)* that allows you to ride with no distance limitation for 21 days on all the lines of Denmark, Sweden, Norway, and Finland. It costs $240 for first class, and $140 for second class. The same ticket can be bought for one month. This ticket gives a 50 percent discount on some shipping lines between Denmark and Sweden. You can get this discount through Crown Line Tours, 545 Fifth Avenue (Suite 408), New York, NY 10017, telephone (212) 883-0274 (only if you fly Scandinavian Airways).

There is also a special ticket, *Midtuke,* valid for 7 days as long as you don't travel on Friday.

Swimming

Truly, we warn you for your own good. Refreshing and everything —but the river basins are affected by sea currents, so you must respect two conditions: Don't stay out longer than 5 or 10 minutes and don't swim even two or three strokes where you can't stand. It can be anguishing to feel your muscles suddenly cramp.

The Sauna

Of Finnish origin, there are different types of saunas. In the cities there are hotel and motel saunas, public saunas, saunas in apartment buildings, private saunas, or those in clubs. In the countryside, farms and resorts have their saunas near the water. They are often found on campgrounds and even in youth hostels.

The idea of a sauna is to increase blood circulation by alternating between hot and cold. At first, heat from 175° to 215° F (80° to 100° C), until you perspire; water thrown on the hot rocks increases the heat. To cool off quickly, you dive into a lake or the sea, or take a cold shower. The sauna is always built of wood with steps at different levels. A stove of high quality is essential. The circulation of air and degree of humidity must be carefully regulated. A sauna that is too hot or too dry should be avoided. A sauna bath is not an endurance contest but an excellent means of relaxation.

Useful Addresses in New York

—SAS: 638 Fifth Ave., New York, NY 10020. Telephone (212) 657-7700

—Air France: 666 Fifth Ave., New York, NY 10103. Telephone (212) 841-7301

—Sabena: 16 West 49th St., New York, NY 10017. Telephone (212) 961-6200

—Swissair: 608 Fifth Ave., New York, NY 10020. Telephone (212) 990-4500

Entry Formalities

None in particular. Don't forget your passport and, if you are driving into Scandinavia, your international driver's permit, along with the right papers for the vehicle. Otherwise, your troubles will start at the border.

Distances Between Some Cities

Rødby–Copenhagen	92 miles (147 km)
Malmö–Göteberg	179 miles (287 km)
Malmö–Stockholm (route E4)	393 miles (629 km)
Stockholm–Kiruna	833 miles (1,333 km)
Göteborg–Oslo	204 miles (326 km)
Stockholm–Karlstad–Oslo	346 miles (554 km)

DENMARK

So tender and smiling a country, so calm and tolerant, how can one think of such a revolution in the modes of life? Denmark is savored with the bouquet of old Europe, a province between Great Britain and Switzerland, a country where cleanliness is customary and the foliage is domesticated. Still the country of Andersen, melancholic moralists, of elves and trolls who populate dreams and chase the blues away. Copenhagen, with its round-cheeked, healthy girls, the tranquil smiles on its inhabitants, the coziness of its houses, and the red frock coats of the mailmen, has its idyllic allures, like cities in operettas. Everything seems too sure, too perfect. That is the question.
—Pascal Dupont

The Country

Denmark, the smallest of the Scandinavian countries, is composed of several islands, of which the most important are:

—Fyn, specially known for Odense (birthplace of Hans Christian Andersen).

—Zealand, with Copenhagen.

—Lolland, Falster, Møn . . . and a large peninsula, Jutland.

It's also the country that voyagers in a hurry (the ecologically minded going up to Norway or backpackers fantasizing about Sweden) sometimes cross too rapidly. Assuredly, they're mistaken. Denmark hides its own ecological marvels, and its guys and girls are the liveliest and warmest in Scandinavia. Take time to discover this country which, if it doesn't offer great natural curiosities, proffers thousands of others, more discreet, around each bend, in each city. Rent a bike; hundreds of miles of bike routes facilitate discovering this land, the rhythm of Danish nature, so sweet, so enervating.

The Great Danes

Denmark is one of the most egalitarian nations in Europe, with the best social laws (even through the rich still exist, of course). Repression in any form is rare. Many prisons don't have bars, and conjugal visitation is allowed. The presence of police in the street is almost nonexistent, and youth really reigns. The Danes are very modest and often refuse to show any exterior sign of wealth. Does this all mean that everything is hunky-dory (like social democracy)? No, of course not. Tolerance and the refusal to make distinctions can lead to a certain uniformity of customs and behavior, resulting in a discreet boredom. The providential nature of the state risks anesthetizing all desire to struggle. Instead of eliminating capitalism, the Danes have rendered it livable and as little oppressive as possible. All the better for them!

Useful Addresses in New York

—*Danish Consulate General:* 280 Park Ave., New York, NY 10017. Telephone (212) 697–5101.

—*Danish National Tourist Office:* 75 Rockefeller Plaza, New York, NY 10019. Telephone (212) 582–2802.

Where to Sleep

—*Youth Hostels:* It's less expensive to buy a card in the U.S. If that's not possible, you can buy it at: Herbergs-Ringen, 35 Vesterbrogade, 1260 Copenhagen.

—*Sleep-in:* They furnish only mattresses on the floor, except at *Titan*. Good atmosphere in general, but watch out for your belongings . . .

—*A great many campgrounds:* Often very well arranged. Danish or international card required. It is possible to obtain a temporary card at the first official campground visited. This card costs 17 Kr (which adds to the cost if you stay only a short time in Denmark).

—Sleeping under the beautiful stars is also possible. But sometimes you can be chased away, for camping in nonspecified areas is forbidden.

—How about exchanging your house or apartment for the equivalent in Denmark during your vacation period? An excellent deal that allows you to live in a small city, and see how the Danes live. For information or for more details, write to the National Tourist Office.

—Denmark can supply a list of 65 typical and very comfortable inns, spread out around the country, which can accommodate tourists at good prices through the program called "check-inns." This check gives you the right to a bed in a double room and breakfast, and includes service charge and taxes. You can also reserve a room in an inn of superior category, paying an additional $2 or so. On the other hand, if you want a room without a bath or shower, the inn will return the difference of $2 or $3. Note that the price of each "check-in" is between $15 and $27 (140–250 Kr) in tourist class and an additional $8 (minimum) for an extra bed.

Things That Are Good to Know

—*National Holiday:* June 5

—*Business hours:*

Offices: 8 or 9 A.M. to 4 or 5 P.M.

Banks: 10 A.M. to 3 P.M. Closed Saturday.

Post office boxes: To send, simply write: *Poste Restante,* the name of the receiver, the city, and the country.

—*Language:* English and German are widely spoken.

—*Museums:* 50 percent student discount.

—In Denmark, in Copenhagen in any case, everything is closed for five days at Easter: Holy Thursday, Good Friday, Holy Saturday, Easter Sunday and Monday. Even the cops stay home. One exception, though: the store at the Central Station.

Meals

The noontime meal in Denmark is eaten at noontime! (Original.) The evening meal is eaten between 6 and 7 P.M. Breakfast is sometimes difficult, for the Danes never eat breakfast out. There are 566 restaurants spread out across Denmark that have joined to offer *Dan Menu,* consisting of a typical Danish menu of 2 dishes, at about 56

Kr; it is also found on certain ferries, for example on the train-ferry from Grand Belt. A guide listing all these addresses has been published.

What to Eat and Drink in Denmark

Right off the bat, you didn't come for the gastronomy, that's clear. However, the country offers some delicious specialties. Costly enough, it's true, but you must at least taste them.

—*The smørrebrød:* The national dish that consists of small slices of rye bread covered with herring, smoked meats, sometimes salmon *(laks),* accompanied by hardboiled eggs, pickled beets, salad, and onions. Can range from a very elaborate *smørrebrød* of a fancy restaurant to a very simple affair at a café to a snack composed of three little *canapés.* They drink beer or *aquavit* (which must come from the freezer).

—*Herrings (sild):* Found in all kinds of sauces (one more delicious than the next): marinated, in madeira, cherry, curry with cream, and so forth.

—A cold platter composed of herring, fish fillets, pâté, and morsels of meat and cheese. The most elaborate platters can include smoked eel, shrimp, salmon, pork or duck, and several types of cheese.

—Some typical dishes: curried pork roasted with potatoes and prunes *(stegt svinekam med cebler og svesker),* salted lamb *(spraengt lam),* and *frikadeller* (a type of meatball).

—Laws concerning the purchase of alcohol are much less strict than in other Scandinavian countries, where they strictly enforce the *Bolaget* system in which the state stores keep draconian hours. However, forget about anything that carries the name of wine in restaurants; they're way overpriced. Settle for the excellent Carlsberg or Tuborg beers whose reputations say it all. The best berry brandy is *Aalborg Export* (good to drink ice cold, we repeat!).

Movies

Great! All the films in Denmark are in the original language with subtitles! If you want to hear some English, go see the latest *Star Wars.* Some Danish films have English subtitles. See the newspaper listings.

Purchases

Everything is expensive here, with the exception of electromechanical equipment (turntables, amplifiers, speakers, electronic pocket calculators, and so forth).

Note: Foreigners are entitled to a discount amounting to the sales tax and up to 20 percent of the sale price, on the condition that the merchandise is shipped.

How to Travel in Denmark

Hitchhiking: It is tolerated, we can say with assurance. But it is relatively difficult due to opposition from the natives and the increasing popularity of camping (cars are often jammed with equipment,

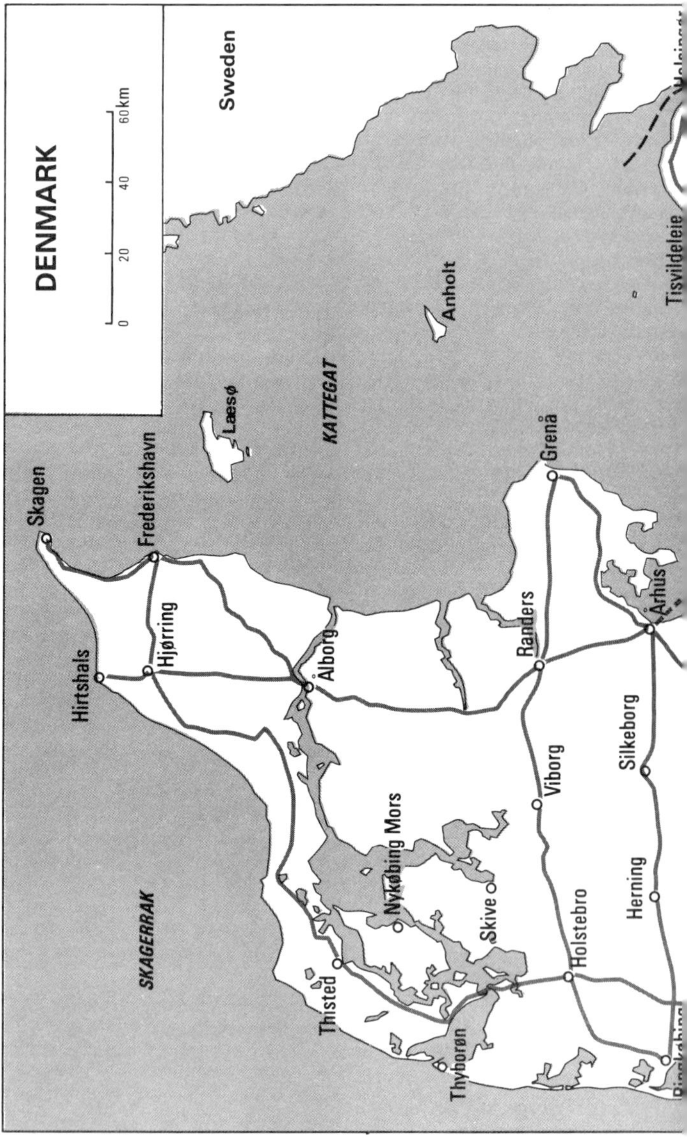
DENMARK
0
20
40
60 km
Sweden
Skagen
Frederikshavn
Hirtshals
Hjørring
Ålborg
Læsø
KATTEGAT
Anholt
Grenå
Randers
Århus
Viborg
Silkeborg
Nykøbing Mors
Skive
Herning
Holstebro
Thisted
Thyborøn
SKAGERRAK
Tisvildeleje

DENMARK • 51

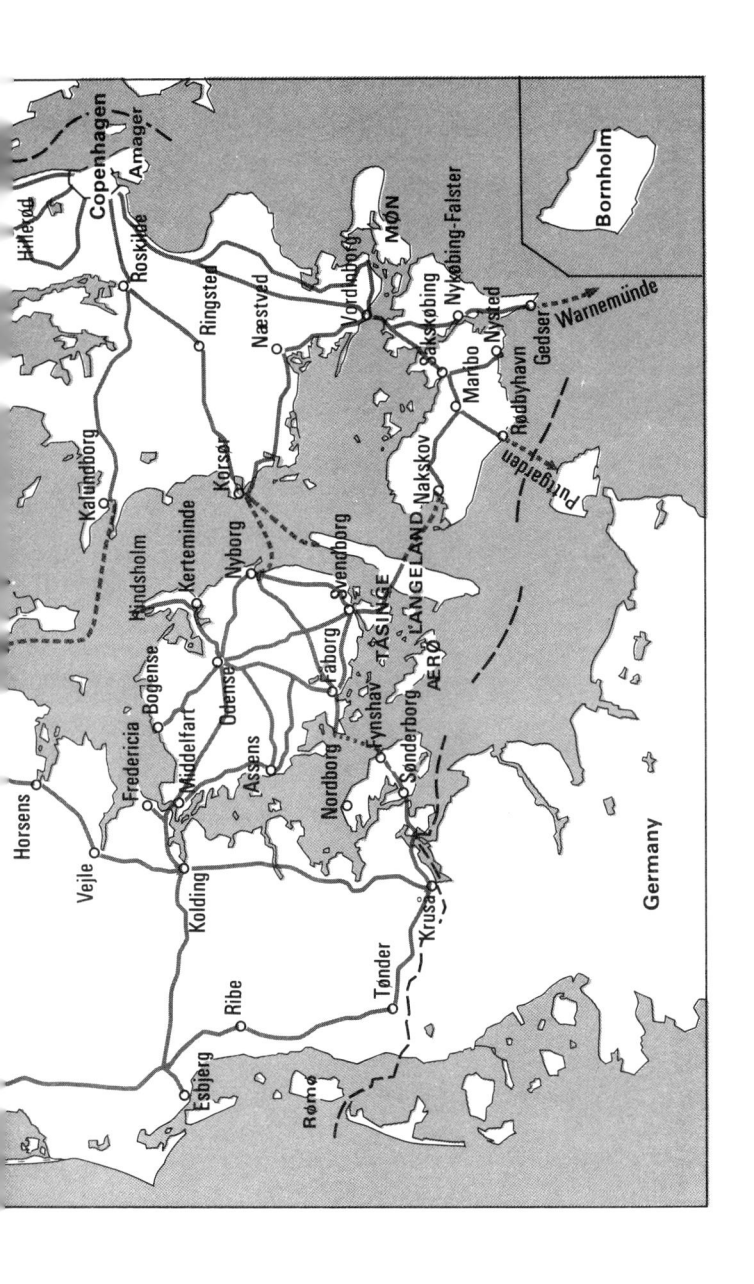

therefore no room). However, if you are patient, you can go wherever your heart desires without any problems. To cross the different branches of the sea and avoid paying for the ferry each time, which gets expensive after a while, ask truck drivers to take you in their truck cabs; they also benefit by a reduced rate for the truck.

—*The private car* is ideal if there are several of you. Carry what you need for cooking and arrange the car so you can sleep in it. Living is relatively expensive in Scandinavian countries, so fill your backpack or car with canned goods and other foodstuffs.

—*Bicycle rentals:* You can rent bikes in some train stations. Otherwise, Tourist Information can give you addresses of local renters. A deposit is required as a guarantee, along with some I.D.

—*Train:* 10-day passes and monthly passes are available on all Danish trains. The *Rover* ticket is valid for 17 days on trains, buses, and ferries operated by Danish Government Railways.

The Inter-Rail pass is not valid on the Pottgarden-Rødby or the Helsingør-Helsingborg ferries.

To get to Denmark, the D.S.B. (Danish Railways) offers tickets at reduced prices.

—*Remarks concerning the border:* For those who go from Amsterdam to Denmark and pass the border between Nordhorn and Danekamp, there is a bank open until 10 P.M. and a truckers' restaurant where you can eat your fill and not empty your wallet.

Don't exchange money at the Flensburg border crossing between Germany and Denmark; it's 10 percent less than the exchange 6 miles (10 km) from the border.

An Itinerary

At Krusa (Denmark–German border) take road A8 toward Sønderborg. Arriving on the island of Als, which has pretty beaches in the southeast, continue on A8 to Fynshav. From there, a ferry takes you to Bøjden in 45 minutes. Take the road that runs along the coast, from Bøjden to Svendborg. Between these two you can visit Faborg, a very old and pretty city. The rustic homes have thatched roofs and wooden walls.

From Svendborg, take A9 toward Rudkosing. You arrive on Langeland island. At Spodsberg, take the ferry to Tars (45 minutes). At Tars, go toward Maribo. Then take highway E4 that leads to Copenhagen.

COPENHAGEN

This city alone is worth the trip to Denmark. It's lovely and it's vivacious. You realize that Denmark is the heart of Scandinavia. The streets are lively, the people very open. In short, Copenhagen is first-rate. But avoid arriving on Sunday when everything is closed.

Useful Addresses

—*Tourist Information:* 22 H. C. Andersens Boulevard. (There is also a kiosk at the Central Station in the arrivals hall.) Telephone 01–111–415. A nice greeting—lots of free brochures and maps of the city.

—*Central Bureau of Telecommunications:* 37 Kobmagergade. Open from 7 A.M. to midnight.

—*U.S. Embassy:* 24 Dag Hammarskjöld Allé. Telephone 01–42–31–44.

—*American Express:* 12 H. C. Andersens Boulevard. Telephone 12–23–01.

—*VISA Card Headquarters:* 24B Østergade. Telephone 14–65–45.

—*DIS:* 28 Skindergade. Telephone 11–00–44. Open from 9:30 A.M. to 5 P.M. Closed Saturday. Trains and charters for youths and students.

—*Transalpino:* 6 Skoubogade. Telephone 14–46–33. Discount train tickets for those under 26. Open Monday to Friday from 9 A.M. to 5 P.M. On Saturday from 10 A.M. to 1 P.M. in June and July.

—*Central Post Office:* 37 Tietgensgade. Open Monday to Friday from 8 A.M. to 7 P.M. On Saturday until 1 P.M. *Post Restante.*

—*Airport:* By S.A.S. shuttle bus (14 Kr) or city bus #32 that you get at Rådhus (4 Kr).

Money Exchanges

—*At the airport:* Every day from 8 A.M. to 10:30 P.M.

—*At the Central Station:* Every day from 7 A.M. to 10 P.M. They take an enormous commission (nearly 20 Kr).

—*American Express:* 18 Amagertorv. Saturday until noon.

—*Handelsbanken* allows you to withdraw money with a European VISA blue card.

—*Privatbanken i Kjøbenhaun, Den Danske Landmansbank,* and *Kjøbenhavns Handelsbank* each ask for the VISA blue card.

"Use It"

We really must talk about it on its own because it's great, and ever since we discovered it, we're jealous of the Danes.

They give information on *everything:* Festivals, where to eat, "in" spots. You can leave luggage there, for free, although you have to leave a deposit of 10 Kr which is returned when you pick up your belongings.

They organize concerts, show you where you can play music without being picked up by the cops, help you if you have drug problems: This is a gift to travelers from a country where nothing is given away! And that's not all! They hand out brochures and a map of the city where everything is located by numbers; offer a bulletin board for messages; find you a ride if you're hitching or hitchhikers if you're driving; hand out a large notebook with hitchhiking tips; write in yours; and give a post office box! Yeaa, lovely . . .

The address for the post box is: *P.R. Use It,* 14 Magstraede, DK 1204, Copenhagen K, Denmark.

And that's not all, folks! In their building, which is called HUSET, there's a restaurant *(Spisehuset),* a café-rock concert club, a small theater . . . Alas, we don't have room to include everything they have there! Go to 14 Magstraede. Telephone 15-65-18. Open from 10 A.M. to 8 P.M. from June 15 to September 14. The rest of the year from 11 A.M. to 5 P.M., Tuesday and Thursday until 7 P.M.

They are a little busy in the summer. Before heading to the

counter consult their bulletin boards where most of the information is posted. Closed at Easter.

A small detail: It's subsidized by the city.

Another detail: They have a sense of humor, evident from their brochure. They are *very nice.* If you think of it, send us their brochure because it's terrific. That's all. That's not bad.

Public Baths and Showers

Yeah, showers and saunas are rather pleasant. And, since wanderers get filthy trekking in Denmark, it's useful to have these addresses. Open Monday to Friday from 8 A.M. to 6:30 P.M., on Saturday from 8 A.M. to 3 P.M. You can shower for 3 Kr at 12 Borgerkade and at 12 Sjaellandsgade. Swimming pool, shower, and sauna for 10.75 Kr at 35 Frankrigsgade, the same hours as above.

Emergencies

—*Hospital: Riegshospitalet,* 9 Blegdamsvej. Telephone 39-66-33. Buses #3, #10, #43, and #84. In principle, if you're not Danish, you must pay for your treatment in the hospital, but in fact it's rare. Ask first. Open 24 hours a day.

—*Kommunehospitalet:* 5 Øster Farimagsgade. Ditto. Telephone 15-85-00. Buses #14, #40, and #43. Also treats venereal diseases.

—*Emergency:* Dial 000 without putting in any coins.

—*Emergency Dental Care (Tandlaegvagt):* 14 Oslo Plads. Monday to Friday from 8 to 10 P.M. Saturday, Sunday, and holidays from 10 A.M. to noon. (Don't ask "why these hours?") You must pay a little.

How to Get Around

In the central area, there is a system of common fares allowing transfers between buses and trains within a certain periphery and during certain hours. Stations and HT kiosks sell books of tickets at reduced fares for 10 trips. Bus drivers also sell them. Your ticket must be "punched" upon entering the bus and station platforms.

—*Buses:* Tickets are valid for 1 hour. Cheaper by the book.

—*S-Train:* Same price as the bus. Inter-Rail passes are valid on the S-Trains.

—*Bikes:* Cheap rentals: Cykelborsen, 157 Gothersgade. You can also rent them at stations (20 Kr a day).

Where to Sleep

The "P" Kiosk at the Central Station has information for finding lodging. Open from 9 A.M. to midnight in the summer.

—If you stay long enough in Copenhagen (more than a week), it's a good idea to rent a room in a *pension,* as long as you're not flat broke. See *Use It.* Ditto for lodgings at a native's home.

—Hotels are not for you.

—But rest assured—there are still plenty of places for you. We have arranged them by neighborhood so that you can easily find a place, even when you're traveling in a pack.

- **North—Lyngby Area**
   —*Lyngby Vandrehjem:* Rådvad 1. Telephone 80-30-74. About 9 miles from the center of town. You can make reservations over the phone. Sheets required; can be rented. Careful: The doors close at 11 A.M. The desk is open from 7 A.M. to 1 P.M. and again from 4 P.M. to 9 A.M. Youth hostel card required. 94 beds. To get there: S-Train to Lyngby, then bus 187 to Radvad. You can eat here.

- **Northwest—Brønshoj area**
   —*Bellahoj Vandrerhjem:* 8 Herbergsuejen. Telephone 28-97-15. 3 miles from the center of town. Sheets required; can be rented. Doors close at 1:30 A.M. Desk is open until 10:45 P.M. Youth hostel card required. 324 beds. To get there: Bus #2 from City Hall. Plaza Stop at *Fuglsang Allé*. Cafeteria. Open all year.
   —*Bellahøj Camping:* 2400 Hvidkildevej. Telephone 10-11-50. Summer only, June 12 to August 22. 3 miles from the center of town. To get there, bus #8 from City Hall Plaza. Stop at the campgrounds. They are immense but not especially nice; they're in the middle of housing projects and many roads.
   —*Copenhagen Sleep-in:* 6 Per Henrik Lings Allé. Telephone 26-50-59. Open from July 9 to September 5. Buses #1 and #6 from Radhuspladsen. Stop at Idraetsparken. By the S-Train: A, B, and C lines; get off at Nordhavn station. Closed from noon to 6 A.M. but open all night long. 40 Kr. a night with breakfast included. And all with music!

- **West**
   —*Absalon Camping:* 132 Korsdalsvej, 2610 Rødrove. Telephone 41-06-00. Open all year. 6 miles from the center of town. To get there: S-Train from the central station toward Tastrup, to *Brøndbyøster*. A half mile from the station, on the right. Easy to reach for camping by Inter-Rail. For cars, get off E4 at Rodoure Brøndbyøster, take a right at Roskildevej, then a left at the Mobil station. Somewhat expensive. Have to pay for shower, too. A bit like a factory.

- **South**
   —*Copenhagen Hostel:* 55 Sjaellandsbroen. Telephone 52-29-08. Bus #37 from Holmens Bro. Get off at Sjaellandsbroen. 3 miles from the center of the city. 2 or 4 beds per room. Sheets required. Open all year. Closes at midnight.

- **City Center**
   —The penniless are going to frown—the station is closed at night from 2 A.M. to 5 A.M.
   —*Youth Hostel Vesterbro Ungdomsgard:* 8 Absalongsgade. Telephone 31-20-70. Count on a 10-minute walk from the Central Station or buses #6, #28, and #41 toward Alholm Plads and Rodoure. In the Vester Brod area.
   —*Kfuk:* 19 Store Kannikerstaede. Telephone 11-30-30. For women only. 3 rooms and 16 beds. Take the S-Train to Norreport.
   —*Activ University:* 40 Olfert Fichersgade. Telephone 15-61-75. In the old city near Kongens Have park. Rather filthy. Dormitory by sex. There are 100 beds and a free sauna. No card required. Employees as friendly as prison guards. Closes at 1 A.M. Get there by walking or bus #10 to *Solvgade*. *Use It* mentions it but does not recommend it.

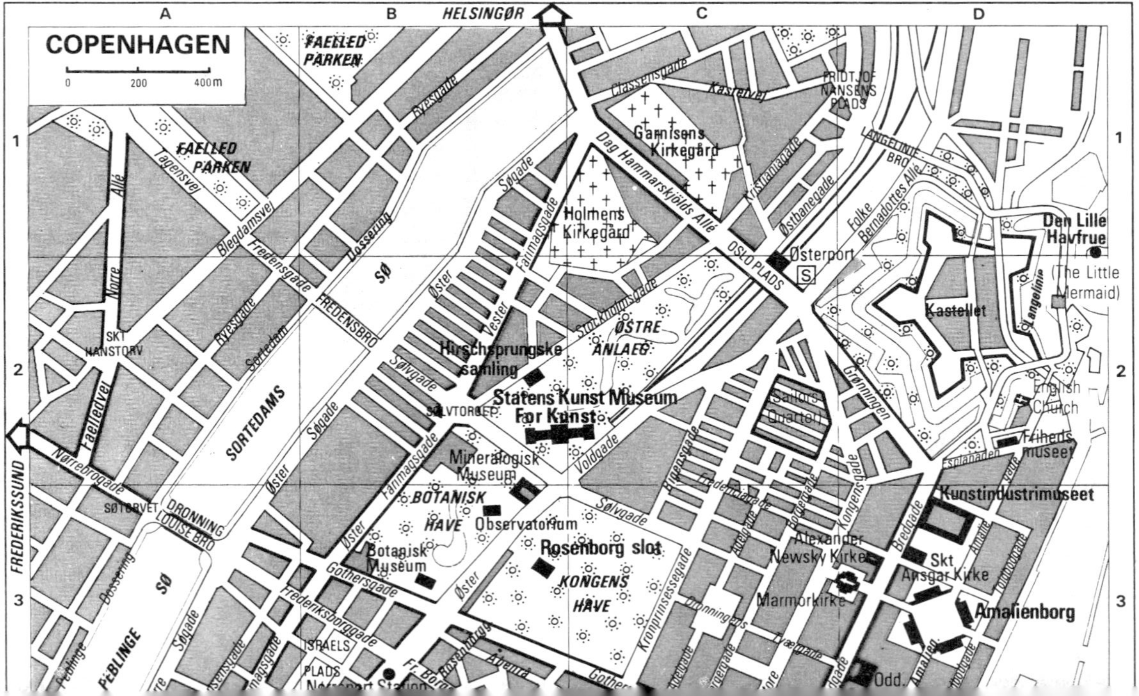
COPENHAGEN
0
200
400m
A
B
C
D
1
2
3
HELSINGØR
FREDERIKSSUND
FAELLED PARKEN
FAELLED PARKEN
Tagensvej
Allé
Nørre
Bledamsvej
Fredensgade
Ryesgade
Ryesgade
Dossering
SØ
FREDENSBRO
Sortedam
SORTEDAMS
SKT HANSTORV
Faelledvej
Nørrebrogade
SØTORVET
DRONNING LOUISE BRO
Dossering
SØ
PEBLINGE
Peblinge
Søgade
Søgade
Øster
Søgade
Øster
Vester
Sølvgade
SØLVTORVET
Farimagsgade
Farimagsgade
Classensgade
Kastelvej
Garnisons Kirkegård
Holmens Kirkegård
Dag Hammarskjölds Allé
PRIDTJOF NANSENS PLADS
Kristianiagade
Østbanegade
LANGELINIE BRO
Folke Bernadottes Allé
OSLO PLADS
Østerport
S
Stockholmsgade
ØSTRE ANLAEG
Hirschsprungske samling
Statens Kunst Museum For Kunst
Voldgade
Mineralogisk Museum
BOTANISK HAVE
Observatorium
Botanisk Museum
Øster
Gothersgade
Frederiksborggade
ISRAELS PLADS
Nørreport Station
Rosenborg slot
KONGENS HAVE
Sølvgade
Kronprinsessegade
Den Lille Havfrue
(The Little Mermaid)
Langelinie
Kastellet
Grønningen
Sailors' Quarter
English Church
Frihedsmuseet
Esplanaden
Kunstindustrimuseet
Bredgade
Skt Ansgar Kirke
Amalienborg
Alexander Newsky Kirke
Marmorkirke
Kongensgade
Dronningens
Odd.

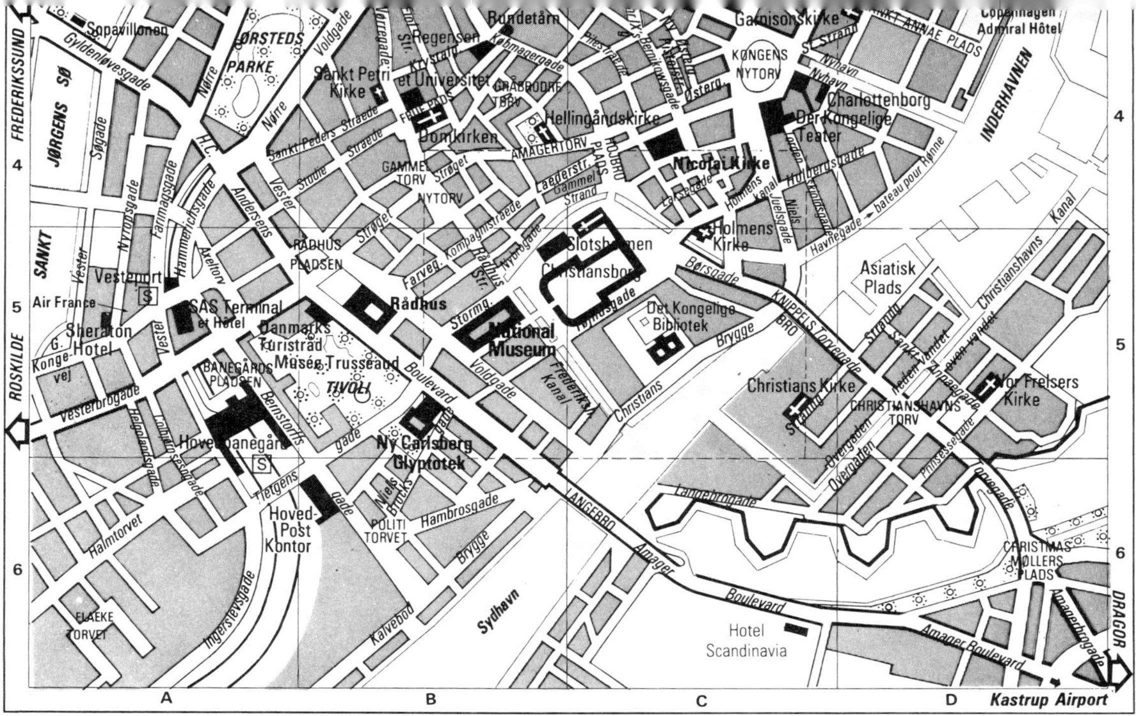
FREDERIKSSUND
ROSKILDE
DRAGOR
Kastrup Airport
Copenhagen Admiral Hôtel
INDERHAVNEN
Kongens Nytorv
Garnisonskirke
Charlottenborg
Det Kongelige Teater
Nyhavn
Nicolai Kirke
Holmens Kirke
Hellingåndskirke
Rundetårn
Regensen
Universitet
Sankt Petri Kirke
Domkirken
Gammeltorv
Nytorv
Amagertorv
Højbro Plads
Ørsteds Parke
Jørgens Sø
Sankt
Sopavillonen
Vesterport
Air France
Sheraton Hotel
SAS Terminal et Hôtel
Rådhus Pladsen
Rådhus
Danmarks Turistråd
Musée Trusseaud
Tivoli
Banegårds Pladsen
Hovedbanegård
Ny Carlsberg Glyptotek
Hoved-Post Kontor
Politi Torvet
Flaeke Torvet
Slotsholmen
Christiansborg
National Museum
Det Kongelige Bibliotek
Frederiksh. Kanal
Asiatisk Plads
Knippels Bro
Christians Kirke
Christianshavns Torv
Vor Frelsers Kirke
Christmas Møllers Plads
Hotel Scandinavia
Sydhavn
Langebro
Amager Boulevard
Amagerbrogade
Vesterbrogade
H.C. Andersens Boulevard
Bernstorffsgade
Halmtorvet
Ingerslevsgade
Kalvebod Brygge
Havnegade
Christianshavns Kanal
Torvegade
Langebrogade
Børsgade
A
B
C
D
4
5
6

—*Hotel Regina:* 6 Reventlowsgade. Telephone 31-78-50. Next to the station.
—*Hotel West:* 8 Dannebrogsgade. Telephone 24-27-61. Single and double rooms.

Where to Eat

Many restaurants stop serving meals after a certain hour but continue to serve drinks to customers. Those that display the sign *Dan Menu* serve 2 good dishes for 56 Kr, everything included.

• In the Center of Town

—*Café Sorgenfri:* 11 Brolaeggerstrade. Good smørrebrød at decent prices, served from 11 A.M. to 9 P.M. An inviting setting with its cellar room, low ceilings, and checkered tablecloths.

—*Det Gronne Kokken* (The Green Kitchen): 10 Larsbjørnsstraede. Third floor. You eat good vegetarian food in a pleasant, fresh environment with green plants. Open from Monday to Saturday from noon to 10 P.M.

—*Restaurant Natural:* 12A Larsbjørnsstraede. Another vegetarian restaurant with original decor. Salad buffet (half price with a main dish).

—*Universitet Café:* 2 Fiolstraede. Old tavern. Wooden interior decorated with front pages from old newspapers. Student ambiance (obviously, with such a name). Open from 11 A.M. to 5 A.M., but complete menu only until 7 P.M., then sandwiches, onion soup, Chili con carne, and so forth.

—*Klaptraet:* 13 Kultorvet. Open from 2 P.M. to midnight. Decorated with old movie posters and projectors. Excellent rock music. In cahoots with a small movie house upstairs. Various salads and good chocolate cakes. Young clientele with a lively atmosphere.

—*Rådhus Kroen:* 21 Longangsstraede. Telephone 11-64-53. Open from 10:00 A.M. to 4:30 A.M. Moderately priced dishes.

• Around Kongens Nytorv Place

—*Petersborg:* 76 Bredgade. A little further than Amalienborg Palace. Telephone 12-50-16. Open, except on Sunday, from 10:30 A.M. to 9:00 P.M. Conservative atmosphere for business people and traveling salesmen, in a refined interior of wood and engravings. Delicious *Petersborg Platten* for two.

—*Vita:* 25 Store Kongensgade. Large brasserie in *fin-de-siècle* style with faded red velvet and glass bead chandeliers. They serve inexpensive but not overly generous portions of food, but all night. Open every day. A hangout for the down-and-out in the wee hours of the morning.

—*Café Victor:* Østergade and Hovedvagtsgade. Recently opened. All white, sparkling and gaudy. To have tea or grab a bite. No intimacy, yet frequented by rather clean and well-combed young people.

—*Skindbuksen:* 4 Lille Kongensgade. Open from 11 A.M. to 2 A.M. Good *smørrebrød*. In the style of the Brown Cafés of Amsterdam, with a lively air and cheerful folks. A good place to come and have a drink at any time in a smoky dive. No food on Sundays.

• Near the Station

—The supermarkets and the kiosks in the station are open until midnight daily.

—*Axelborg Bodega:* 1 Axeltorv. 3 minutes from the station. A large quiet pub, rather nicer than the other places around the station. Some small snacks.

—*DSB Cafeteria:* In the station. You can get a good meal for 30 Kr. The one on the second floor is more expensive and has less variety. Open from 10 A.M. to 10 P.M.

—*Kanal Cafeen:* 18 Frederiksholms Canal. Next to the National Museum. Telephone 11-57-70. One of the best restaurants in Copenhagen, but you'll pay dearly. For hitchhiking millionaires or at the end of your trip. Having said that, the decor is superb, not at all touristy and frequented solely by the Danish. Taste the *gravad laks* with *dilddressing* (salmon with a sweet mustard sauce). Delicious!

• *In the Norrebro Area*

This is a workingclass neighborhood in the northwest, a little distance. However, it's very interesting for those who want a more realistic impression of social life in Copenhagen. Many inexpensive little restaurants. Take bus #7 or #17 from Kongens Nytorv to Stengade.

—*Pepino:* 32 Sankt Hans Torv. Bus #17 to Faelledvej. One of many bistro-restaurants in the area. Pleasant atmosphere and very decent eats. Moderate prices. Open from noon to 3 P.M. and from 6 P.M. to 9 P.M.

• *In the Christianshavn Area*

—*A Christiania:* We prefer the large restaurant which is all white, with arches and a large fireplace in the back. Across from Green Hall. More room, less smoke, and good vegetarian dishes.

—*Faergecafé:* Strangade and Christianshavn Canal. Meals from 11 A.M. to 2 P.M. and from 5 P.M. to 7:30 P.M. Reasonable prices. Delightfully situated north of a canal and in a calm and colorful area. A stroll all around is wonderfully pleasant.

Where to Down a Few

—*Pilegärden:* 44 Pilestraede. A lot of Tuborg can be quaffed in a joyous and noisy atmosphere. Good blues and background music. Open until 2 A.M. Cover charge.

—*Rosa Luxembourg:* 13 Huset Rådhus Straede. A great little pub. Needless to say, given the name of this place, the owner is a bit leftist, and not just around the edges. And the walls are covered with posters and tracts. Truly congenial. Birds of a feather with *Use It,* if you catch our drift. Open from noon to midnight.

—*Dan Turell:* 3 Store Regnegade. Open from 11 A.M. to 2 A.M. We don't know what the young people find in this roadside dive, but they've made it one of their favorite hangouts. Bright fluorescent lighting, plastic and Formica. Nothing pleasant about it.

—*Ernst Hviid:* 19–23 Kongens Nytorv. Established in 1834. Many rooms, low ceilings, engravings on the walls. The customers are young, upwardly mobile types, with a sprinkling of tourists.

—*Sofiekaeldren:* 32A Overgaden Oven Vandet. Open every day from noon to dawn. Located in Christianshavn. Marginal bistro with good rock music. A café on the second floor.

—*Folkets Hus:* 50 Stengade. Good atmosphere and sometimes folk music.

—*Hand I Hanke.* 20 Griffenfeldtsgade, at Nørrebro. Open every day from 2 P.M. to 1 A.M. A popular kind of pub where the neighborhood young folks get together in a pleasant atmosphere.

Where to Listen to Music

—*Montmartre:* 41 Nørregade. Telephone 11-46-67. The best jazz club in Copenhagen. Has a very good reputation in Scandinavia. Open from 8 P.M. to 2 A.M. Dancing on Friday and Saturday from 1 A.M. to 5 A.M.

—*Loppen:* In Christiania. Mostly rock. Operates from Thursday to Sunday, 9 P.M. to 3:30 A.M. Cover charge.

—*Musikanten:* 15 Vacrnedamsvej. Open every night from 9 P.M. to 5 A.M. Bring your own instruments.

To See

• *Christiania*
Ah, yes! Christiania still exists. Even if it no longer corresponds at all to the original conception, the experience continues. . . .

A little history: In 1971 the army abandoned these barracks located at Christianshavn—55 acres of land and concrete buildings in the capital. The opportunity was too sweet to pass up. A squatters' movement developed, and soon hundreds of young people were occupying the place, fixing up the barracks, creating workshops, and boutiques, and establishing an alternative lifestyle. The public powers-that-be allowed them to live out this social experiment for 3 years. After these enthusiastic years, Christiania underwent its first crisis when the government wanted to arrest and expel the occupants because of the drug problem and a certain decline in the experiment. An extraordinary drive, pressure, and petitions, culminating in a demonstration of 30,000 people in front of Parliament, reversed the decision. At the same time, the residents of Christiania brought legal action against the eviction decision.

Democracy functions particularly well at the workshop or district level. There's no central administration to speak of. Each resident pays 250 Kr rent. Half of this is given to the municipality for community expenses. Many residents work outside, but Christiania employs about 100 people. Here the right to use is more important than property rights. No one can sell his/her house or leave it for more than 6 months.

Recently, the inhabitants lost in 2 trials pending against the eviction notice but over the years the 2 sides established friendly relations, and the government no longer mentions eviction. If utopia has deserted Christiania, its inhabitants are no less determined to defend their "privileged" way of life. The problem of drugs continues; 5 years ago, we must mention, the majority of Christianites fought against the dealers and tried to eliminate them. The experiment continues. You will obviously be in the somewhat embarrassing position of a voyeur when you arrive. You can't visit the barracks or apartments as you can a zoo. Try to hook up with a resident in a restaurant or a store in Christiania, or it would be better yet if you already had a contact. You can't pitch a tent or live there. Christiania does not have the technical and sanitary means to put up the thousands of visitors who arrive each summer. We must make this very clear: Instead of wanting to change the world, the Christianites want to preserve their own way of life, which is understandable. Anyhow, you will come across different activities in Christiania's public places and meet the interesting inhabitants, and that in itself is very important.

• *Monuments*
—*Amalienborg Place:* Beautiful architectural grouping of 4 eighteenth-century palaces. The palace of Christian IX today belongs to the Queen. When she is in Copenhagen, there is a parade of the guard every day at noon.

—*Slotsholmen* (the castle on the small island): Located across from the National Museum and surrounded by canals. A group of buildings constituting the historic heart of the city. They are:
- *Christianborg Castle,* built in 1745. Burned several times; only the two wings of the stables still stand. The current building dates to the beginning of the century and houses the Folketing, the Danish parliament (visits every day except Saturday from 10 A.M. to 4 P.M.
- The ruins of the first medieval citadel: *Absalon.* The entrance for a guided tour is on Slotsplads; at 10 A.M., and 11 A.M. except Monday.
- The *former exchange:* One of the prettiest buildings in the city. Observe the fancy gables and the high golden spire composed of four dragon tails.
- *Thorvaldsen Museum:* Exhibits the works of the greatest Danish sculptor who was influenced by Greek classicism. He left a considerable legacy. The tomb of the artist is in the courtyard. Open from 10 A.M. to 4 P.M. every day. (Closed on Tuesdays and at 3 P.M. on the other days from October to May.)
- *Theater Museum:* For those who are interested in this artistic domain, collections of costumes, souvenirs from famous actors from the sixteenth century to today. Open Wednesday, Friday, and Sunday from 2 to 4 P.M.

—*Rådhus* (City Hall): Built at the end of the nineteenth century. Its style is partially Middle Ages, partially Nordic, partially Lombard Renaissance. Inside, view the World Clock, the paintings, and the sculptures. A 340-foot tower with a great panoramic view of the city. The Rådhus is open all week except Sunday from 10 A.M. to 3 P.M. (Saturday till noon). Visit the tower Monday to Friday from 11 A.M. to 2 P.M., Saturday till 3 A.M.

—*Kongens Nytorv:* The aristocratic center of Copenhagen, with famous cafés, big stores, Hotel of England, as well as:
- The Royal Theater.
- Charlottenborg Palace, one of the most important baroque monuments in Denmark. Built at the end of the seventeenth century, it later became the Royal Academy of Fine Arts.

—Cruise on the canals and the port: Gammel Strand. From May 1 to September 15; several departures a day.

• *Churches*
—*Vor Frue Kirke* (cathedral): On Nørregade. Rebuilt in the neoclassical style in 1811. In the nave, a statue of Throvaldsen. The interior decoration is not too interesting, but the acoustics are extraordinary. Try to attend Mozart's *Requiem* or another concert with choirs. Open from 8 A.M. to 5 P.M.

—*Marmor Kirken* (Marble Church): 4 Frederiksgade. Broke a record for length of time in construction. Started in 1746 but not completed until 1894. Circular shape with a 150-foot-high cupola. Many statues of famous people all around. Open from 9 A.M. to 4 P.M. but on Wednesday until noon. Closed on Sunday.

—*Vor Fresers Kirche* (Sankt Annaegade): At Christiania. Baroque-style church of the seventeenth century that deserves a visit (and it's right next to Christiania). Lovely steeple with a spiral staircase on the exterior; the spire is surmounted by a "man on the globe," measuring 208 feet in height. On the inside, an Italian baroque-style altar in marble and wood and a remarkable organ. Open every day from 10 A.M. to 4 P.M., Sunday from noon to 4 P.M. Possible to clamber up to the top of the tower and benefit from a beautiful view of the port. (Lazy bones stay away . . . more than 400 steps).

• *Some Interesting Sections*

Of course you will be led to discover some places by chance during your own strolls, but here are some others—isolated or simply with a small, intimate charm that allows you to appreciate once again the diversity of Copenhagen.

—*Strøget:* A long pedestrian street that links Rådhus Pladsen to Kongens Nytorv. Luxury stores, crafts boutiques, cafés with terraces, and the crowds of Fifth Avenue. Super touristy in the summer. Strøget crosses Gammeltorv, a pretty place bordered by several baroque- and Renaissance-style homes, then extends to the Holy Spirit Church which dates back to 1672. Farther on you'll find one of the oldest mansions in the city which houses the royal manufacturer of porcelain and on the second floor a small porcelain museum. The route ends up at Østergade, which preserves the memorabilia of the intellectuals who lived there: Andersen, Kirkegaard, Drachmann, and Strindberg the Swede.

—*"Latin Quarter":* A few pedestrian streets around the university and the cathedral. Lovely old homes bathed in pink and purple tones. At the corner of Nørregade and Studie Straede, *Sankt Petri Kirke,* the oldest church in the city, still thrusts its beautiful spire into the sky.

On Købmargergade you will discover what is probably the oldest university residence in the world—Regensen—dating from the mid-seventeenth century. From there, you can go to the Round Tower, erected during the same period; it has served as an observatory for university astronomers. You can climb up to enjoy a marvelous view of the city. The whole neighborhood has an old-fashioned charm, perfect for romantic evening strolls.

—*Nyhavn:* One of the liveliest neighborhoods in the city, and in the summer one of the busiest. Rows of old houses, from one end of the canal to the other, frequented, unfortunately, by rather unsavory types. A lot of charm with all those boats, most of them moored permanently. Sailors still go there to mingle with the locals and the tourists. Crowds of unemployed sailors, prostitutes, and drunks. Hans Christian Andersen lived for about 20 years at #67. Toast to his memory at the International Bar at #25. Take a peek at #63, a handsome building with an interior court dating from 1756. This is also the district for tattoo parlors. If that's your idea of a good time, go see *Tatoo Jack* at #37 Nyhavn.

• *Christianshavn*

Past the Knippels Bro bridge, you will discover this peaceful section of fishermen who seem to have been untouched by the passing of time. The boats rock gently in the canals lined with small low homes and warehouses. Enjoy a stroll on the Strandgade, Christianshavn canal, and especially Gaden Oven Bandet, which boasts beautiful mansions, former homes of ship captains, and now a small local history museum—*Brøstes Samling*, at #10. Open every day from 10 A.M. to 4 P.M. At 4 Strandgade there's another small museum dedicated to boat construction. Film lovers must visit the *Det Danske Filmuseum* on Store Søndervoldstraede. This film museum shows movies from Monday to Friday, noon to 4 P.M. Free admission.

• *Nørrebro*

Working-class neighborhood in the north of Copenhagen that is of no interest except to those who love popular neighborhoods and small, friendly cafés, where they squeeze close together on rainy days, and for those who want to see how the Danes really live, without pretense.... In the new housing projects, like small islands in the middle of real estate developments, there are many young people of the *Nå* generation, a vague term that means "neither yes nor no." It's the generation that is unemployed and has no perspective. Some squatters on Korsgade succeeded in establishing an astonishing connection with the aged in the neighborhood who refuse to be evicted. At Nørrebro you'll find many good inexpensive restaurants, shops, health food stores, and so forth. Don't forget to hoist a few at Håand I Hanke on Griffenfeldtsgade. To get to Nørrebro take bus #7 and then #17 to Kongens Nytorv.

• *Vesterbro*

The porn district that wraps around Istedgade, behind the station. Sorry flesh and glum surroundings. When you think there are people who come for this, the real thing is definitely a dirty trick.

• *Museums*

—*Glyptotek:* Dantes Plads, next to Tivoli. Open from 10 A.M. to 4 P.M. except Monday. Free on Wednesday and Sunday. After Carl Jacobsen made the entire world drunk with his famous Carlsberg and became rich, he donated many exquisite works of art. Very well endowed section of Egyptian, Greek, Roman, and Etruscan antiquities. Magnificent Impressionists, especially Gauguin, Renoir, Sisley, and so forth. The Gauguin collection is probably one of the most beautiful in the world. The Danish collection is also interesting. Upon entering there is an unusual atrium, decorated with palm trees and in a turn-of-the-century style. Truly a must-see place.

—*Kunstindustrimuseet:* 68 Bredgade. Next to the Amalienborg palace. Telephone 14-04-52. Danish-ornamented works from the Middle Ages to the present times, some rare pieces including a tapestry from Tournai, a reliquary, and the most important collection in the world of Toulouse-Lautrec posters. Open from 1 P.M. to 4 P.M. except Monday. Admission is 7 Kr in July and August; free the rest of the year.

—*Rosenborg Castle:* On Øster Voldgade. A handsome castle from the seventeenth century; houses all the royal collections of art, jewelry, and silverware of the last 300 years. Open every day from 10 A.M. to 3 P.M. In autumn and winter, Tuesdays, Fridays, and Sundays from 11 A.M. to 1 P.M. Admission is 12 Kr.

—*National Museum:* On Frederiksholms Canal, between Tivoli and Christianborg. See the fascinating wing of Danish prehistory. The section on the Bronze Age is particularly rich with arms, tombs, bodies, and clothes—all well preserved, discovered in peat bogs. Stones covered with obscure runes (the oldest Nordic inscriptions). The display of clothes, domestic objects, dishes, furniture, and so forth, from the Middle Ages to the nineteenth century is a little old-fashioned, but the collection is large and colorful. Don't leave without visiting the ethnology section devoted to the Eskimos. All facets of their existence are exhibited in an attractive and realistic way. Open every day from 10 A.M. to 4 P.M. except Monday. Certain sections are open later. Free admission.

—*Statens Museum For Kunst* (Museum of Fine Arts): Sølvgade. One of the most important museums in Copenhagen. Remarkable collection of foreign paintings, some from the "golden century of Holland," and an exceptional collection by Matisse, drawings and paintings exploding with colors. Danish painting is brilliantly represented, especially the school of Skagen. Open from Tuesday to Saturday from 11 A.M. to 5 P.M. Free admission.

—*Tøjhusmuseet* (Military Museum): 3 Tøjhusgade. Telephone 11-60-37. In this building, constructed around 1600, are exhibits relating to military history: arms, uniforms, international trophies and so forth.

Besides these, there are many other kinds of museums: Wax, beer, medicine, post office, and so on. There's even a pipe museum. Information can be obtained at the Tourist Office.

• *Even More...*
—*Tivoli:* Famous amusement park near the station with pantomime theater, concert halls, games, roller coasters, et cetera. Fireworks 3 times a week including Sunday. Expensive restaurants. Tourist trap. We prefer the one at Bakken, more popular and free. S-Train to Klampenborg.

—*Visit the breweries:* Carlsberg, 140 Ny Carlsbergrej. Bus #6 or #18 for Val by Langgade. Free guided tours from Monday to Friday, at 9 A.M., 11 A.M., and 2:30 P.M. The visit to Tuborg, which is less known, seems more complete to us: 54 Strandvejen. Monday to Friday, from 8:30 A.M. to 2:30 P.M. Bus #1.

—*The Little Mermaid:* Even though it's nice, you could pass it up. A postcard suffices. Departures from Gammel Strand every half hour from 10 A.M.

Leaving Copenhagen

• *Hitchhiking*
—Toward the north (Sweden and Norway): Buses #6, #24, #27, and #84 to Hans Knudsens Plads.

—Toward the south (Germany): Bus #16 to Folehaven (Ring II) or S-Train to the Ellebjerg station (line A).

—Toward the west: S-Train to Roskildevej. Stop at Tastrup.

• *By Train and Plane*
Two companies offer tickets at reduced prices under certain conditions:

—*Transalpino:* 116 Vester Voldgade. Telephone 14-46-33. Open from 9 A.M. to 6 P.M., Saturday until 1 P.M.

—*Dis Rejser:* 28 Skindergade. Telephone: 11-00-44. Open from 9:30 A.M. to 5 P.M. Closed Saturday.

—You can also get information from *Use It.*

• **By Boat**

—To Sweden by hydrofoil: from Havnegade to Halmö. Every half hour daily from 6:15 A.M. to midnight. By boat, 3 times a day.

—To Oslo: From Kvaesthusbroden. Every day at 5 P.M.

NORTH ZEALAND

A synthesis of all that characterizes Denmark. Many castles, superb churches, dainty cities. From Copenhagen to Helsingör, the road follows the Danish "Riviera." On the way you pass the deer park of Klampenborg and Louisiania.

LOUISIANIA MUSEUM OF MODERN ART

Telephone (03)-19-07-19. One of the most beautiful museums in Europe, located just before the small city of Humlebaek. It's truly worth the trip. Very happy marriage of art and nature. Statues are scattered all over a magnificent park, and the paintings are hung in galleries linked by glass rooms; thus, not for one moment do you leave nature, and everything is bathed in an unbelievable light. The Calder mobiles stand out against the sea and the horizon. Truly well conceived and superbly shown.

The important collection of Giacometti's works and the temporary shows reveal the richness and healthy state of young Danish painting. Open from 10 A.M. to 5 P.M. Admission charge.

HELSINGØR/ELSINORE

The fishing and commerce port closest to Sweden. The city makes a fortune now, on tolls, which were formerly collected at Øresund. The city center is pretty and has many old homes from the seventeenth and eighteenth centuries. At the corner of Bjergegade and Stengade there's a handsome gabled home that houses a reasonably priced cafeteria. Stroll around Stengade, Strangade, and Sankt Olaigade streets to inhale the air of the past. (It is, after all, the home of Hamlet!)

Visit the fifteenth-century Sankt Mariae Church. The cloister is one of the best preserved in Europe. Visits at 11 A.M., 2 P.M. and 3 P.M. Admission charge.

—*Tourist Office:* 93 Strangade. Telephone (03)-21-13-33.

Where to Sleep, Where to Eat

—*Youth Hostel,* Moltke *Villa:* 24 Strandvej. Situated north of the city, near the sea, next to the beach. Telephone (02)-21-16-40. Bus #340. More than 200 beds.

—*Hornbaek Camping:* at Hornbaek, about 8 miles north of Helsingør. Telephone (02)-20-02-23. In a very pleasant little area near the sea. Dunes and pretty beaches.

—*Kalorius:* 8B Svingelport. A sociopolitical restaurant with proletariat prices. Near the entrance to the city coming from Humlebaek. Near the former fire station. Chance to meet a lot of people. Open evenings.

—*Salat Caféen:* 48 Stengade. Fresh and pleasant decor. Small, quiet courtyard for eating delicious salads. Open from noon to 6 P.M.

To See

—*Kronborg Castle:* A mile or so north of the city. Very imposing. Superb fortifications bordering the sea, evidently strategically placed. The fort was built in 1585 in Renaissance style. Where Shakespeare set the action for *Hamlet* . . . though he had never set foot in the area. See the chapel's choir stalls, pews, pulpit, and altar of sculpted golden wood. The knights hall is rather impressive—75 yards long with huge beams and a beautiful marble floor. A tour of the casemates allows you to see the statue of the national hero, Holger Dansk (Holger the Dane), who pretends to sleep and wakes up each time the nation is endangered.

FREDENSBORG

A castle located on the road between Helsingør and Hillerød, along Estrom Sø lake. Built in 1720 to celebrate the peace agreement between Denmark and Sweden. The Queen lives here from April through November, except July. During this month you can visit this elegant white-and-green residence, along with the royal apartments. Her park is open to the public all the time. The site was well chosen and offers a good opportunity to stroll.

In front of the castle stands the famous *Storekro* inn. It is very refined in decor and serves high-quality Danish food. For worldly hitchhikers.

TISVILDELEJE

Seaside resort frequented by the inhabitants of Copenhagen. Superb sandy beach. The whole coast is boardered by a forest of oaks and beech trees planted 200 years ago to prevent soil erosion. The little village of Tibirke, 2 miles from Tisvildeleje, was engulfed by sand. Only the church remains. Pleasant countryside with hills and woods.

Where to Sleep

—*Youth Hostel of Frederiksvaerk:* "Stranbo," 30 Strangade. Telephone (02)-12-07-66. Open at Easter and from April 1 to October 31.

FREDERIKSBORG

An extraordinary castle constructed in 1620. Situated on the coast of Hillerød. Elegant red-brick buildings in Renaissance style, covered with green-gray roofs, and clock towers. The main building was partially burned in 1859 but was superbly restored. The castle is located on the edge of a lake in a pretty wooded region. Up until 1848 the castle was a residence for Danish kings, and all the coronations took place there. Today it serves as the National History Museum. A must-see.

To See

—*Chapel:* Spared by the fire, it contains 2 floors of richly ornamented galleries. The altar and pulpit are ebony with silver decoration. Organ from 1610.

—*Hall of Honor:* Sumptuous. Crazy coffered ceilings and tapestries carefully restored after the great fire of 1859.

—On 2 floors, nearly 50 rooms of the most beautiful Danish furniture, paintings, royal portraits, and art objects. Admire the remarkable exhibition of miniatures and portraits in lockets from a time when photo booths did not exist. Frederiksborg is open from May 1 to September 30, from 10 A.M. to 5 P.M.; from 11 A.M. to 4 P.M. during the rest of the year.

ROSKILDE

When it was a royal city, it was a first-rate commercial and religious town; Roskilde has preserved its undefinable distinction and great nobility, represented by the tapered spires of its cathedral. Don't miss this pleasant city which has so much to offer.

Useful Addresses

—*Tourist Office:* Fondens Bro. Telephone 35-27-00. Right next to the cathedral.

—*Trains and Buses:* 1 Jernbanegade. Telephone (02)-35-23-48.

—*Post Office:* 3 Jernbanegade. Telephone 35-88-33.

—*Bike Rentals:* JAS Cykler, 3 Gullandsstraede.

Where to Sleep, Where to Eat

—*Youth Hostel* (Hørgåden): 61 Hørhusene. Telephone (02)-35-21-89. To get there, bus #604 or #601 which stops 10 minutes away by foot. Open from January 15 to December 15. Large and lovely house in the countryside.

—*Camping Vigen Strandparks:* Veddelev. Telephone 75-79-96. The closest to the city, it's 2 miles to the north. Very well kept. The water is cold, but the view of the fjord is superb. Open from mid-April to mid-September.

—*Camping Borrevejle:* DK-4060 Kirke Såby. Telephone 40-01-40. Open all year. Very far from the city.

—*Svogerslev Kro:* Svogerslev. Telephone (02)-38-30-05. The least expensive hotel in the city, but a ways from the city, toward the west.

Pretty, well-equipped cottage, at 250 Kr for a double and 130 Kr for a single.

—*Hos Mester:* 42 Algade. Meals served from 11 A.M. to 2 P.M. and from 5 P.M. to 8 P.M. Inexpensive food and a pleasant terrace.

To See

—*Domkirke* (Cathedral): This immense church happily links the Roman and Gothic styles, and its interior is splendid. The sovereigns of Denmark are buried here: 38 tombs in all. Some are in a gaudy, heavy baroque style; others are masterpieces of intricate stonework. The handsome shelf above the altar (the retable) in Renaissance style dates from 1580. The wooden stalls were sculpted in 1420. Behind the altar, Queen Magrethe I lies in her tomb of black and white marble. A dozen chapels encircle the nave. Linger around the tomb of Christian IV (1620)—unforgettable baroque richness, carved sarcophagi, epitaphs, frescos, and superb iron-forged gates (1618). It is too much! Open every day.

—*Former Episcopalian Palace:* Right next to the cathedral. Harmonious 1733 construction in orange and white tones. Here, royalty stayed for funerals. Attached to the cathedral by the Absalon arch. Some paintings and furniture. Open from 1 P.M. to 5 P.M.

—*Museum of Viking Boats:* Built on the wharf next to the water. Complete carcasses, more or less, of five boats that sailed in the Roskilde fjord around the year 1000 to prevent foreign invasion. They were patiently rebuilt by experts from thousands of pieces of debris found in 1957. After all that time in the water, the wood could not stand being dried out. Several hundred pounds of a type of liquid, (glycol), were injected into the "pores" of the wood. Among the boats there is a *knarr* (a high-seas merchant vessel), another merchant vessel, a *drakkar* (a warship powered by 24 rowers), a ferry, and a 92-foot ship used for long expeditions. The presentation is very didactic. An interesting film on the raising of the ships. Open November to March from 10 A.M. to 4 P.M.; in April, May, September, and October from 9 A.M. to 5 P.M. Summer months from 9 A.M. to 6 P.M. Admission charge. Information: Telephone (03)-35-65-55.

—*Museum of Roskilde:* 18 Sankt Olaigade. Telephone 36-60-44. Regional museum presenting collections of peasant costumes (pretty embroideries), folklore costumes, and so forth. Open from 2 P.M. to 5 P.M.

—*A pleasant stroll around the port and the Skt. Jørgensberg area:* Old row houses and winding streets. In the summer, tours in the fjord with the old "steam-veteran" *Skjelskor* at 2:30 P.M. and 4 P.M. every Saturday and Sunday.

Festivals

Every year at Roskilde, on the first weekend of July, a 3-day festival takes place, a sort of mini-Woodstock. If you like music, don't miss it. Plenty of Norwegians, Swedes, Danes, and other travelers.

Around and About

—*Research Center of Lejre* (Oldtidsbyen): Located about 5 miles southwest of Roskilde. These iron- and stone-age villages were reconstructed in a pretty area of rolling hills; they offer multiple activities and archaeological finds. The promoters try to duplicate the mode of life in the long-gone days of the first trades and craftspeople. During the school year, all the students of the country go there at least once to learn how to make fire (in case of war); to maneuver a canoe, dug out from a tree trunk, on a pond; to grind grains; to prepare a prehistoric meal, and so forth. Finally, history lessons among the hills, presenting every aspect of domestic life during the iron age, with lively and detailed explanations. Truly interesting tours. Open every day from 10 A.M. to 5 P.M. from May to September. Telephone (02)-38-02-45. Admission is 20 Kr and 7 Kr for students. Rather difficult to reach by hitchhiking. Take the Roskilde–Lejre train, then the bus from Lejre. Bus schedule: 8:43 A.M., 9:43 A.M., 12:43 P.M., and 5 P.M.

Possible side trips within a circumference of a few miles:

—*Ledreborg Castle:* A baroque residence from 1740 with an English park. Open in the summer from 10 A.M. to 4 P.M.

—*Gammel Lejre:* Small, typical Danish village with thatched-roof cottages. Small museum.

—Near Øm, right next to it, a tomb with a 5000-year-old subterranean passage. Bring a flashlight.

KØGE

A small, peaceful city that will please lovers of old and pretty timber-framed houses. The oldest house in Denmark is here.

—*Tourist Office:* 1 Vestergade.

Where to Sleep, Where to Eat

—*Youth Hostel "Lille Køgegard":* Ølbyvej. Telephone (03)-65-14-74. Open from May 15 to September 1. Located 2 miles from the station, outside the city.

—*SDR Strands Camping:* Bodevej. Telephone 65-07-69. Located 100 yards from the sea and near the town center.

—*Vallø Camping:* South of the city at Vallø. Far enough but located in the woods near a very pretty beach. Telephone 65-28-51.

—*Ritchers Gaard:* 16 Vestergade. Telephone 66-29-49. In a splendid timber-framed house from 1644. Count on 60–70 Kr per meal.

To See

—*Old Houses:* Particularly on Kirkestraede: 20, the blacksmith's house, and 13, assumed to be the oldest in the country (1527). And #7 and 11 (play those numbers) Vestergade and #16 Brogade. Also on Nørregade: # 4 (a museum) and #31.

—*Regional Museum:* 4 Nørregade. Telephone 65-02-62. Superb exhibit of the history of the city through its costumes, furniture, domestic objects, and so forth. Køge was a great merchant port for a long time, and into it flowed merchandise from all over Europe. A must-see. Open in the summer every day from 10 A.M. to 5 P.M.

Around and About

—*Vallø Castle:* 5 miles southeast of Køge. The park is open every day. Elegant brick building with a pretty dome rising above round towers.

ISLAND OF MØN

The travelers who rush from Rødby to Copenhagen often have a tendency to forget this island. Too bad. Møn is a veritable ecological jewel, a happy compromise between the gentleness of Belle-Île off the Brittany Coast and the charm of Ireland, a paradise for geologists. . . . Here you find the *Grinjaegers hoj,* the most important prehistoric graves in the country. There are also nearly 200 mounds from the Bronze Age. For cyclists, small country roads, sinewy hills and dales allow you to discover the riches of the island. Bicycle rentals at Stege and Magleby.

How to Get There

- From Copenhagen: Train to Vordingborg, then a bus to Møns Klint, four times a day, from May 27 to September 27.
- From Falster Island: Ferry from Stubbekøbing at Bogø.

• *The Road of Churches*
On your way to Møns Klint you will find some of the most beautiful rural churches in Denmark.

—*Keldby:* A lavish selection of frescos by the master from Elmelunde. Camping.

—*Elmelunde:* The oldest church of the island. Frescos portraying scenes from village life. All white, on a little hill, it formerly served as a landmark for fishermen. Unfortunately, these days it's often closed. Camping.

—*Borre:* Magnificent exterior architecture.

—*Magleby:* Rather austere red-brick construction, dating from 1200, with Roman influences.

• *Møns Klint*
On the eastern point, 20,000 years ago, the sudden freezing of the waters elevated the chalky depths of the sea, creating these high cliffs, sprinkled with needles and steep slopes. This geological curiosity is know as Møns Klint. Erosion did the rest. Different rock formations appeared, along with millions of shells and animal fossils. You can walk for 5 miles at the foot of the cliffs, and even swim. In the evening there's a superb spectacle of the sun playing on the white cliffs, enhanced by the hues of green from the bordering forest of beeches.

Where to Sleep

—*Sømarke Youth Hostel:* 18–19 Stendyssevej at Somarke. Telephone (03)-81-21-42. Adorable youth hostel in the middle of nature. The manager is very kind. The bus coming from Stege stops 1½ miles

away. Some prehistoric stones nearby on the road from Magleby (Sømarkdyssen).
—*Lodging at the farm near Stege:* The home of Alice and H. J. Rasmussen, Skovsgärd, Klintevej 15. Kitchen, bathroom, recreation room, TV, for 45 Kr per person.
—Campgrounds at Liselund and on the cliffs.

To See

—*The cliffs:* Reached by a stairway; at its foot there's a small exhibition on the local geographical discoveries. The "Queen's Chair" is 416 feet high.
—*Liselund Castle:* Stunning 1795 mansion with a thatched roof. Overlooks a magnificent English garden that is open to the public. Tours from May 1 to October 31 at 10:30 A.M. and 11 A.M. and 1:30 P.M. and 2 P.M. Tours on Sunday also at 4 P.M. and 4:30 P.M. Pretty furniture.
—*Klintholm:* Large park with wide roads, ponds, and a neo-Renaissance-style manor house. The park is open daily. Also a small port and pretty beach.

• South of the Island of Møn

—*Fanefjord Church:* A true picture book. All the arches are covered with frescos portraying episodes from the Bible, made for the peasants who were illiterate.
—*Prehistoric graves of Gronjaegers Høj,* with three "rooms" and more than 100 stones around it.
—*A 1½-mile dam* links Møn to the small island of Bofø. Pretty church with some Roman influences and an old Dutch windmill (1852). Ferry from Bøgo to Stubbekøbing on Falster Island.

Where to Sleep, Where to Eat

—*Mønsbroen Campgrounds:* At Koster. Telephone 81-40-70.
—*Verstmøn Campgrounds:* At Harbølle. Telephone 81-72-77.
—Campgrounds at Bogo.
—*Fanefjord Grobpavillon:* 1½ miles from the Fanefjord church, past the small village of Vindebaek. Inn is in the middle of a forest. Good kitchen and *Dan Menu.* Accessible only by car.

FALSTER ISLAND

Flatter, less secret than the Island of Møn, but it does offer some pleasant landscapes. At Stubbekøbing, a motorcycle museum which is interesting. More than 100 models and some old scooters.
—*Tourist Office:* 9 Havnegade. Telephone 84-13-04.
The road that follows the coast to Nykøbing crosses the small, charming fishing port of Hesnoës. The walls of the houses are covered with wicker, in accordance with the local custom. Some cliffs at Pomlenakke and a mansion and large forest at Korselitze.
At Nykøbing there is yet another pretty red-brick church. Inside see the family trees painted in 1627 with an extraordinary feeling for detail.
—*Youth Hostel:* Open from May 1 to September 15.

LOLLAND ISLAND

A hopelessly flat island on which you start walking while debarking at Rødby. The inhabitants of Møn smilingly say that when you stand on a case of beer you can see the whole island of Lolland. And then you can see that there are some sites to visit.

NYSTED

The southernmost city in Denmark. Right next to it is Alholm, a lovely castle with a park that is open to the public. Half a mile away, on the road to Rødby, is the largest automobile museum in Northern Europe. Fabulous. More than 300 models, from the 1901 Delauney–Belleville to the 1938 Bugatti, and in between the magnificent 1922 Pierce Arrow. Telephone 87-15-09. Free admission.
—*Tourist Office:* 67 Adelgade.

MARIBO

A really carefree, small, provincial city, with a colorful flowered street leading to the cathedral. However, don't waste your time if you're in a hurry.
—*Tourist Office:* Jernebanegade. Telephone 88-04-96.

Where to Sleep, Where to Eat
—*Youth Hostel:* 19 Skelstrupvej. Telephone (03)-88-33-14. Far enough from the town; 3 miles from the station.
—*Hotel S. Hansen:* Jernbanegade and Museumgade. Near the station. Meals served from 10 A.M. to 10 P.M.
—*Maribo Campgrounds:* 25 Bangshavevej. Telephone 88-00-71.

To See
—*Cathedral:* A splendid 1470 Gothic church. The interior is whitewashed with limestone, accentuating the 1641 Baroque retable and the pulpit. Open from 9 A.M. to 6 P.M..
—*Diocesan Museum:* Jernebanegade. Collection of regional antiques and paintings. Many tacky items, but a small section of contemporary paintings, notably some canvases by Paul Janus Ipsen. Don't miss the room devoted to Christ on the cross. While it's from the Middle Ages, some of it has an astonishingly contemporary style.
—*Frilands Museum* (open-air museum): Meinckesvej. You can see farms and houses typical of Lolland, with their furniture, decoration, and domestic objects.

Around and About
—*Knuthenborg:* 3-4 miles form Maribo, a photo-safari park of 1,500 acres with miles of interior roads to observe the "wild beasts" roaming freely. A superb wild zoo for those who like that. Car required. Open every day from 10 A.M. to 6 P.M. Admission fee. In the

summer, an old retired locomotive and wagons link Maribo to its port, Bankholm.

—*Birket Church:* 12 miles west of Maribo. A pretty church with a steeple of a different kind of wood. The only example of this in Denmark. Of interest only to the motorized aesthetes of religious architecture.

FYN ISLANDS

Comprised of 4 principal islands: Langeland, Tåsinge, Aero, and Fyn, 4 small smiling faces that are a required sight on a serious visit to Denmark. You can get to Langeland by ferry from Lars to Spodsbjerg in 45 minutes. 1 crossing an hour all year. In season from 6:45 A.M. to 11:45 P.M. (weekends, 9:45 P.M.). All the other islands are linked by bridges (except Aero).

LANGELAND

The longest and least known of the 4. Round, hilly landscapes covered with windmills, white limestone churches, and small woods and high forests licked by the sea.

To See

—*Tranekaer Castle:* About 8 miles north of Rudkøbing. Free admission to the exterior park with moats. A great blood-red structure built at an angle on top of a hill overlooking the small, charming villages.

—*Bøsrup Church:* A few miles up from Tranekaer. Multilayered roofs and very old granite figures inlaid in the walls. The small cemetery and the old cottage next door are charming.

—*Rudkøbing:* The "capital" of the island. Pretty timber-framed houses around Smedegade, Brogade, and Østergade streets. See 15 Brogade, the old pharmacy and its little medicinal herb garden. The regional museum of Langeland, 12 Jens Winthers Vej, displays interesting collections and temporary exhibitions.

Where to Sleep, Where to Eat

—*Youth Hostel of Rudkøbing:* Dyrskuepladsen. Telephone (09) 51-18-30. Open from May 15 to September 15. Has 2 rooms for families.

—*Tullebølle Kro:* At Tullebølle, a little before Tranekaer. Telephone 50-13-25. Single or double rooms. Reasonably priced restaurant.

—*Tranekaer Gaestgivergard:* At Tranekaer. Telephone 59-12-04. An old inn from the nineteenth century; somewhat luxurious. Breakfast included. Good Danish kitchen. For honeymooning hitchhikers.

—*Campgrounds:* At Bagenkop, Lohals, Tranekaer, Rudkøbing, and Spodsbjerg.

TÅSINGE

When a bridge linked it to Svendborg, Tåsinge lost much of its autonomy but not its seduction. Pleasant to explore on bike.

To See

—*Troense:* A small, very touristy port with neat houses. The local maritime museum, in an old school dating from 1790, is amusing with its ship models, paintings, drawings, and all sorts of souvenirs. Sea-related.

—*Valdemar Castle:* A few miles from Troense. Built in 1756 in baroque style. On either side of the castle are pretty, yellow-and-white farmhouses with bell towers, and there is a large pond in front. Valdemar became an annex of the maritime museum, with an emphasis on the furniture and collections of the former landowner, an admiral who made his fortune in naval battles. Rather high admission fee.

—*Bregninge:* The main village has an interesting hilltop church, the focal point of the island, with a beautiful head of Christ dating from 1200 and some ship models from the eighteenth century. If the church is closed, you can still climb the exterior staircase to the belfry for a great view of the area.

A small museum of local interest in an 1826 building. Some writing (in Danish only, unfortunately) about the tragic end of Elvira Madigan and her lover. This famous dancer, immortalized in many books, is buried in the cemetery in Landet, a few miles away.

AERO ISLAND

The prettiest of the Fyn Islands, perhaps because time seems not to have touched it. Its smartly colored seventeenth- and eighteenth-century houses continue to enliven the varied landscapes. Super-touristy in the summer. To rent a bike is not just an idea but a necessity. (In Aeroskøbing at Pielbaekken.)

—*Ferry* from Svendborg to Aerokøbing: 10 times a day; 1 hour and 15 minutes.

—*Tourist Office:* Det Gamle Rådhus, Torvet. Telephone (09)-52-13-00.

To See

—*Aeroskøbing:* The "capital" offers some charming places to visit: a collection of boats in bottles at 22 Smedegade; a small regional museum in Brogade, consist of the former pharmacy and some furnishings, goods, and clothes, evoking life on this island for the past 3 centuries. The house of the sculptor Hammerich at 22 Gyden can be toured. The city boasts Denmark's oldest post office (1749) on Vestergade. Open in the summer for the sale of stamps from 1 A.M. to 4 P.M., Monday to Friday.

—*Bregninge:* A Romanesque church with frescos and a magnificent triptych by Claus Berg (1530)

—Go see the small port of *Søby* and numerous prehistoric remains. A list can be obtained at the Tourist Office.

—*Marstal:* Had been one of the most important ports in Denmark; even today, in spite of its decline, its life revolves around the sea.
—*Tourist Office:* 25 Kirkestraede. Telephone (09)-53-19-60.

You can visit the Church of Sailors; touching, with its votive lights. Also the Museum of Marstal at 4 Prinsengade. Objects and memorabilia from all over the world, with a great collection of miniatures of boat models, arms, etchings, photos, and so forth. Very rewarding.

Where to Sleep

Youth Hostel: 29 Faergestraede. (300 yards from the port.) Telephone 53-10-64. Open from May 1 to September 1.

Other Ferries

—*Rudkøbing–Marstal:* 5 times a day. Telephone 53-17-22.
—*Faborg–Søby:* 5 times a day. Telephone (in Faborg) 61-14-88.
—*Monmark* (Jutland)–*Søby:* from mid-June to mid-August, 4 times a day. May and September, 2 times a day. No boats off-season. Telephone 58-17-17.

FYN

An island that has not rejected industrialization but still maintains an ecological miracle. The prettiest Danish countryside, hidden villages, sharp hedgerows, windmills, forests, and timber-framed houses. It is not surprising that many people choose to live their retirement years here.

SVENDBORG

A great port for many years, Valdemar the Victorious and the pirates of the Baltic Sea came to quench their thirst and sacked the city from time to time. In spite of that, a great number of houses survived, and a stroll through the small streets is super. Lively and many young people. What more could you want?

Useful Addresses

—*Tourist Office:* 20 Møllergade. Telephone 21-09-80. Can change money in a pinch.
—*Post Office:* 11 Klosterplads. Telephone 21-52-07.

Where to Sleep

Youth Hostel Villa Søro: 3 Bellevuevej. Telephone 21-26-16. Located about a mile from the station. Bus #201. Past the Kellogs factory on top of the hill. Very quiet, wooden, with a view of the sea. The manager is a nice guy. Open from March 1 to November 30.

—*Fåborgvej Campgrounds:* 21 Ryttervej. Telephone 21-36-10. Open from May 15 to August 30. Near enough to the center of town.

—*Hotel Royal:* 5 Toldbodvej. Telephone 21-21-13. A few minutes from the station and the least expensive in town. Single and doubles.

Where to Eat and Where to Down a Tuborg

—*Jazz 79:* 79 Møllergade. Telephone 21-50-89. Open every day from 2 P.M. to 3 A.M., Friday and Saturday until 5 A.M. Meals served until 9 P.M. Discothèque.

—*Kloster Moster:* Klosterplads. Open every day from 10 A.M. to 2 A.M. Friday and Saturday until 3 A.M. Frequented solely by young people and students. Great atmosphere. Light meals served in the evening. At 10 P.M. every day, rock and funky music bands.

—*Bøg Café:* 22 Grubemøllevej. Telephone 22-02-10. A bit out of the city. Open from Tuesday to Thursday from 10 A.M. to 5:30 P.M., Monday to 2 P.M. and Friday to 7 P.M. Cafeteria, bookstore, and laundromat. Frequented by the young and unusual.

To See

—*Regional Museum:* 3 Fruestraede, near the market. Telephone 21-02-61. Located in *Anne Hvides Gård*, an old house (1560) that is very pretty. Collection of domestic objects and dishes from the seventeenth and eighteenth centuries.

—*Notre-Dame Church:* Dominates the market place. Of Romanesque origins, it has been considerably renovated in the Gothic style. Rather austere interior, with a pulpit from 1598 and a Renaissance-style altar from the beginning of the seventeenth century. The 27 bells chime at noon and 4 P.M. At 10 P.M., they ring one last time to remind "the good people" that it's beddie-bye time, perpetuating the Middle Ages custom of the "town crier."

—*Saint Nicolas Church:* Gerritsgade. The oldest church in the city. Lovely red-brick structure. Light and bright interior.

—*Timber-framed houses:* On Bagergade, Gaasestraede, and Møllergade. See the magnificent Wiggers Gaard, at the market place, which houses a large store.

EGESKOV CASTLE

Located about 12 miles from Svendborg on the road to Odense. Justly considered one of the most beautiful European Renaissance castles. Built on a lake, it stands on oak posts. The park, with its baroque gardens and 200-year-old trees, is open to the public from 9 A.M.–6 P.M. Admission fee. A cafeteria is in one of the former stables of the castle. At the other end of the park is the "veteran" museum: old cars, motorcycles, and some fighter planes, as well as a remarkable collection of different types of carriages—bench, face-to-face, country hearses, buggies, coupés and so forth. Admission fee.

Where to Sleep

Youth Hostel Midtfyns Fritidscenter: Floravej. About 6 miles north of Egeskov, at Ringe. Bus stop half a mile away. Telephone 62-21-51. Opens June 1.

ODENSE

Pronounced "Wensay." A typical ultra-touristy city, but it would be a shame to miss. Home of Hans Christian Andersen, who made millions of kids cry with his story of the little match girl. For a long time the city was a hot spot for pilgrimages honoring Saint Knud, the king assassinated in 1086. Some beautiful churches remain.

Useful Addresses

—*Tourist Office:* On Rådhuset near Vestergade. Telephone (09)-12-75-20.

—*Central Station:* Østre Stationvej. Telephone 12-01-48.

—*Central Post Office:* 1 Lille Gråbrødrestraede. - Telephone 12-04-83.

—*Telephone and Telegraph:* 3 Klosterbakken.

Where to Sleep, Where to Eat

—*Youth Hostel Kragsbjerggården:* 121 Kragsbjergvej. Telephone (09)-13-04-25. 1 mile from the station. Bus #6. Open all year except from December 20 to January 2.

—*Hunderup Campgrounds:* 102 Odensevej. Telephone 11-47-02. Bus #1. Pleasantly located and right next to the city.

—*Blommenslyst:* 494 Middelfartvej. Telephone 96-76-41. Rather far west of the city.

—*Målet:* 17 Jernbanegade. Telephone 11-82-44.

To See

—*Andersen House:* 45 Hans Jensens Straede. Open in season from 9 A.M. to 7 P.M. All the souvenirs, photos, letters, and objects that belonged to Andersen. Their presentation is impeccable and lively. Full of interesting things that truly lets you enter the world of this storyteller: drawings, sketches of voyages, collages he did while bored, and so forth. Afterwards you'll understand better how Andersen, who was enormously slow at school and often among the "dunces," was able to write the adorable tale of "The Ugly Duckling." The entire neighborhood has been superbly renovated, but it is obviously very touristy. You can also visit his birthplace, 3–5 Munkembøllestraede.

—*Saint Knud Cathedral:* On Flakhaven. Open from May 1 to August 31 from 10 A.M. to 5 P.M., Sunday from 11:30 to 12:30. One of the most important Gothic churches in the country. Look at the remarkable triptych retable with 300 figures sculpted by Claus Berg, the Odense master. Baptismal fonts date back to 1720. Those who like religious architecture should visit *Skt. Hans Church,* with its exterior pulpit, and *Frue Kirke,* with its copper roof and baptismal font and pulpit sculpted by Mortensen (circa 1600).

—*Møntegården:* 48 Overgade. Open from 10 A.M. to 4 P.M. Group of old houses: Møntegården (1646), Ejler Rønnow (1547), and Østerbye house (1631). Furniture, dishes, domestic objects, and clothes from that period.

—*Fyn Museum of Art:* 13 Jernbanegade. Open every day from 10 A.M. to 4 P.M. and Wednesday from 7 to 10 P.M. All movements of

Danish art, particularly the school of Fyn painters. A section of the museum is devoted to the prehistoric period of the island.

—*National Danish Railway Museum:* 24 Dannebrogsgade. On the north side of the Central Station. Open from 10 A.M. to 4 P.M. You guessed it . . . an interesting collection of old locomotives.

—*Falck Museum:* 28 Klostervej, 300 yards from the station toward the southwest. A museum for future ambulance drivers only. They'll see all the emergency vehicles one could imagine from the eighteenth century on.

—Lovers of old houses will stroll the Jernbanegade to see the *Grabrødrekloster* (Monastery of the Gray Friars) from 1279, Abani Torv and the "convent for young noble ladies from Odense" (circa 1500), and Overgade.

—*Fionian Village* (Hunderup Skov): Sejerskovvej. Telephone 13-13-72. Bus #2. Open in April and May from 9 A.M. to 4:30 P.M.; from June through August 15 from 9 A.M. to 6:30 P.M.; in October to 3:30 P.M.; from November to March on Sundays only from 10 A.M. to 3:30 P.M. Consists of about 20 farms and rural homes that have been renovated, along with a windmill, forge, tile shop, and so forth. An inn serves delicious (but a little expensive) Fyn dishes. In the summer there are popular dances on Sundays and small plays adapted from Andersen's tales.

—You can visit a glass blower, *Holmegaard A/S*, 20 Lille Glasvej. Telephone 11-44-17. Closed in July. Tours at 10:30 A.M. and 1:15 P.M..

—*Market:* Wednesdays and Saturdays at Sortebrødretorv.

KOLDING

A stopover during your visit to Jutland, with an imposing fort that you can visit.

—*Tourist Office:* 18 Helligkorsgade.

—*Youth Hostel:* 10 Ornsborvej. Telephone (05)-52-76-84. Closed from December 15 to January 15.

BILLUND

This city has no interest unless you're traveling with your kids or you want to photograph blonds. Isn't it the ideal place for kids? This is where they manufacture the famous Lego games. An amusement park provides games, a western city, models of castles, villages made with Lego sets, and even an imitation of Mount Rushmore . . . assembled with 1,500,000 Lego bricks. Familiar, tacky, and touristy. Open in season from 10 A.M. to 8 P.M.

Where to Sleep Around Here

—*Billund Camping:* 3 Nordmarklveg. Telephone 33-15-21.

—*Youth Hostel Mørsbol Skolevej:* 24 at Grindsted. Telephone (05)-32-26-05. Closed from December 20 to January 6.

—*Youth Hostel Gl. Landevej 80 at Vejle:* 2 miles from the station. Telephone (05)-82-51-88. Bus #1 stops 200 yards away.

ÅRHUS

The second city of Denmark is also a large university. Once upon a time this was an important Viking city because of its strategic location, then a flourishing commercial port for centuries, before becoming a large industrial city surrounded by forests. Århus has a certain charm that we like almost as much as Copenhagen. The area around the port and the cathedral is laced with peaceful little streets lined with decrepit old houses. The hangouts are full of students and are particularly lively (less in summer, of course). To keep you busy during the day, there are some interesting museums. Then how come you're not yet in Århus?

Useful Addresses

—*Tourist Office:* Rådhuset. Telephone 12-16-00. Open from June 15 to August 31, from 9 A.M. to 9 P.M., the rest of the year from 9 A.M. to 5 P.M.
—*Post Office:* Central Station plaza.
—*Bus:* For information Telephone 12-86-22.

Where to Sleep

—*Youth Hostel Pavillonnen:* Østre Skoveej, 8240 Risskov. Telephone 16-72-98. Well located. Only 2 miles from the center of town, near the beach, and surrounded by forest. Open all year. Bus #1 or #2 from Central Station to the *Marienlund* terminal.

—*Blommenhaven Campgrounds:* In an ideal spot in the forest. Spread out on terraces above Århus Bay. Follow the forest road along the beach, about 3½ miles south. Bus #19 from Central Station directly to the campgrounds, (limited summer service) or bus #6 to Hørhaveveg. Open from mid-May to mid-September. Telephone 27-02-07.

—*Århus North Campgrounds:* On A10/E3 in the direction of Alborg (5 miles to the north near Lisjborg). Telephone 23-11-33. Pleasant place with a swimming pool. You can rent a wooden cabin. Open all year. Bus #54 from the bus station to Lisbjerg.

—*Strautrup Campgrounds:* Ormslevvej in Stautrup (4½ miles west of Århus). Telephone 28-33-40. Bus #55 from the bus station. Open all year.

—*Hotel Sømandshjem:* 20 Havnegade. Telephone 12-15-99. Very centrally located and one of the least expensive in the city.

Where to Eat

—*Tio Pepe:* Fiskergade and Fredens Torv, 300 yards from the cathedral. Spanish restaurant, a meeting place for young city people. Lively and warm atmosphere. Fish and meat dishes. One of the least expensive in the city.

—*Varme Stuen:* Mejlgade. Near the cathedral. For the broke, it's the Salvation Army. Decent grub for a few Kr.

—*Garveriet:* 14 Mejlgade. Danish dishes around 35 Kr. Very vital.

Where to Down a Few

Here are a few addresses that, indubitably, will enable you to make some interesting acquaintances:

—*Fronthuset:* 53 Mejlgade, not far from the cathedral. A great place for drinking, eating, or just discussing. It's a former factory converted cooperatively by a hundred students. Various activities. Nice, not expensive, and very good for meeting people. Find out if it still exists.

—*Huset:* 15 Vesteralle. Telephone (06)-12-26-77. A kind of cultural center for youths in the middle of the city with lots of activities. Every evening at 9 or 10 there's a rock or folk concert. Also has a café-theater with small tables and a warm atmosphere.

—*Alsken:* 8 Arnholtsgade, a small street parallel to Nørregade. On the top floor of an old building. You'll find nothing but neighborhood youths; there are no tourists because it's not easy to find. Intimate and pleasant atmosphere. Open every evening until midnight and Saturday until 1 A.M.

—*Café Himmelha:* Mejlgade and Skt. Olufs Gade. The kind of café you find in every city that attracts some young people: bright lights, gaudy paintings, old moleskin seats, movie posters . . .

To See

—*The Old City* (Den gamle By): One of the most popular curiosities of Denmark, with 60 timber-framed houses brought from all over the country. Block by block, stone by stone, they reconstructed these private homes, commercial houses, shops, workshops, small industries, windmills, customs house, post office, and so forth. In the market place, in the heart of the "Old City," you'll find the mayor's office, the best of the museum; 400 years old, it contains magnificent furniture, like that formerly owned by wealthy Danish families. Bus #3.

—*Prehistoric Museum:* In the Moesgård mansion south of Århus. Bus #6 to the terminal or bus #19 to the beach, then walk to the museum. Exceptional location and one of the most beautiful museums in Denmark (and we need to say no more). Complete explanations of the different periods. Skeletons, domestic objects, jewelry, and so forth, are placed exactly how they were found in the earth or in stones. Enlarged photos show the placement of homes, people, and animals, and the jewelry photos are magnified at least 10 times. Magnificent runic stones. See one kind of natural phenomenon—the Grauballe man—dating back to the iron age and found intact in a peat bog. They determined that he was born in 80 B.C., lived for 30 years, and suffered from arthritis. He was surely an intellectual of the period (long, refined hands) who the day he died had eaten some porridge (barley and oats) mixed with dozens of culinary herbs. The iron content in the soil gave him a reddish tint, and the tannic acids preserved him. There are many other things to see, such as votive lamp stands, carved cauldrons, and a remarkable section on Eskimo life. You can top off the visit with a walk through the forest following a marked path past megalithic stones, dolmens, circles of stones, and reconstructions of prehistoric homes. Great.

—*Cathedral:* A magnificent work in the shape of a cross with a tapered spire. Has the longest nave in Denmark and many treasures: baptismal fonts from 1481, an altar from the sixteenth century, and an especially extraordinary retable by the master of Lübeck, Bernt Notke. Open from 9:30 A.M. to 4 P.M.

—*Kunstmuseum* (Fine Arts Museum): Vennelyst Park, along Nørrebrogade. Open from 10 A.M. to 4 P.M., Saturday and Sunday to 5 P.M.; closed Monday. All the Danish painting movements, with a particularly seductive contemporary section. Look at the works by Wilhelm Lundstrøm bursting into different styles, from Expressionism to Cubism; those by Jens Søndergaard, whose landscapes show his obsession with death; those by expressionist Harald Giersing (*Dancers 1920*); and the posters by Thor Bøgelund. Full of equally interesting small bronzes.

—*Museum of Danish Firemen:* Bus #1 to Dalgas Avenue. Open every day from May 1 to September 30. Nearly 60 vehicles from the Vikings to the present. It's the most important museum of its kind, so we thought we should mention it.

—*Library:* Møllenparken. Many books in many languages, including English. Open from May to August, from 10 A.M. to 8 P.M.

—*Århus Festival:* Each year at the beginning of September a festival gets under way with jazz concerts, improvisations in the street, marionettes, old-type fairs, and sports matches in the "old city." If you vacation in Denmark in September, start here. You won't forget it.

The Road from Århus to the Mols Region

For the motorists and those not in a rush, a chance to wander on small roads searching for rural churches and castles, to whet your appetite before arriving in the Mols region.

—*Todbjerg Church:* On the road from Lisbjerg to Mejlby. Made of granite in the twelfth century. Lovely stone lions at the door. The interior has the remains of some original frescos.

—*Hornslet:* This church contains some remarkable treasures, such as baptismal fonts and a retable by Jutland master Claus Berg. Pretty frescos from the fourteenth century in astonishingly vivid and fresh colors. Very lively combat scenes. Rather surprising when you think of the frescos from the same period in Yugoslavia, often so dark and heavy. There are 14 generations of the Rozenkrantz family buried here.

—*Rosenholm Castle:* Small, charming, Renaissance-style castle with grand roofs, small, domed towers, moats, and a large park. Tours every day from June 19 to August 8, from 10 A.M. to noon and from 1 P.M. to 5 P.M. Admission fee. Pretty 300-year-old Flemish tapestries and a collection of domestic objects rediscovered 20 years ago while cleaning the moats.

—*Thorsager Church:* The only round church in Jutland; constructed around 1200 in brick, with 4 support columns for 9 arches.

MOLS REGION

One of the prettiest regions in Denmark. The topography appears somewhat accidental, with a pleasant effect. After Vrinners, there's a magnificent panorama of Århus Bay and the Mols Hoved peninsula. The countryside is spotted with small white farms spread out across impeccable green round hills. If you have the time to go to Ebeltoft, take the coast road by Vrinners and the charming little port of Knebelbro rather than the direct route. See, near Knebel, the dolmen of *Posk aer Stenhus.*

—*Sølystgaard Campgrounds:* On the Sletter Hage peninsula on the road from Helgenaes.

—*Youth Hostel Kalo:* 2 Kaløvej in Rønde. Telephone 37-11-08. On the outskirts of the city going toward Grenå. Open from April 1 to September 30.

EBELTOFT

This could be called a small city or a large town. Full of charm, providing pleasant walks on cobblestone streets with old timber-framed houses. One of the oldest cities in the country, it received its charter in 1301. Truly worth the trip. Stores and museums close at 5 P.M.

—*Tourist Office:* 9 Torvet. Telephone (06)-34-14-00.

—*Youth Hostel:* 43 Søndergade. Telephone (06)-34-20-53. Open all year except from December 1 to January 6. Well located not far from the city.

—Six campgrounds offer pleasant locales, including *Elsegårde* and *Draby* on the east coast.

To See

—The former town hall of 1567 was converted into a small museum, comprising 3 sections:

• A small archaeological section.

• The museum of Siam: original and rather unique. Thygesen Havmøller, a native of Ebeltoft, left at a young age to work in Siam as a forester, staying there 20 years. A victim of malaria, he returned with this surprising collection (he died in 1940). We highly recommend a visit for those who anticipate a visit to Thailand. You will see a jumble of old photos full of mystery, an unbelievable collection of exotic birds, snakes, bats, iguanas in jars, artwork, daggers, rare swords, and so forth. All the ambiguous charm of "the good old days."

• A small ethnological section, with furniture and domestic objects. Observe these 2 curious traditions that have disappeared today: hair jewelry by Swedish craftsmen (several Ebeltoft artists wove flowers, necklaces, and earrings into ladies' hair) and a collection of condolence cards for the deceased, more moving than today's simple cards, with drawings done with flowers, homey writings, poems placed under glass and framed, and so forth.

Be aware that to find the ethnology section you must leave the Siam museum and go to the building that was the town hall, 25 yards from the corner of the street. The same ticket is valid for both places.

—*Jylland Frigate:* Built in 1860, although now demasted, it remains the oldest war boat in the world still afloat. Tours from May 7 to September 30, from 11 A.M. to 5 P.M. Admission fee.

—*Old dye works of the seventeenth century:* Open from 10 A.M. to 5 P.M. Closed Monday.

—Walk to discover the often charming interior courtyards and disjointed cobblestone streets with their old houses, like *Den skaeve Bar* in Overgade.

The Road Toward the North of Jutland

You can continue to journey along the coast of Djursland by Grenå or head directly to Randers, Hobro, and Ålborg. It's a question of time, of course, and possibly an overdose of churches and castles.

—*Rural churches* with frescos at Draby and Hyllested.

—*Rugård Manor,* from 1590. You can't visit it, but the road by there is pleasant. It follows the contours of a pond in a pretty village that was witness to actions that were more than questionable. Around 1682, the lord of these lands, Jørgen Arenfeldt, believing himself to be persecuted by witches, appealed to God to unmask them. The women suspected of sorcery were brought to the pond; those who came back up to the surface revealed their culpability, and those who stayed at the bottom were declared innocent. The simplicity of the good old days!

—*Alsø Church:* A cute romanesque church; a prettily designed crenelated steeple. On the inside an altar and stalls from 1597. *Katholm Manor,* 4 miles before Grenå, is not open to the public, but it offers an appealing architecture with towers and gables from 1600.

GRENÅ

A modern port with several old streets and half-timbered houses. On Søndergade there's a regional museum in a large merchant's house dating from the beginning of the eighteenth century. Open from 10 A.M. to noon and from 2 P.M. to 5 P.M.

—*Tourist Office:* Markedsgade. Telephone (06)-32-12-02.

—*Campgrounds near Fornaes:* North of the city. A long beach of several miles, obviously much frequented in the summer.

—Ferry for Hundested in Zeeland and Varberg in Sweden.

—Ferry for the island of Anholt at 2:45 P.M. (4½ miles), where you can walk or cycle. This island, with its 160 inhabitants, is cited because of its unique landscape and its lighthouse from 1780. In the center is the *Orkenin,* a landscape of rocks, dunes, and quicksands. Lodgings in the homes of residents and camping at the port.

Where to Sleep

—*Youth Hostel Djursvold:* 9 Dyrehavevej. Telephone 38-41-99. Located 6½ miles north of Grenå. Bus stops nearby at Gjerrild. The whole area is very pleasant. Forests and changing countryside. A pretty beach at Nordstrand, 1 mile away. In the village church, a retable, a pulpit entry with coats of arms, and frescos from the seventeenth century. In the same area there is also the Sostrup Castle, built in 1599. Upon request, certain rooms can be visited. Restaurant and coffee shop that you get to by a strange spiral staircase.

—*Albertinelund Campgrounds:* On Bønnerup Strand. Telephone 38-62-33. Near the small fishing port of Bønnerup.

On the Randers–Hobro Road

—*Løvenholm Manor:* Between Bønnerup and Auning. A beautiful park open to the public.

—*Gammel Estrup Castle:* A bit beyond Auning. Renaissance-style house dating from 1500. From May 1 to October 31, open every day from 10 A.M. to 5 P.M. The rest of the year open Tuesday to Sunday from 11 A.M. to 3 P.M. Tour. An agriculture museum is in the estate's former small farm. Very interesting.

RANDERS

In the middle of the "green heart of Jutland," with charming old houses and lively cafés. For a long time an important crossroads where maritime routes crossed 13 overland routes. For the Danes the first act of resistance against German invasion took place in this city when Niels Ebbesen killed Count Holstein in 1340.

—*Tourist Office:* Helligandshuset, 1 Erik Menveds Plads. Telephone (06)-42-44-77.

—*Youth Hostel Ved Campingpladsen i Fladbro.* On the way to Silkeborg, 4 miles from the city. Telephone 42-93-61. Open from April 15 to October 1. Has 20 small, rustic cabins. Camping in the same area.

To See

—*The old houses:* Helligaandshuset (the house of the Holy Ghost) on Erik Menveds Plads. It dates back to 1490 and presents an elegant exterior gallery. Stork's nest on the roof. A curiosity: Rådhus, built in 1778 . . . put on tracks and moved 10 feet to improve traffic flow. Great Danes. . . . On Brodregade and Storegade, other pretty timber-framed homes.

For fans of modern architecture, see the Cultural Center at 2 Stemannsgade which houses the city's cultural history and fine arts museums. Free admission. Rare etchings by Rembrandt and a fine selection of furniture in reconstructed interiors. Works by Jutland artists.

—*Sankt Mortens Church:* On Kirkegade. Baptismal fonts and a pulpit from the seventeenth century, and a baroque retable.

In the Area

—*Clausholm Castle:* 8 miles south. Pretty baroque-style edifice with sumptuous rooms. The chapel has the oldest organ in the country. Park with terraces. Open from Easter to the end of October on weekends, and from May 15 to September 15 every day from 10 A.M. to noon and from 2 P.M. to 5:30 P.M..

HOBRO

Haa do wot i Hobro? (Have you ever been to Hobrow?) An angry Dane abruptly addressed one of his acquaintances in this way, while punching him. It was during a lively discussion in which each offered his opinion on the prettiest city in Europe. This scene took place in Zurich, Switzerland, and was reported in Denmark. A famous clown used the reply in his repertoire, and the saying became popular. With this said, if Hobro is not the most beautiful city in Europe, it's still pleasant, nestling at the base of the longest fjord in Denmark, at the gates of Himmerland. It is known in particular for Fyrkat, an exceptional Viking fortress, located in the delicious countryside.

—*Tourist Office:* 2 Vestergade. Telephone (08)-52-18-47. Located in a great spot on the north bank of the fjord.

—*Gattenborg Campgrounds:* 2 Gattenborg. Telephone 52-32-88. Superb view of the city and the fjord.

To See

—*Fyrkat Fortress:* 2 miles southwest of the city. 1 of the 4 most important Viking fortresses in the country, along with Trelleborg, Nonnebakken, and Aggesborg. Around the year 1000, it commanded the Onslid River (which must have been larger at the time) and from there controlled the whole fjord. The Vikings knew how to combine strategy and the art of living, for the site is superb. Green undulating hills, forests and streams . . . The citadel measures almost 400 feet in diameter. Its circular ramparts are 40 feet wide and 14 feet high, pierced by doors at the 4 chief points. The central area is divided into 4 parts, each comprising 4 buildings laid out in squares and each able to lodge 50 warriors. Therefore, the fortress held 800 to 1,000 men. You can visit in the summer. Ask at the Tourist Office.

—*Archaeological Museum:* 21 Vestergade. Situated in an old timber-framed house. It holds most of the objects found in the Viking fortress as well as those discovered from ancient graves in the area.

MARIAGER

A small, charming medieval city, perfect for strolling the promenade along the fjord. Has streets coarsely paved with round stones and old timber-framed houses. At 7A Østergade is a house with a highly decorated door. A massive white church overlooks the city. Regional museum at 4B Kirkegade in a beautiful building, the former residence of a merchant.

—*Tourist Office:* 4 Torvet. Telephone 54-13-77.

—*Langengen Motel,* just on leaving the city for Hadsund. Telephone 54-11-22.

—An official campsite, but you can pitch your tent along the fjord a little bit further than the motel. Super quiet and a good evening guaranteed.

Here and There

—An old folkloric slow trains runs on Sunday between Mariager and Handest. Round trip is 24 Kr. Runs from June 6 to August 29.

—*Overgård Castle:* Located at the mouth of the fjord. Those who go from Ebeltoft to Hobro by the coast road will certainly come across it. Only the park is open to the public. Beautiful Renaissance-style structure with a round tower in the middle and a recessed dome. One of the closest advisors to King Francis I, Jorgen Likke, moved here upon his return from France. The rural church of Udbyneder, with a pulpit from 1650 and frescos, is 2 miles away.

HIMMERLAND

A vast stretch of deserted land, of hills covered with shrubs and forests, of wastelands like the swamps of Lille Vildmose in the northeast. You cross *Rold Skov,* Denmark's largest forest, to get to Rebild National Park, a curious forest to which the local population attributes singular powers. For instance, in the part called the "enchanted forest" there are some trees with twisted forms whose trunks developed in two branches and then grew back together, leaving an "eye" which can cure certain illnesses. Many people come from far away to slide their children through the eye of the magic tree to be cured. A little before Skørping, the *Den jyske Skovhave* has a selection of the various kinds of trees that grow in Denmark.

REBILD NATIONAL PARK

Established in 1912 on 500 acres of Rold Skov by Americans of Danish descent. The Fourth of July is celebrated there each year by the Danish–American community. A wild and more varied landscape than anywhere else and rather unique for Denmark. The youth hostel is well located at the beginning of the road that crosses the park. The rather small size of the site makes for a wonderfully pleasant stroll as the sun sets. On one of the hills in the park there's a replica of Lincoln's first home, built with logs from each state of the United States. It houses a small immigration museum.
—*Youth Hostel Cimbrergarden:* 23 Rebildvej. Telephone (08)-39-13-40. Open from January 20 to December 20.

ALBORG

The other large city in Jutland along with Århus. This great commercial and industrial center suddenly pops up from the vast expanses of Himmerland and Vendsyssel. An extraordinary city that, thanks to its system of highways, allows you to be in the countryside in a few minutes but also tolerates enormous polluting cement factories at its edge. Fortunately this city features old streets and neighborhoods that are among the most charming in the country and especially one of the most beautiful museums of modern art in the world.

Useful Addresses

—*Tourist Office:* 8 Østeraagade. Telephone (08)-12-60-22. Open from June 22 to August 16, from 9 A.M. to 9 P.M.; on Saturday from 9 A.M. to 3 P.M. and 7 P.M. to 9 P.M.; and on Sunday from 10 A.M. to noon and 7 P.M. to 9 P.M.
—*Post Office:* 42 Algade.
—*Emergency Pharmacy—Budolfi Pharmacy:* Vesterbo-Algade. Telephone: 12-06-77.
—*Car rental:* Avis, 45 Gammel Gugvej. Telephone 16-27-77.

—*Train station* (Telephone 12-02-06) and *Bus Station* (Telephone 12-63-33) on J. F. Kennedy Plads.

Where to Sleep

As in all large Danish cities, hotels are too expensive. A good solution is to stay at the home of a local. Get information at the Tourist Office.

—*Youth Hostel:* 18 Kornblomstvej, south of the city. Telephone 13-00-48. Large youth hostel, barracks-style, but not too far from town. Bus #7. The back door is open all night. Open from May 11 to August 31.

—*Mølleparken Campgrounds:* Near the zoo. Telephone 13-33-89. Open from May 1 to September 15.

—*Strandparken:* Right near the outdoor swimming pool, on the banks of the Limfjorden, in the northwest. Telephone 12-76-29. Open from May 15 to September 1.

—*Turist Hotel:* 36 Prinsengade. Near the station. Telephone 13-22-00.

• Two youth and student centers plan to have lodging during school vacations. Telephone ahead.

—*Fjerde Maj Kollegiet:* 8 Hasserigade. Telephone 12-12-82. Buses # 3 and #5.

—*Teknisk Kollegium:* Kollegievej. Telephone 14-32-52. Buses #8, #20, #21.

Where to Eat

Most of the restaurants and fast-food joints are on Jomfru Anegade, a very touristy street.

—*Caffeen:* 8 Jomfru Anegade. Apparently it's the best. Simple decor and *Dan Menu* for 48 Kr. Reasonable.

—*Geva:* 5 Ved Stranden. Telephone 12-46-50. Very central. Popular restaurant without any special character suggests very simple dishes, like breaded fish filets and potato salad. One of the cheapest in the city.

—*Tempo:* 111 Vesterbro. Serves some reasonable dishes from 11 A.M. to 10 P.M.

Where to Have a Quiet Drink

Night life in Alborg ain't happening. Nevertheless, here are a few lively joints.

—*Duus Vinkaelder:* Østeraa, a kind of chic café in the vaulted cellars of the Jens Bang Hotel. Open from 11 A.M. to midnight. A few hot dishes served. Closed Sunday.

—*Western Saloon Rio Bravo:* 27 Østeraa. You might not like the cowboy style, but the bar doesn't close until 2 A.M., and they serve reasonably priced food until midnight, which assures at least some action. An adjoining, tacky club closes at 4 A.M.

—*Socialistisk Bog Café:* 17 Vestera. Leftists keep a bookstore with exhibits in the window on local struggles. For those who wish to venture further in their knowledge of the city. Open during the day only—and not always then!

To See

—*Sankt Budolfi Church:* On Algade. You can't miss it, with its beautiful baroque steeple and immaculate walls. A cathedral since 1554, it owes its name to the English Saint Botolph. A few frescos still stand in the entry. Lovely painted rostrums and carved pulpit from the seventeenth century. Some baroque influences (twisted columns of the retable). Rococo-style organ preserved in its original handsome case. If you come when it opens, you might hear the organist rehearsing.

—*Holy Ghost Cloister:* Right near the cathedral on C. W. Obelds Plads. Dates from—get a hold on yourself—1431 (it's written on the vault). The place is always astonishingly peaceful and pleasant. You can visit the cloister and the chapter house. Frescos from the fifteenth century. Ask at the Tourist Office.

—*The former Rådhus and Jens Bang mansion:* 9 Østeraa. Standing side by side, the small building is the old city hall, a pretty 1762 baroque edifice, and the large one was built in 1623 by a rich merchant. Splendid Renaissance facade.

—*Aalborghus:* On Slots Pladsen, across from the port. A pretty group of three timber-framed houses around a courtyard paved with round stones. This graceful, peaceful haven is 100 yards from the frenetic activity of the port. Notice the small recesses carved in each window frame for birds, which transform the courtyard into a permanent concert.

—*Old streets* that harmoniously overlap with the modern streets in residential and commercial neighborhoods. A charming little street of steps behind the cathedral, Latinergyden, leads to Gravensgade, at the bottom of which Jomfru Ane Gade starts, a small street lined with timber-framed buildings that house many chic restaurants and discothèques. Super-touristy, but very lively at night. At 6 Maren Turis Gade you'll find *Jørgen Olufsen's Gaard,* a superb Renaissance-style home. From the interior courtyard you will come out on Østeraagade. Farther up, you should stroll around Notre Dame Church (see *Frue Kirke,* especially, at Hjelmerstald and Møllegade), one of the rare L-shaped streets that still exists. On Nørregade there are other interesting groups of houses, especially #18. Then follow Østergravensgad, Søndergade, Klokkestøbergade, and Niels Ebbesensgade. We can't mention all the charming homes and gardens nearby.

—*Historic Museum:* Øn Algade. Telephone 12-45-22. Open every day from 10 A.M. to 5 P.M. Free admission. Prehistoric collection and regional antiques. Period rooms including Alborg Hall of 1602. Exceptional crystal collection.

—*Jutland Art Museum:* 50 Christians Allé. Telephone 13-80-88. Open every day from 10 A.M. to 5 P.M. One of the most beautiful museums of modern art—and we wouldn't kid you. Vast and light rooms. Great light thanks to the type of light wells (similar to Knossos in Crete). Exterior architecture by Alvar Aålto, the Finnish master. Jens Søndergaard's morbid and poetic landscapes, Wilhelm Lundstrøm's perpetual swinging between Expressionism and Cubism, Harald Giersing's expressionist paintings, works of the Cobra group, Jacobsen's sculptures . . . Temporary exhibits that are always very attractive and rich in artistic temerity. All right, we won't say any more so that you can have the pleasure of discovery. Be nice—if you send us helpful tips on the city, write them on a postcard from the museum, and this will plunge us back into blissful daydreaming.

Other Curiosities

—*Animal Market:* The biggest in Scandinavia, on Nyhavnsgade. Tuesday and Friday from 9 A.M. to noon. For those who have never seen such a spectacle, here's your chance. Thousands of beasts change hands in a few hours. You must see the bulls refusing to be weighed, charging into the herd of panic-stricken cows. The sights and smells, the cries of the dealers, the various rituals . . . an unusual happening in a large city.

—*Flea Market:* During the summer on C. W. Obelds Plads, on Saturdays from 9 A.M. to 1 P.M.

ON THE ROAD TO THE NORTH

NØRRESUNBY

On the other side of Limfjord. An industrial city linked to Ålborg. An old Viking city. They found *Lindholm Høje* (or *Vikingepladsen*), an important cemetery from that period. More than 682 tombs surrounded by stone circles in the form of ships, and the foundations of a Viking city. The site is great. Very interesting tour. Bus #8.

DRONNINGLUND

A castle located about 20 miles from Alborg. The most interesting part is the adjoining church. Together they create a harmonious architecture. Look at the shape of the windows. In the church the frescos are uplifting, with a great variety of tones. Also battle scenes (among others, Alexander the Great on an elephant). The retable dates to circa 1600. Splendid lordly rostrum and carved stalls with painted coats of arms. See Voergård Castle, 16 miles north, a pretty Renaissance residence. Rich interior decoration. Tours on the weekends in the summer. Interesting rural church nearby at Voer.

SAEBY

Small seaside resort with low, dainty houses and abundant flowers. Don't miss Saint Marie Church, the former chapel of a long-gone monastery. Admirable sixteenth-century frescos. On one of the walls there's a rich epitaph praising the benefactors of the church, plus their portraits. Stalls from 1500 on which, curiously, you'll find many engravings, and a retable from the Dutch school of the same period.

—*Tourist Office:* 1 Krystaltorvet. Telephone (08)-46-15-19.

—*Youth Hostel Saebygårdvej.* Telephone (08)-46-36-50. A new youth hostel . . . all modern. Well thought out and functional.

FREDERIKSHAVN

The largest city of Vendsyssel and the focal point of tourism by boat in Scandinavia. Pleasant by itself, Very interesting tour of Bangsbo Manor, 2 miles southwest (therefore, it's before you reach the city if you're coming from the south).

Useful Addresses

—*Tourist Office:* 1 Brotorvet. Telephone 42-32-66.
—*Post Office:* Skippergade.
—*Youth Hostel:* 6 Buhlsvej. Telephone 42-14-75. Open all year; 1 mile from the station. Well marked and located in a pleasant setting. Rooms for families.
—*Nordstrand Campgrounds:* On the road from Skagen, 2 miles on the right.

To See

—*Bangsbo Manor:* Dronning Magrethesvej. The present buildings date from 1700. They house a good museum divided into several sections: a section on local and regional history: engravings, paintings, dishes, and furniture; a picturesque collection of hair "jewelry"; then a maritime section, with prows of vessels, models, onboard instruments, and so forth. Nearby, there's a section devoted to the Danish Resistance during World War II, remarkably exhibited. And, finally, another building houses the remains of a Viking boat. Ah, yes, all this for one price! All around the manor is a lovely park for picnics or strolls.

—*Laesø Island:* A small island off Frederikshavn. The roofs of most of the fishermen's homes are preserved with seaweed. In the summer there are several departures each day from the port.

Sea Links

There is a boat from Frederikshavn to Oslo: 10 hours on the water. Reasonably priced. It is better to cross in daylight. Leaves at 10 A.M. Entering the fjord at Oslo at sunset is enchanting. And we're usually blasé concerning conventional sunsets.

Boat to Narvik (Narvik Line): Sleeping on the *Peter Wessel* is manageable. Take a down bag. The cushions in the saloon and cafeteria are comfortable and fought for.

Note: There's a private railway line between Skagen and Frederikshavn (no discounts with Inter-Rail pass).

SKAGEN

The northernmost city in Denmark. You shouldn't miss getting there to soak up the pervasive solitude of Vendsyssel—at the extreme point of Jutland, at Grenen, where violets grow in the dunes and where two seas meet in one wave perpendicular to the land. This region has always attracted artists. Visit the municipal museum. See the paintings of Michael Ancher and Krøyer who have captured the particular radiance of Skagen, where sun, white dunes, and sea comingle in pearly blue hues.

The city is very pleasant with its old fishermen's homes with yellow walls. See the little port with its picturesque red-and-white warehouses. Good seafood restaurants.

—*Tourist Office:* 18 Lavrentivej. Telephone (08)-44-13-77.

—*Youth Hostel:* 32 Gammel Skagen Højjensvej. Telephone 44-13-56. About half a mile before the city, on the left. Well located ⅓ mile from the beach. Open from March 15 to October 31.

TVIND

Very interesting experiment near Ulfborg, on the west coast of Jutland. It's a school where theory and practice are equal, where the professors and students truly have the same power, where there is no sexual discrimination, and where, especially, studies are centered on a trip to a third-world country. After the trip, the students prepare for a teacher's diploma. A school that tries to be different: solar houses, windmills . . . You must see it. Be aware that in the summer there are no students, only welcoming hostesses.

Boats from Jutland

—*From Jutland to Copenhagen:* You can board at Grenå. More expensive than the Stena line, but you economize on gas. No tourists, only laughing Danes.

—*The Hirtshals–Kristiansand link* by the Fred Olsen line is more expensive than the Kristiansand–Hanstholm link by Scanline. In Hirtshals, you can sleep at the youth hostel, a very quiet place on the sea.

—*Hanstholm–Kristiansand:* The trek takes 4½ hours. Hanstholm is on the peninsula of Thy, north of Thisted.

—*Frederikshavn–Larvik* (Norway): One boat a day on Larvik lines. Telephone (08)-42-14-00. The voyage lasts 6 hours in the daytime, 9 hours at night. Count on $25 per person and $35 for a car.

—*Frederikshavn–Göteborg:* At least 6 boats a day on the Stena line. Lasts about 3½ hours.

—*Frederikshavn–Oslo:* Daily from June 18 to August 20. Leaves 9:30 A.M. and arrives at 7:30 P.M.

SWEDEN

What strikes you first, upon arriving in Sweden, after Denmark and Germany, is the light traffic on the roads. The density of population is very low here. They don't jostle each other; moreover, they're not the type to do so. Therefore, you will have immense forests and innumerable lakes all to yourself.

Useful Addresses in New York

—*Swedish Consulate General:* 825 Third Avenue, New York, New York 10022. Telephone (212)751-5900.

—*Swedish National Tourist Office:* 75 Rockefeller Plaza, New York, New York 10019. Telephone (212) 582-2802.

Currency

The unit of currency is the crown (krona), abbreviated as Kr. It is divided into 100 ore, with a value slightly different from the Danish and Norwegian crowns.

If you buy traveler's checks, take large denominations, for the banks take a commission on each check cashed. Banks are generally closed on Saturday and Sunday. In an emergency you can go to the major post offices (on Saturday) and some train stations.

Where to Sleep

—*Camping:* In Sweden there is an ancestral custom that goes right to our hearts (always individualistic by inclination). It's *Allemansratt,* which literally means "each person's right." In practice, this tradition allows you to pitch a tent just about anywhere you want, sail or swim, gather berries or mushrooms, draw water from any well, spring or lake, and make a campfire at night. This unique charter, in its way, gives you the right and the option to enjoy life in the great outdoors. With this said, the rules of elementary courtesy are still in operation. Therefore, it is always good to ask permission from the owner of a field to pitch your tent, if he's around.

But there are about 580 official campgrounds, principally in the south and on the coasts. The complete list is in the *Guide to Swedish Camping.* At half of the campgrounds you can rent a wooden bungalow *(hytter)* with 2 to 6 beds and equipped with a kitchen; a *hytter* is much less expensive than a hotel. You must bring your own sheets or sleeping bag. Be aware: the *hytters* are fairly packed in the summer.

Several campgrounds rent boats and place at their visitors' disposal golf courses, saunas, swimming pools, bicycles, tennis courts, horses, and canoes. For the most part they also provide special equipment for the handicapped. (Non-Swedish campgrounds could learn some lessons.) Finally, sometimes there are special prices for cyclists. Don't hesitate to ask.

—Sweden also has 150 youth hostels and 80 family inns (called *Vandrarhem*). Generally, sleeping bags are forbidden; therefore, you need a sleep-sack. You need a membership card for the youth hostels, the other inns are open to everyone, but the card gives you discounts.

Be aware that some youth hostels are in schools and are closed after August 15.

—Finally, hotels are rather expensive, even the Salvation Army inns. When Amnesty International organized a congress at Stockholm, some delegates were lodged there; that says something! Note: The police can hassle you if you sleep in the parks of large cities (especially Stockholm); these things are simply not done here.

There are now *Check-Hotels* which are accepted in 270 places throughout Sweden and which offer a discount of 20 to 40 percent off the normal price. There are 2 categories: the Quality Check-Hotel that is valid in all first-class establishments and the Budget Check-Hotel for middle-category hotels. The prices in 1983 for Check-Hotels for one night were 145 Kr for Quality and 100 Kr for Budget. We advise you to buy these discount checks before your departure. They also allow you to make reservations at no charge from the hotel where you're staying for the next night at another hotel. Check the Swedish Tourist Office in New York.

Business Hours

Banks and stores operate on Western European hours. Stores open from 9 A.M. to 6 or 6:30 P.M., but they stay open somedays until 8 or 10 P.M. In a city like Arvidsjaur, stores close 3 times a week at 9 P.M. and are open on Sunday from 1 P.M. to 9 P.M.

Banks open at 9:30 A.M. and close at 3 or 6 P.M., according to the size of the city; the banks at Arlanda Airport stay open from 7 A.M. to 10 P.M.

Post offices are open from 8 A.M. to 6:30 P.M.; on Saturday from 9 A.M. to 1 P.M. In Göteborg, Stockholm, and Malmö, the post offices are open on Sunday morning for simple transactions.

Gas

Gas is less expensive in automatic self-service stations *(automat)*. You must have a supply of 10 Kr notes, the only denomination accepted by the machines. You have a choice of three octanes—93, 95, and 99 (99 is "super")—without a substantial difference in price. Give a taste to your hotrod, and it'll tell you what it prefers. Be aware that the automatic pumps generally don't give change; therefore, know exactly what you need before putting in the right amount of bills.

Hitchhiking

Given the scarcity of cars off the main drags, you guessed it: hitching is difficult. In addition, the car is a sign of wealth and respectability for Swedes (including the young), so those who don't have them are considered outsiders. But with perseverance and the wearing of a foreign flag . . . The old red, white and blue may help you, though the maple-leaf design may be less obtrusive. . . .

Driving Rules

You must drive with your headlights on day and night. It's not the car that's passing that must move over; the car that is being passed must drift over to the edge. Anyway, Swedish roads were designed for this. You will find a booklet in English on Sweden's driving rules.

At railroad crossings, a white light blinks constantly. The red light signals an oncoming train. If the white light is not blinking, be careful—something is evidently out of order. A very intelligent system.

Distances Between Swedish Cities (in Miles)

	Göteborg	Haparanda	Helsingborg	Jönkoping	Kalmar	Kiruna	Kristianstad	Luleå	Malmö	Stockholm	Uppsala
Göteborg	X	890	142	96	249	1036	171	806	176	310	281
Haparanda	890	X	998	884	914	232	988	86	1027	674	629
Helsingborg	142	998	X	153	188	1147	66	918	40	361	392
Jönkoping	96	884	153	X	146	997	142	776	183	210	238
Kalmar	249	914	188	146	X	1060	123	834	178	265	314
Kiruna	1036	232	1147	997	1060	X	1134	213	1173	820	775
Kristianstad	171	988	66	142	123	1134	X	909	55	356	381
Luleå	806	86	918	776	834	213	909	X	947	618	549
Malmö	176	1027	40	183	178	1173	55	947	X	393	425
Stockholm	310	674	361	210	265	820	356	618	393	X	45
Uppsala	281	629	392	238	314	775	381	549	425	45	X

Railways (S.J.)

Swedish railways offer a *Lagpriskortet* card which, for 115 Kr (1983 price), gives a 45 percent discount on all trains within Sweden. It is valid every day except from 5 A.M. on Friday to 5 A.M. on Saturday and from 5 A.M. on Sunday to 5 A.M. on Monday. In the stations, ask for the free part of the train schedules *(Snabbtåg).*

Reservations (10 Kr) are required on all trains marked "R" including Inter-Rail.

A new idea has been introduced concerning the transportation of travelers—the notion that reduced fares are in the public's interest; therefore, discounts can amount to 15 or 40 percent in off-peak hours. In the north of Sweden, trains are frequently an hour late. On the other hand, the train has a lot of ground to cover and each stop is completely indispensable. A reservation must be made and paid for in advance for most trains. A fine is levied if you board a train without a reservation. The S. J. railway company also operates buses almost everywhere in Sweden. They are clearly cheaper, so take the bus.

By Plane

You can travel standby (without a reservation) on flights within Sweden. This ticket cost 120 Kr in 1983; it is not applicable on all trips but only from or to Stockholm. It's called *Hundra Lappen* and is only for those under 26.

Food

You can find some reasonable restaurants on one condition: Never drink anything resembling wine or beer. It's a guaranteed rip-off.

In almost every restaurant you can order the special of the day *(Dägens Rätt),* served from 11 A.M. to 3 P.M. It's the least expensive item.

Those who want to save should buy their food at *Tempo* or *Domus,* supermarkets throughout Sweden belonging to the same chain. This chain is managed by a consumers union and thus has the lowest prices.

There are pizzerias that are less expensive than restaurants (and good for local color!). On the road the food is not expensive, but disgusting.

The food at campground supermarkets is often sky-high. Don't encourage them—buy elsewhere.

Something cheap to eat: Cheese in a tube. Not bad, and it's filling. As for fruit, there are huckleberries, *smultrons* (wild strawberries), and *hjorton* (a kind of yellow mulberry that is found only in Lapland and is served with sour cream).

Drinks

The rules concerning alcohol are worthy of Queen Victoria. In food stores you can buy only low-proof beer.

Lattol (number 1) is beer without alcohol. *Falkol* (number 2) resembles French beer. *Starkol* is the strongest and most expensive. In bars ask for *Falkol;* otherwise they'll serve you *Starkol,* to the disgruntlement of your taste buds.

The strongest beer (number 3), wine, and other alcoholic beverages are sold exclusively in state stores. No need to tell you how expensive. These stores are closed on Sunday, obviously. On other days they open at 6 P.M. and on Saturday at 1 P.M. Which explains why the Swedes stand in line on Friday evening to buy their supplies of artificial paradise for the weekend. Having obtained their treasure, some don't resist getting drunk from Friday on.

The laws concerning alcohol forbid babas au rhum and mackerel in white wine. Carry your own provisions so that you aren't caught short.

A tip: In Esso service stations they serve coffee with free refills. In the coffee and pastry shops (Konditori), you can also refill several times.

So . . . Swedish Women?

There is a widely dispersed myth in Latin countries concerning the morals of Swedish women. It's well supported by porn films and by those who return from Sweden. Human nature is weak, causing individuals to exaggerate or invent exploits.

There is a tradition in some nightclubs that can rouse certain fragile spirits: *Varannan dans damernas*—women invite men to dance. But this tradition is not as common as you'd think and when examined is just kids' play. Yes! Like all good Lutheran countries, Sweden is puritanical. Therefore, stop fantasizing. But one fantasy is real: Swedish women are incredibly beautiful, far exceeding the norm. We assure you, so are the Swedish men.

Vocabulary

yes	*ja*
no	*nej*
excuse me	*ursäkta mig (uchekta mey)*
pardon	*Förlat*
please	*var så god*
thank you	*tack*
see you soon	*vi ses*
very good	*mycket bra (muken bra)*
river	*flod (floude)*
lake	*sjö (cheu)*
street	*gatan*
tent	*talt (telt)*
room	*rum*
train	*täg (tog)*
airport	*flygplats (flugplats)*
working days (Monday to Friday)	*vardagar*
holidays	*held-dagar (elydagar)*
one	*ett*
two	*tvä*
three	*tre*
four	*fyra*
five	*fem*
six	*sex*
seven	*sju*
eight	*åtta (otta)*
nine	*nio*
ten	*tio*
eleven	*elva*
twelve	*tolv*
thirteen	*tretton*
fourteen	*fjorton*
fifteen	*femton*
sixteen	*sexton*
seventeen	*sjutton*
eighteen	*arton*
nineteen	*nitton*
twenty	*tjugu*
thirty	*trettio*
forty	*fyrtio*
fifty	*femtio*
sixty	*sextio*
seventy	*sjuttio*
eighty	*åttio*
ninety	*nittio*
one hundred	*hundra*
two hundred	*tva hundra*
one thousand	*tusen*

The definite article (the) is formed by a suffix, *en, n,* or *et,* at the end of the word. Examples:
en gata = a street = *gatan*
ett hotel = a hotel = *hotellet*
ett universitet = a university = *universitetet*

MALMÖ

This is often the first stop for a hitchhiker in Sweden. The city itself is not fantastically interesting, with the exception of the Grand Palace *(Stortorget).* In fact, the Renaissance-style buildings remind us of the wonderful square in Brussels. Don't miss *Apotex Lejonet,* the oldest pharmacy in Sweden, open since 1571. Alongside it is *Lilla Torg,* a small residential neighborhood with old timber-framed houses, antique shops, and outdoor cafés.

—*Tourist Office:* 1 Hamngatan, facing the Central Station, on the other side of the canal.

To See

—*San Petri Church:* Started in the beginning of the fourteenth century. It's famous for its sumptuous retable above the main altar.

—*Muzik Puben:* Across from San Petri Church. One of the liveliest evening spots.

—*American and foreign newspapers:* Stomakeragatan, at the corner of Södergatan. Near the large square. You can even find *Pravda.*

Where to Sleep

—*Youth Hostel Södergatan:* 18 Backvagen. Telephone 040-822-20. South of the city. Bus #36 from Central Station. Rather expensive. Game room, TV, free sauna, washing machine, volley ball. You can cook in a well-supplied kitchen. Closed from 10 A.M. to 4 P.M. and from midnight to 6 A.M. Some inconveniences: very far from the arrival of boats to Denmark, from the bus, from the market, and everything. Also, it's next to the highway, on an ugly street, and not far from an enormous factory with 5 gigantic smokestacks. Why not sleep at the youth hostel of *Ystad* (located in a very pleasant area)?

—*Hotel Hembygden:* 7 Isak Slaktargatan. Telephone 11-97-47. In the heart of things, near the prettiest place in the city (Lilla Torg). It's 150 Kr for a nice room for 2.

Where to Eat

—*Restaurant B and B:* Inside the Saluhallen market which is next to Lilla Torg Square. Affordable dishes.

—*Margareta Restaurant:* 63 S. Promenaden. Another good inexpensive place.

LUND

A ravishing university city that is indisputably among the most beautiful in Sweden. And everything noteworthy is within walking distance of the cathedral! You will be astonished by the charm of this place, with its cobblestone streets and old houses, the prettiest ones right behind the cathedral.

SWEDEN (SOUTHERN)

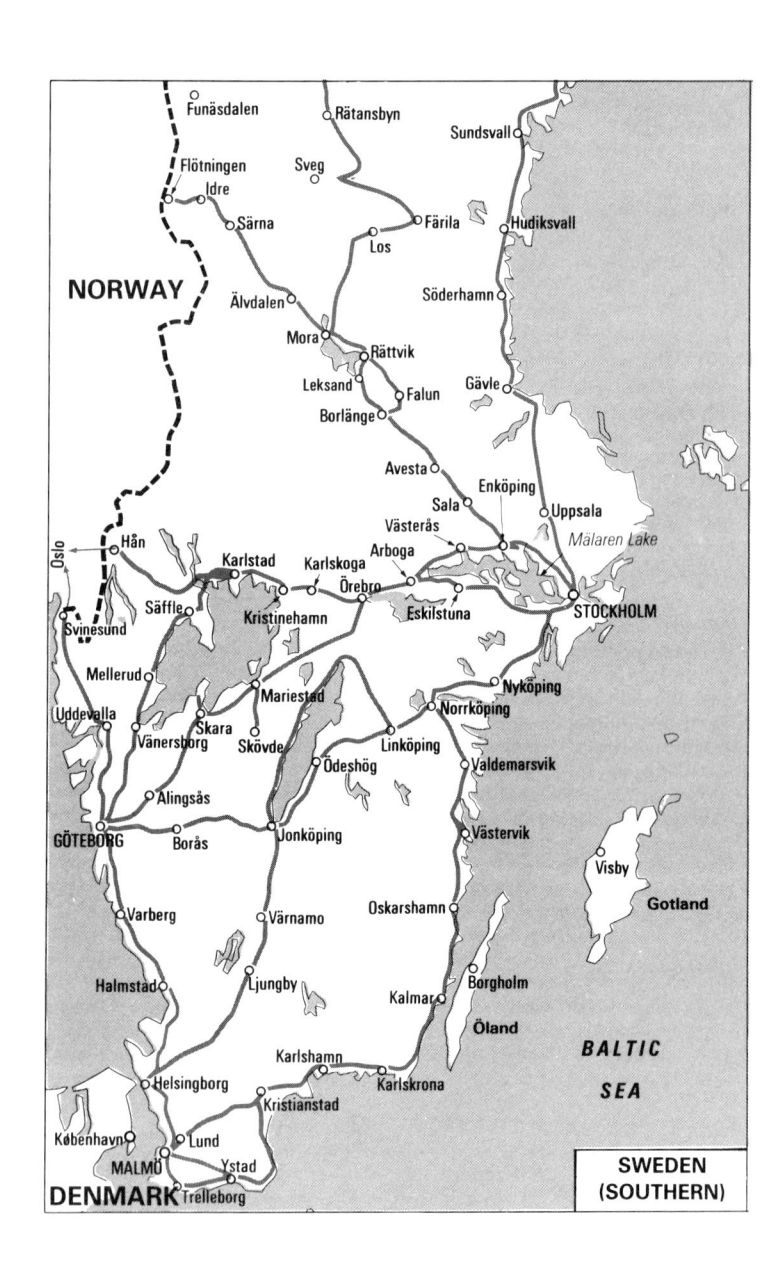

Useful Addresses

—*Tourist Office:* 4 Saint Petri Kyrkogatan, near the station.
—*Exchange* at the main post office, across from the station.

Where to Eat

—*Chongren Cafeteria:* Behind the cathedral. Restaurant connected to the university with a large terrace where you can eat. Not expensive. Interesting people.
—*Domus:* A large store on Mortenstorget that has an affordable self-service eatery.
—*Café and Krog:* 6 Mortenstorget. Small restaurant and pub overlooking a small pleasant interior court.

Where to Sleep

—*Youth Hostel* (Hotel Sparta): 39 Tunabagan. Telephone 046/12-40-80. It's actually a university residence that accepts travelers in the summer. A large modern building next to a supermarket, east of the city. Bus #1 from the station. Price is slightly higher for nonmembers. Double rooms. Open day and night. Self-service restaurant with tables outside as soon as the sun appears.

To See

—*Cathedral:* The oldest Episcopal church in Scandinavia, founded in 1080. Romanesque style. Don't miss the fourteenth-century astronomical clock: It has 2 dials between which the 3 kings of the Magi appear carrying their offerings. This display occurs every day at noon and 3 P.M. (Sunday at 1 P.M. and 3 P.M.). A stairway to the right of the altar descends to the crypt, the oldest in the country. Each of the 28 pillars represents a legendary character. There are the tombs of nobles.
—*Kulturhistoriska Museet:* Museum of art and popular traditions, but also an outdoor museum like the Skansen in Stockholm. Open from 11 A.M. to 5 P.M. Archaeological rooms, several of which have runic stones. A traditional village has been reconstructed in the garden.

YSTAD

One of the best preserved medieval villages in Sweden. Nearly 300 timber-framed houses give it much charm. Some are hidden, so the Tourist Office gives out a small brochure that helps you to visit from the center of town on foot. The old city surrounds the Saint Marykyrkan Church. This church is famous thanks to its guardian who, faithful to medieval tradition, rings the bells every 15 minutes. Not far away is Saint Petrikyrkan Church, the former church of the cloisters. It is encircled by a very lovely plaza with well-preserved houses. From there, get a drink at the Backahsten restaurant, right nearby and wonderful. Tables outside. Closes at 6 P.M..
—*Youth Hostel:* Just as you leave the city. A large house overlooking the beach. Truly great, with a well-equipped kitchen, rooms for

two with sink, TV, and a nice innkeeper. A 30-minute walk from the station along a well-marked road bordering an immense pine grove. A few minutes away there's a campground where you can buy food. It has an immense beach with fine sand, but the water is a little cold.
—*Camping:* Near the youth hostel, next to the main road.

HELSINGBORG

One of the entry ports of Sweden. In fact, a very important port. A modern city without much interest.
—*Tourist Office:* Rådhustorget, on the left when leaving the station, in a red-brick building.
—*Thalassa Youth Hostel:* 3 miles north of the city. Certainly the prettiest youth hostel in the country. Imagine an all-white mansion on top of a hill overlooking the sea. From the terrace you can see Denmark. Small wooden castles have been built in the park. Bus #16 from in front of the harbor station to the last stop. Closed from 10 A.M. to 4 P.M.
—*Camping:* 3 miles south of the city on the road from Råå. next to the sea. A swimming pool and hamburgers. We were a little crowded. Take a walk to Råå, 1 mile south of the city. A pleasing little port with several fishermen.
—*Sauna and indoor pool:* 60 Södergatan. In the center of town. Buses #20, #21, #22, and #23. Inside, superb mosaics by Hugo Gehlin.
—See the *Folk Parken,* outdoor museum with old houses, stores, and so forth. Admission: 4 Kr. Bus #14 or #15.

MÖRRUM

A small industrial city famous for its salmon fishing, which opens April 1. You can buy a fishing permit good for one day (50 Kr). Difficult to find lodgings.

RONNEBY

A small city known for its Holy Cross Church (*Heliga Korskyrkan*). Built in the twelfth century, it is uniquely fortified. Pretty frescos on the inside, including one that represents a macabre dance. Remarkable old houses in the area.
—*Youth Hostel:* In the Ronneby Brun area. Truly fantastic. An immense old building, all in wood, next to the forest. Closed from 10 A.M. to 5 P.M. Across from it there's a glass blower establishment that is open to the public.
—*Camping:* Near the youth hostel, in a pretty park near a forest.

KARLSKRONA

Both a naval base and an important fishing port, Karlskrona is an airy city, divided by large thoroughfares.

To See

—*Marin Museet:* Note the hours: Open every day from noon to 4 P.M.; in July from noon to 8 P.M. An exceptional museum with naval cannon, superb ship models, an interesting section on the handicraft aboard ships—knots, ropes . . . One room is full of impressive prow figures. Reconstructed cabins, naval instruments, and so forth.

—*Amiralitetskyrkan:* Not far from the naval museum, this is the wooden church where the families of sailors came to pray. It is in the form of a Greek cross. In front is the painted wooden statue of old Rosenbom, known by all Swedes. It awaits a sign from a passerby that a sailor is in trouble.

—*Bjorkholmen:* The oldest section of the city, with great well-restored wooden houses. Across from it lies the island of Ekholmen.

KALMAR

Rather lively seaside resort located across from Oland Island.

—*Gas refills:* Elmer Svenssons at Tjärhovet, in the gas port. Standard exchange of 3 kg bottles (6.6 pounds). Open from 7 A.M. to 4 P.M.

Where to Sleep

—*Youth Hostel:* North of the city, on the road that leads to Oland Island. Recent construction with a pleasant cafeteria overlooking a small branch of the sea.

—*Camping:* Near Kalmar Castle.

To See

—*Cathedral:* An imposing building with greenish-bronze cupolas. Strangely built in Italian baroque style.

—*Kalmar Castle* (Slottet): Practically intact and protected by strong ramparts, it borders the sea. Inside there's a museum in which you can visit the queen's chambers, the chapel, and various ornate halls with furnishings of the period and royal portraits.

—*Large market:* Saturday morning in front of the cathedral.

Around and About

—*Lessebo:* 37 miles west of Kalmar, on the road from Växjö. This small city has one of the oldest paper mills in the world. It was recently reopened to the public, so you can see the different stages of making paper and then buy some. Free tours from June to August, at 10 A.M., 1 P.M., 2 P.M. There is also a glass factory in the city.

JÖNKÖPING

By Wattern Lake. The city itself is pretty, but most interesting is the old city.

—*Tourist Office:* 9 Västra Storgatan.

—In the station, a *supermarket* open from 8 A.M. to midnight.

—*Match Museum:* The history, a film in English, and insane match boxes.
—*Departmental Museum:* Great. Superb reconstruction of workshops.
—Swimming pool, showers, and sauna for 8 Kr at the *Badhus.* Along the lake, to the left when leaving the station.

Where to Sleep

—The youth hostel is nice and has a lovely view of the lake. In fact, it's a youth center that is transformed into a youth hostel for the summer. Mini-kitchen.
—*Motorcycle Club Campgrounds:* In a pine forest near a beach. Not expensive. Open to all. Bus #25-27 for Bankeryd. Ask the driver for the "camping" stop. Closed after August 15. We advise against Rosenlund Campground near the station; it's much more expensive.

VADSTENA

A small town along Vattern Lake. Rather touristy, yet has kept its medieval flavor.

Where to Sleep

—*Youth Hostel:* Large, new building not far from the town center. Impeccable.
—*Kungs Starby Inn:* 1 mile south on Route 50. A small mansion transformed into a hotel. Rather expensive, but an exceptional setting. Live a little. Some rooms in the annex are less expensive.
—*Camping:* On the beach at Vättervik.

To See

More than the monuments, it's the city in general that is pleasing: low houses, cobblestone streets, and everything Swedish clean.
—*The Castle:* Overlooking the lake, this imposing structure is one of the most beautiful examples of Dutch Renaissance. The moats connect directly with the lake. Tours of the castle upon request of the Tourist Bureau.
—*Rådhus:* Built in the fifteenth century, it's without a doubt one of the oldest courthouses in the country. Recognizable by its powerful square tower. Free admission.
—*Saint Brigitte Abbey:* An interesting tour, especially the superb group of medieval sculptures.

LINKÖPING

The old city (*Gamla Stan*) is nice to visit. An artist, craftsperson, or small museum occupies each house. Very pleasant forests on the outskirts.
—*Municipal Campgrounds:* Very well equipped with washing machines, heaters, dining rooms . . . for 18 Kr a night.

—*Hamlet:* Restaurant good for the broke as well as the moneyed. Pretty setting.

—Bus #50 in the old city will take you to Mantorp (12 miles west of Linköping), from 6 A.M. to 1 P.M. only. Craftsmen work with glass there. You can even blow your own bottle.

STOCKHOLM

Superbly located, Stockholm collects contradictions: a terrific old city (principally from the eighteenth century), entirely pedestrian, neighboring a particularly disorderly ultra-modern center. Immense and almost wild parks next to an infernal network of urban highways and idiotic crossovers that transform this city into an exasperating labyrinth for the inexperienced driver. A visible ecological concern makes Stockholm perhaps the only capital in the world where you can swim in the sea without fear of contracting typhoid fever. With a little luck, perhaps you will see some fishermen tickling salmon at the foot of the Royal Palace.

Useful Addresses

—*Tourist Information:* House of Sweden, 27 Hamngatan. Telephone 22-70-00. Open from 9 A.M. to 5 P.M., except Saturday and Sunday from 9 A.M. to 3 P.M.. In summer, open every day from 8:30 A.M. to 6 P.M. The House of Sweden also welcomes students. Don't forget to ask for the brochure entitled *This Week in Stockholm* to check out free concerts. Ask them to telephone the youth hostel to see if there is a room available and so avoid that hassle.

—*Information on hotels and youth hostels:* On the lower level of the main train station, near the entrance to the subway T-Centralen. Open in the summer from 8 A.M. to 9 P.M., on Saturday from 8 A.M. to 5 P.M., and Sunday from 1 P.M. to 9 P.M. Be aware that they hand out maps of Stockholm, but some are expensive.

—*Main Post Office:* 28–34 Vasagatan. Telephone 781-20-05. Open from 8 A.M. to 8 P.M., on Saturday from 9 A.M. to 3 P.M. They have *Poste Restante* which is free (how rare!). Practically right across from the station.

—*American Express:* L. B. Resebyra, 8 Sturegatan.

—*U.S. Embassy:* 101 Strandvahem. Telephone (08)-63-05-20.

—*Exchange:* Open every day until 9 P.M. in the large hall of the Central Station.

—*S. J. Bus:* The office where you can buy tickets is next to the Central Station: 3 Vasagatan; make a left upon exiting. Remember: It's cheaper than the train.

—*Transalpino Train Tickets:* 13 Birger Jarisgatan. Telephone (08) 24-07-10. Subway: Østermalmstorg.

—*Drugstore open 24 hours a day:* 64 Klarabergsgatan.

—*PUB:* A market across from *Konserthuset* where you can find camping gas refills and tent stakes. Subway: Hötorget.

How to Get Around

The Stockholm subway (*Tunnelbana*) consists of 10 lines that go far into the suburbs. They operate until midnight. A ticket is fairly

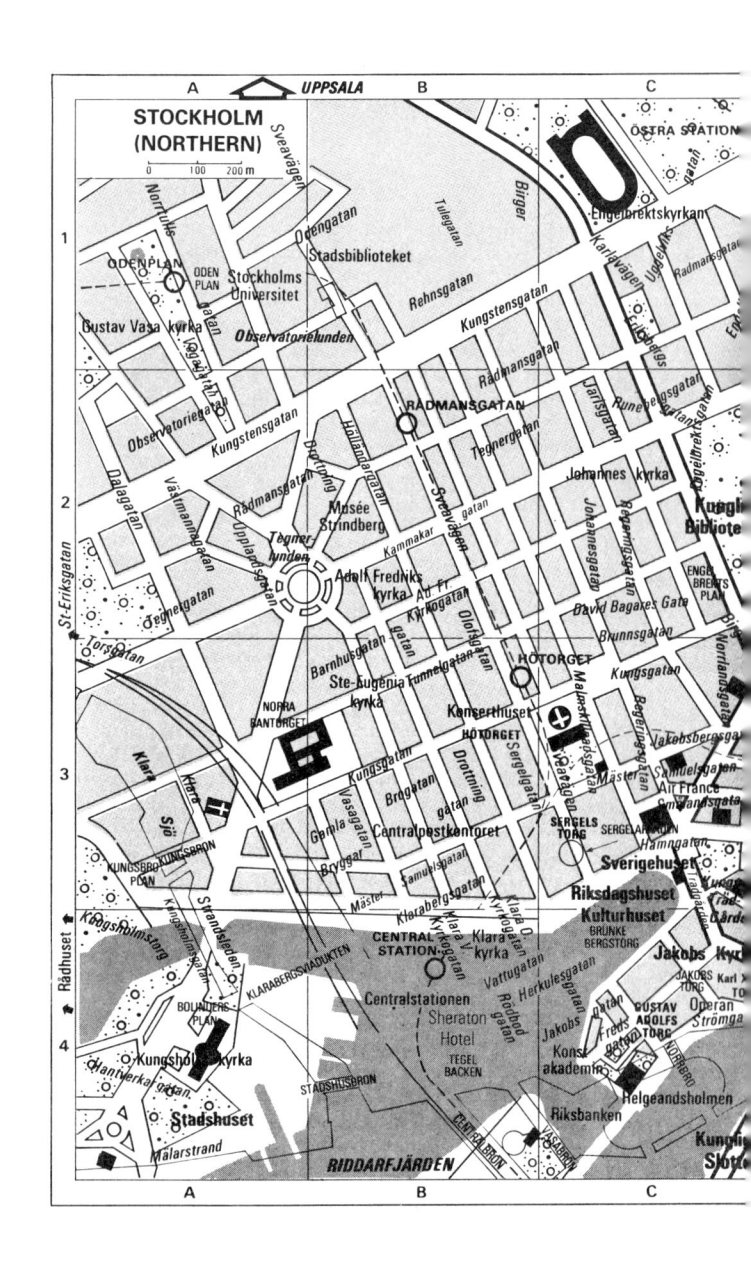

STOCKHOLM (NORTHERN)

D
E
F
1
2
3
Stadion
Lidingövägen
STADION
Tessin
Parken
Dahlbergsgatan
Strindbergsgatan
Valhallavägen
Värtavägen
KARLAPLAN
Karlavägen
Östermalmsgatan
Skeppargatan
Sturegatan
Birger Jarlsgatan
Humlegårdsgatan
Marmorhallarna
ÖSTERMALMSTORG
Hedvig Eleonora kyrka
Armémuseum
Musik Museet
Läkarhuset
Riddargatan
Storgatan
Historiska museet
Narvavägen
Linnégatan
Oscarskyrkan
Strandvägen
Dramatiska Teatern
NYBRO PLAN
Nybropaviljongen
Berzelii Park
Nybrokajen
Blasieholmsgatan
Nationalmuseum
Östasiatiska museet
DJURGÅRDEN
DJURGÅRDSBRON
Nordiska museet
SKANSEN
Djurgårdsvägen
Biologiska museet
ROSENDALS SLOTT
Moderna Museet
WALDEMARSUDDE

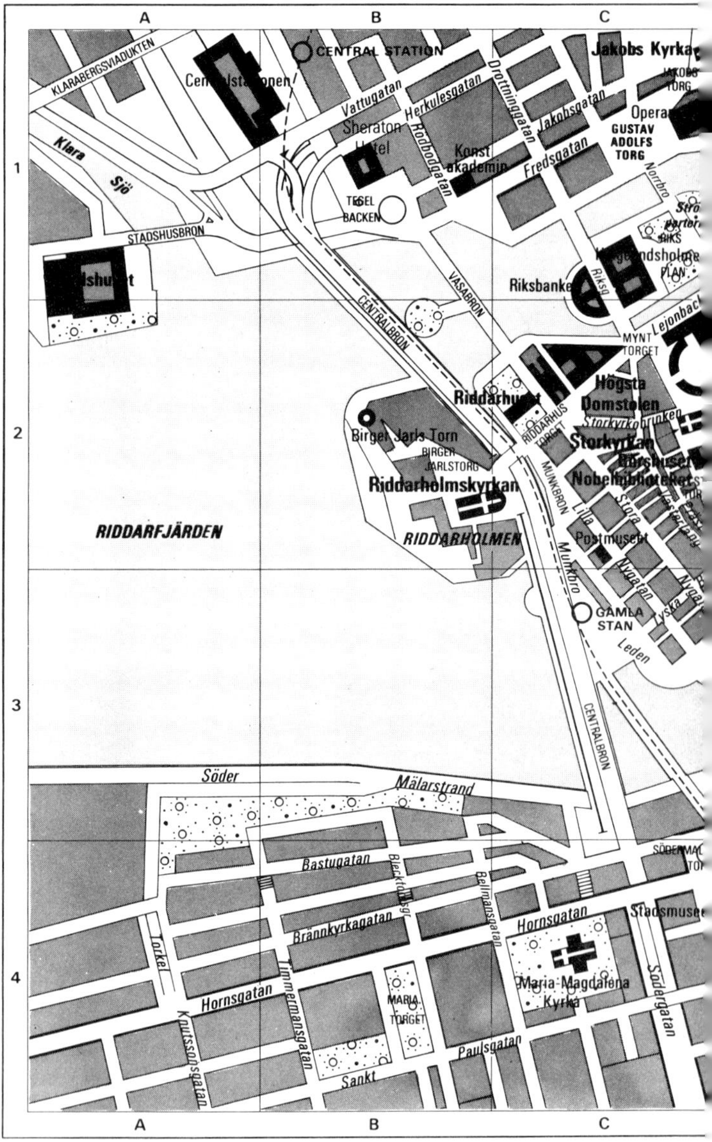
A
B
C
1
2
3
4
KLARABERGSVIADUKTEN
CENTRAL STATION
Jakobs Kyrka
Vattugatan
Herkulesgatan
Drottninggatan
Jakobsgatan
JAKOBS TORG
Opera
GUSTAV ADOLFS TORG
Sheraton Hotel
Rödbodgatan
Konst akademin
Fredsgatan
Klara Sjö
TEGEL BACKEN
Norrbro
STADSHUSBRON
VASABRON
Riksbank
Lejonback
CENTRALBRON
MYNT TORGET
Riddarhuset
Högsta Domstolen
RIDDARHUS TORGET
Storkyrkobrinken
Birger Jarls Torn
BIRGER JARLSTORG
Storkyrkan
Riddarholmskyrkan
MUNKBRON
RIDDARFJÄRDEN
RIDDARHOLMEN
Postmuseet
Munkbro
Nygatan
GAMLA STAN
Leden
CENTRALBRON
Söder
Mälarstrand
Bastugatan
Bellmansgatan
Brännkyrkagatan
Hornsgatan
Maria-Magdalena Kyrka
Södergatan
Torkel
Timmermansgatan
Hornsgatan
MARIA TORGET
Knutssonsgatan
Paulsgatan
Sankt

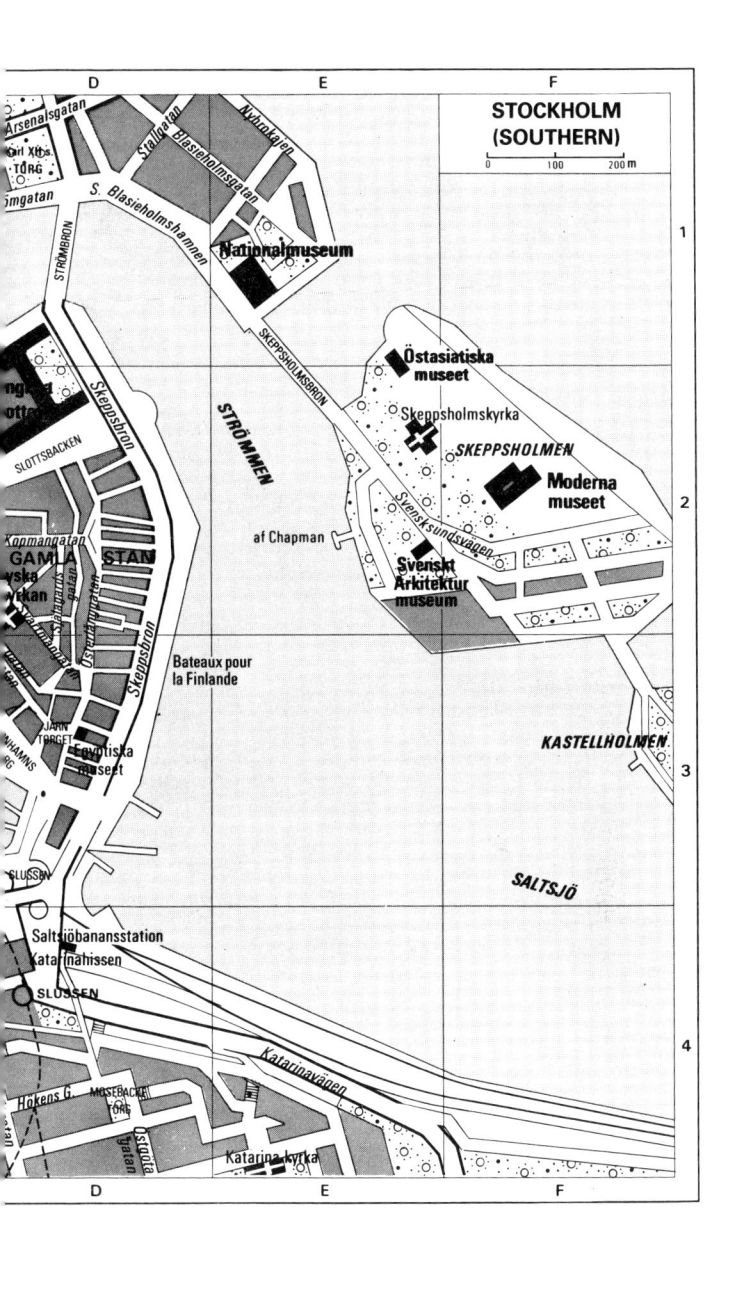

STOCKHOLM (SOUTHERN)

0   100   200 m

Arsenalsgatan
Karl XII:s TORG
S. Blasieholmsgatan
Stallgatan
Nybrokajen
S. Blasieholmshamnen
Nationalmuseum
STRÖMBRON
Skeppsbron
SLOTTSBACKEN
Köpmangatan
GAMLA STAN
tyska kyrkan
STRÖMMEN
SKEPPSHOLMSBRON
Östasiatiska museet
Skeppsholmskyrka
SKEPPSHOLMEN
Moderna museet
Svensksundsvägen
af Chapman
Svenskt Arkitektur museum
Bateaux pour la Finlande
JÄRN TORGET
Egyptiska museet
SKEPPSBRON
KASTELLHOLMEN
SLUSSEN
Saltsjöbananssstation
Katarinahissen
SLUSSEN
SALTSJÖ
Hökens G. MOSEBACKE TORG
Östgötagatan
Katarinavägen
Katarina kyrka

expensive. You can buy a book of 20 tickets. A ticket is valid for 2 trips within 1 hour of the time stamped on it.

Tourists benefit from *Turiskcart*, a card good for 1 day (23 Kr) or 3 days (47 Kr) that allows as many trips as you want, including boats going to Djurgarden and admission to Skansen, Gröna Lund, and the Kaknäs tower. It's really worth it. Stockholm residents also have a monthly commuter card.

The subway line 10-11 is new; its stations have been decorated by artists. Some are well done, for example, Solna Centrum. But, unfortunately, they are beginning to deteriorate—graffiti, broken windows, and so forth.

—There are 2 fine boat lines within the city. The first debarks from the wharf near the Slussen subway, the second from Nybroplan. Both go to Djurgarden (the second only during the summer). Same price as the subway.

Where to Sleep

The Swedes make a subtle distinction between "hotel" and "hostel." The second word means a place that provides beds (often without sheets) and is inexpensive. You must look exclusively for "hostels" or *Vandrarhem*. Hotels are too expensive.

It's not easy to find lodgings in Stockholm, particularly in the summer. Affordable accommodations are spread out over the city, which is why we suggest you consult the *Hotellcentralen* in the lower level of the station. For 10 Kr they'll make your reservations. Open from 8 A.M. to 9 P.M. Monday through Friday, on Saturday, from 8 A.M. to 5 P.M., and on Sunday from 1 A.M. to 9 P.M.

• In the Heart of Things

—*Af Chapman:* Skeppsholmen (Southern Map E2). Telephone 10-37-15. Youth hostel located on a wonderful sailing vessel, formerly used by the Swedish naval school. Perfectly maintained, a real marvel. It's not surprising that it's generally full. If you absolutely *must* sleep here, then you must make a reservation. Closed from noon to 3 P.M. Draconian rules: No smoking. No alcoholic beverages. No staying in the cabins between 10 A.M. and 5 P.M. No sleeping bags. We are not making it up. So if it's full, which often happens in the summer, don't be too sad—you're on vacation, not military duty! Closed from noon to 3 P.M. Cafeteria. In good weather you can eat out on deck, with a pretty view of the city as a bonus. Don't forget that the super cafeteria of the Museum of Modern Art is a 5-minute walk.

—*Mälaren:* Söder Mälarstrand (Southern Map B3). Subway: Slussen. This is also a large ship (red, the first one you'll see in the port) converted into a youth hostel, but it is always open, pleasant, and mixed. Double rooms. Discount for those who have their own sheets. Very clean. Inside, a small self-service cafeteria where you can eat for a reasonable price.

—*Gustau af Klint:* 153 Stadsgårdskajen. Subway: Slussen. Telephone (08) 40-40-77. Open all year. It's 65 or 85 Kr per person with sheet included.

—*Colombus:* 11 Tjärhovsgatan. Telephone 44-17-17. 80 beds. Open from May 1 to September 30. A 15-minute walk from the Mälaren hotel. Subway: Medborgarplatzen. Youth hostel card not required. Closed from 10 A.M. to 4 P.M., but there's no fixed hour for returning at night. 39 Kr a bed.

—*Zinken:* 2 Pipmarkargränd. Telephone 68-57-86. Subway: Hornstull. Discount for those with youth hostel card. You can cook. Bicycle rentals. Closed from noon to 4 P.M.

—*Regent Hotel:* 10 Drottninggatan (Northern Map C4). Telephone 20-90-04. In the heart of things, behind the opera. The elevator isn't very inviting, it seems sort of old, but its okay. Anyhow, we don't know of a cheaper hotel in Stockholm: 210 Kr for 2. Kept by a sweet little old lady.

—*Youth Hostel Dansakademien:* 21 Rehnsgatan. Telephone 31-31-18 or 32-38-36. Subway: Rådmansgatan. The street is right at the subway stop or a 10-minute walk from the station. Open from June 11 to August 14. 35 Kr per person. 10 Kr for sheets.

—*Birka Hostel:* 16 Birkagatan. Telephone 30-50-10. Subway: St. Eriksplan. Open from June 29 to July 24. 25 or 45 Kr per person. 10 Kr for sheets.

—Avoid the *Domus Hotel* which pretends to be a youth hostel but costs 240 Kr for a double room.

• *Far from the Heart of Things*

—*Sundbyberg KFUM:* 9 Ångsstigen. Telephone 98-47-53. Reception open from 7:30 A.M. to 9:30 P.M. and from 5 P.M. to 8 P.M. Telephone ahead, for there are only 30 beds. Located northwest of the city, in a school. Many games: Ping-Pong, darts, and cards. The kindness of the innkeeper will make you forget that the showers are cold. Be aware: Open only from July 10 to August 10. Subway 10 or 11 toward Hjulsta. Stop at Näckrosen.

—*Frescati Hotel:* 13 Professorsslingan. Telephone 15-79-96. Subway: Universitetet, then bus #151. Open from June 1 to August 31. 350 beds in double rooms with private bathroom. Open 24 hours a day.

• *More Chic*

—*Anno Hotel:* 3 Mariagränd. Telephone 42-68-60. Subway: Slussen. A large, entirely renovated building with a certain charm on a small quiet street. 200 Kr for 2. A very full breakfast is included.

—*Gustav Vasa:* Västmannagatan. Telephone 34-38-01. A 10-minute walk from the center of town. Small, old, 3-story hotel. A friendly atmosphere. 170 Kr for 2.

• *Campgrounds*

They're all very far from the center, but 3 are accessible by subway:

—*Sätra* (or Bredang Camping): 6 miles from the center of Stockholm, toward the southwest. Subway: Bredang, then ½ mile on foot. Telephone 97-70-71. Open from May 1 to October 15. Very well equipped (sauna). Crowded in the summer and rather expensive. There's a beach ⅓ mile away on Lake Mälaren.

When there are too many people at the Sätra campground, they bring them to the stadium: bizarre atmosphere and insufficient facilities. Not only that, you pay full price.

—*Ängby:* 8 miles west of the center. Telephone 37-04-20. Open from May 1 to September 30. A pretty spot (wooded hill) next to a lake. Take the train to Angbyplan station toward Hasselby, then a 10-minute walk in the forest.

—*Farsta:* 16 miles south of the center. From Central Station (T-

Centralen), take subway 18 toward Farsta until the end. There, bus #744 or #743. Telephone 94-14-45. Open from May 1 to September 30. On the shore of a little lake. The least expensive of the three. Contrary to what is posted at the entrance, a camping card is not necessary. But the trip is costly.

—We don't recommend the fourth *Flaten;* it's too near the airport.

Where to Eat

You'll find sausage stands everywhere, and they're not expensive. They are also hangouts for young people. Besides those, here are a few restaurants (the others are not in our price range; you'd complain to us about them).

—*Servus:* On the lower level of the Central Station. A supermarket with a large selection of food. Open every day from 9 A.M. to 9 P.M. Good for supplies on a train trip or when arriving late in the evening.

—*Hubertus:* 9A Hollandergatan. North of Hötorget Place. It's self-service and one of our favorite addresses in the city. First, it's very cheap, and second, it's in one of the prettiest areas in Stockholm. In good weather you can eat outdoors under the trees and greenery, surrounded by old houses with tremendous charm.

—*Östermalmstorg:* This place, in the city's center, overlooks a very quaint covered market. Each stall is more stylish than the next. Small tables in the fish section allow you to eat the freshest seafood, especially shrimp and small lobster. Note: This covered market closes at 11 A.M..

—*Modern Museum Cafeteria:* A superb place, for you can eat in the garden that is adorned with sculpture and flowers. Rather expensive, 20 Kr a sandwich. Convenient, espeically for those who stay at Youth Hostel Af Chapman nearby. They serve wine, which hardly spoils anything.

—*Pizzeria Piraten:* Tyska Brinken, at the corner of Lilla Nygatan, in the old city (Gamla Stan). The pizzas are no better than elsewhere, but the interior is wild. Picture an enormous room in which they have reconstructed the deck of a large sailing ship with rigging and masts.

—*Bistro Boheme:* 71A Drottninggatan. Telephone 11-90-41. About 5 minutes from the station. Friendly. About 25 Kr for the dish of the day. Appetizers and fruit juices as you please.

—Lavish breakfast to hold you for the whole day, for 26 Kr at the Grand Hotel. Near Youth Hostel Af Chapman, across from Strömbron bridge. You can even leave your bag at the coat check, and a nice hunter with a cap will lead you to the love-feast.

—*Stadhuskållaren:* On the lower level of City Hall (*Stadshuset*). An incredible little restaurant built into these medieval cellars. Very pretty decor with candlelight. As the setting suggests, it's ultra-chic and certainly not for the purse of a hitchhiker. Yet, our prudent eyes have noticed a very reasonably priced menu. Note: This menu is served only from 11 A.M. to 5 P.M. Very good for acting like the rich. A 5-minute walk from Central Station.

—*Ahlèns Cafeteria:* 50 Klarabergsgatan. A large store in the heart of the city that is a self-service on the third floor. No charm but very reasonable. Note: closes at 6 P.M..

—*Restaurant Graziella:* 5 Birger Jarls Torg, Riddarholmen. It's the little island south of Central Station. Choice of 3 main dishes with appetizers and beverages. Very good prices. You will notice all around you many distinguished people eating in a formal manner. These are judges, and you are dining in their canteen (*Kummerskolliegest*). Go there, but be discreet and well behaved.

—Large covered market where you find everything for eating on Hötorget in front of Konserthuset (Subway: Hötorget).

—*Konsum of Järntorget* (in the old city) is open weekdays from 8 A.M. to 10 P.M. and on Saturday from 10 A.M. to 1 P.M. You can buy salads with bread and butter for 24 Kr.

Museums

First we must talk about this card called *Stockholmskortet* that for 105 Kr gives free admission for 3 days to all urban transportation, museums, and monuments in Stockholm. (Though students already benefit from large discounts at practically all museums.) You can buy it at the Tourist Office, 27 Hamnagatan.

—*Moderna Museet* (Museum of Modern Art): Skeppsholmen (Southern Map F2), 2 steps from Youth Hostel Af Chapman. Open Tuesday to Friday from 11 A.M. to 9 P.M., on Saturday and Sunday from 11 A.M. to 5 P.M. Student discounts. This museum is interesting for the layman, for there are relatively few works. The paintings that are shown are terrific, for most represent the break with a former style or the beginning of a new school. Without going into detail, you'll find very pretty paintings from Expressionists, Fauves, and the Cobra group. A few lovely Picassos and Chagalls. Jackson Pollock is well represented. Free on Thursday. Great cafeteria (see Where to Eat).

—*Skansen:* On Djurgarden Island. Bus #47 from Nybroplan or the ferry from Slussen. The park is open every day from 8 A.M. to 11:30 P.M. It's a type of living ethnographic museum, exhibiting Swedish living quarters from the middle of the nineteenth century. You visit a kind of reconstructed village (very pretty wooden houses) in which craftspeople exhibit their skills at 11 A.M.—and at no other time. The cakes at the bakery are good. In the park there's a zoo with bears (white and brown), wolves, bisons, sea lions, moose . . . and a Laplander in her Lapp tent (she is a Lapp civil servant) plus other attractions. Crowded on Sunday. Don't miss the popular balls in the evening in Skansen. An orchestra plays traditional or more modern dances (fox trot, for example), for Swedes from 15 to 75 years of age. They dance heartily, with good technique and good manners. The gentleman invites the lady and then takes her hand to lead her to the dance floor. At the end of the dance, the scenario is repeated in reverse.

—*Wasavarvet:* On Djurgarden Island (Northern map F4). Open every day from 10 A.M. to 7 P.M. The famous warship *Wasa* that sunk in 1628, the day of its launching (the captain sure must have been chewed out!). The tour is fascinating, for the *Wasa* was considered the most beautiful and luxurious ship of its time. One is immediately struck by the five-story-high poop deck with its numerous wooden sculptures. Don't forget that the boat sank *intact,* that is, with all its furnishings and objects of the period. You even find a . . . skeleton. Next to it, a small museum exhibits all the equipment, the cannon, and so forth. In some instances they have represented life on board. Half price for those staying in youth hostels.

—*Nordiska Museet* (Nordic Museum): On Djurgarden Island (Northern Map F4). On the same island as the 2 preceding museums. Open from 10 A.M. to 4 P.M., from noon to 5 P.M. on Saturday and Sunday. Closed on Mondays in the winter. In an immense rococo building, this Scandinavian folklore museum tries to present an image of Swedish life and the different levels of society. Peasant life is represented by the interiors of traditional homes. For the aristocracy and the upper crust, they have reconstructed entire rooms of certain castles, including dining room tables decorated with Swedish silverware, dolls, and so forth.

—*National Museum* (Northern Map D4): Only the artwork is of interest. Don't miss room 307 for some masterpieces by Rubens, *Saint Peter and Saint Paul* by El Greco, and especially *Saint Jerome Pénitent* by Georges de la Tour. In room 308 there are 3 masterpieces by Rembrandt: *Portrait of an Old Man*, the *Young Cook*, and *Oath of the Batavi*. In room 327 there are some Venetian paintings (Guardi and Canaletto). Room 334 will please Francophiles thanks to some beautiful Delacroix and some interesting Impressionist paintings (Manet, Renoir, and Cézanne). In room 335 glance at some seductive paintings by Carl Larsson that strangely resemble the work of Norman Rockwell.

—*Östasiatiska Museet* (Museum of the Far East) (Southern Map E1): Skeppsholmen. Note: Open only from noon to 4 P.M. Closed Monday. Chinese antiques (remarkably beautiful collection of jade and stunning bronzes). Interesting Buddha and Indian sections. You finish near the Japanese Art Gallery, rich in engravings and erotic prints.

—*Drottningsholms Slott:* On Lövon Island, outside the center. To get there, subway to Brommaplan, then bus to Mälaröarna (any number), or in the summer a boat from Klara Mälarstrand. It's a theater museum. The theater dates from the eighteenth century and has been preserved with all its complicated machinery and sets—and everything works! In the summer, there are presentations of opera from the eighteenth century (musicians in the orchestra even wear powdered wigs). It's rather wonderful. As proof: the king and queen stay here. And they have good taste.

—*Millesgården:* Lidingö. Outside the center. Subway to Ropsten, then bus #205 or #290. Open every day from May 1 to October 15 from 11 A.M. to 5 P.M. Carl Milles is a sculptor unfortunately not recognized elsewhere. This fellow reinvented balance in sculpture. You can visit the garden and the house, which he designed himself to exhibit his work. It's absolutely fantastic. One wonders how many of the statues stand, particularly one of a man flying above a winged horse. The memorial fountain in front of Konserthuset is also his.

Strolls

—*Gamla Stan* (Southern Map D2): The medieval city located on a small island. Many tourists, but you can still find peaceful spots, winding streets, and old gable houses. And a good number of streets are closed to traffic. Rather chic boutiques. The young people go here on Saturday night: small restaurants and well-known nightclubs.

The royal castle is on this island. Changing of the guard at 12:15 P.M., on Sunday at 1:15 P.M. No tour of the castle on Monday. You can also visit the throne room and the room with the crown jewels (*Skattkammaren*).

—*Gröna Lund:* Traveling show imitating the Tivoli in Copenhagen. Large carousels. The popular dance halls have a friendly atmosphere. It's on Djurgarden, near Skansen. Closed in the winter. This amusement park is smaller than the one in Copenhagen but more interesting and less expensive. Fewer tourists and a larger variety of amusements.

—*Kulturhuset* (Cultural Center): Sergels Torg, in the heart of the city. Subway: T-Centralen, exit at Drottningsgatan. A plethora of activities and exhibitions. Newspapers from all over the world, chess games, records to listen to, and so forth. Everything is free. On the ground floor, in the hall, there is a billboard for announcements concerning lodgings, hitchhiking, and all that. It works well. On Monday only the ground floor is open.

—*Langholmen Island.* Subway: Hornstull or bus #54. There's a former prison, now a pretty park, old houses, and a pretty view of the city, ideal for picnics. We give it 3 stars! Stockholm residents come to this beach to swim and sunbathe in their birthday suits. You globetrotters can thank us; pick-up artists will be working there. The girls who go there to sunbathe want to be left in peace. You are forewarned.

Where to Swim Without Freezing Your Buns

Those who have buttocks sensitive to cold water will be happy to know that there are plenty of swimming pools in Stockholm.

—*Erikspalsbadet:* Subway to Skanstull.

—*Karelia:* Birger Jarls Gatan. Subway to Östermalmstorg (exit at Stureplan). A true Finnish sauna as in Finland, with a bonus; a nightclub. For sauna fans, you should know that almost all pools have them.

Where to Down a Few. Where to Shake It.

The down and out are consoled in the evening, for all summer there are free pop concerts and theater, in outdoor locales. Very nice. Get information on the programs in the following spots (there are others): *Langholmen* (subway to Hornstull); Vita Berget (subway to Skanstull, near Sofia Church); Ralamshov (subway to Fridhemsplan).

Otherwise, you'll find many bars with bands where you can dance. In these places you pay a cover charge plus drinks (expensive!). On Saturday night they are full by 9 or 10 P.M.—Swedes do everything early. Often you have to line up on the sidewalk to get in.

—*Engelen:* 59B Kornhamnstorg, in Gamla Stan. Our favorite place as long as we avoid Saturday night, when there's usually a half hour wait to get in. On the ground floor there's a bar with New Orleans jazz. In the back there's a restaurant with several rooms where you can eat for just a bit more than elsewhere. Downstairs is a discothèque in the vaulted cellar, beginning around 11:30 P.M. Filled with young people (average age between 17 and 30).

—*Kurbit's:* 10 Transgund, in Gamla Stan, right near Storstorget. Small cellar that is truly pleasant. Modern music. Bar where the beer flows in floods. Food to boot.

—*Front Page:* 20 Kungsholmsgatan, not far from City Hall (Stadshuset). Subway to Rådhuset. An immense joint with a restaurant on the ground floor and a discothèque below. The hip hangout for the 22–35 crowd. The boss makes enough to open only on Wednesday, Thursday, and Friday.

—*Stampen:* 7 Stora Gramunkegränd, on Gamla Stan. Traditional jazz club. Admission charge plus drinks. The clientele is slightly older, recruited from the higher ranks to go slumming for a night.

—*Piperska Muren:* 14 Scheelegatan. Subway to Rådhuset. Singles discothèque, but the chicks pick up chicks, and the cats pick up cats. (Oh, my goodness!). You can mix and you can dance here: it's very nice.

To Leave Stockholm by Thumb

—Toward the north: Go 2 stops past Wenner Green Center. There, you are right by the expressway. If the police come, you can say you're waiting for the bus which is taking its sweet time.

—Toward the south: The highway starts in the middle of the city near the Liljeholmen subway. A sign with your destination is almost obligatory.

To Go to the Airport

Regular shuttle bus on Vasagatan Avenue (leaves from the sidewalk across from the station). Note: There are 4 bus stops. Some go to Arlanda Airport (international flights) and some to Bromma (national flights).

Boats for Finland

There are 2 companies operating the Stockholm–Turku line daily (also the Stockholm–Helsinki) for the same price.

—*Viking Line:* At the end of Märlastrand, after the bridge and Stradsgarden. You can buy tickets on the day of departure, beginning at 4:45 A.M. Reservations aren't really needed for bridge class. There is a 50 percent discount for Inter-Rail and students. It isn't necessary to go to the Viking LIne office in the center of town to buy your ticket; it's more practical to go directly to the dock, particularly if you're staying at the youth hostel. From the station, take the subway to Slussen, then bus #45.

—*Silja Line:* Stureplan (the same subway as the other). Telephone 22-21-40. A 50 percent discount for Inter-Rail (only for bridge class). For 52 Kr you can feast on shrimp and salmon. We advise you to make a reservation in the restaurant for the second seating, when the waiters are less rushed. Free discothèque. Sauna and swimming pool for a fee. The Silja Line is a little more expensive than the Viking Line.

Mini-crossings to the Aland Islands

Departs every day except Sunday. No need to carry food; the meals on board are reasonable. Alcoholic drinks are much less expensive than in Stockholm. 45 Kr is the cheapest price, and there are 60 beds at this price; therefore, book in advance.

TOWARD SWEDISH LAPLAND

UPPSALA

About 44 miles from Stockholm (one hour by train from the Central Station). A rather nice university city; the atmosphere is reminiscent of Cambridge, with a river and old buildings.

—*Tourist Office:* 44 Kungsgatan. On the right when leaving the station. Bicycle rentals. There is also an annex inside the cathedral.

Where to Sleep

—*Vandrarhem* (youth hostel): At Sunnersa, residential suburb 4 miles south of the city. From the city center, take bus #20 from Östra Agatan (along the river). Lovely middle-class wooden homes in a large park overlooking a pretty lake. Closed from 10 A.M. to 5 P.M..

—*Graneberg Campgrounds:* 4 miles south of the city and a 10-minute walk from the youth hostel. From the city center, bus #20 from Östra Agatan (along the river). The campgrounds are located in a forest, down by the water.

—*Gläntan Vandrarhem* (youth hostel): 46 Norbybag, southwest of the city. Bus #6 or #7 from the square near the cathedral. Open only in the summer. Relaxed here: sauna, TV. billiards, Ping-Pong. But it is clearly less appealing than the Vandrarhem.

—*Uppsala RS-KAR:* Västra Strandgatan. Dormitory and family rooms. In the heart of it all. You can cook. Open from 7 to 10 A.M. and from 4 P.M. to midnight.

Where to Drink Hearty

—*Rackis:* 10 Rackarbergsgatan, in the university enclave. Student cafeteria with beer and good music. The local crowd dances to all kinds of music depending on the band.

To See

All the important monuments of Uppsala are near the cathedral.

—*Cathedral:* Strangely evokes the Gothic cathedrals of France. Burned on several occasions, the structure was rebuilt a little too "new" looking for our taste. On the inside, don't miss the pulpit in sculpted wood that is in the choir stalls, quite ornate, in baroque style. To the left is the treasure of the cathedral, a sacred gold and silver vessel. Royal insignia show that the kings of Sweden were formerly crowned here.

—*Gustavium:* Across from the cathedral. This medieval palace houses an operating room where Dr. Rudbeck did his dissections. The cramped arrangement of the benches around the table is very fascinating. Open Monday to Friday from 11 A.M. to 2 P.M..

—*Carolina Rediviva:* University library. Open every day from 9 A.M. to 6 P.M. except Sunday morning. With more than 2 million books and 30,000 manuscripts, it contains the precious *Codex Argenteus* (or *Silver Bible*), written with silver ink on purple parchment (fifth century).

—*The Castle:* An imposing edifice dominating the city from on top of a hill. A visit inside is superfluous because there is no furniture from that period. Not only that, there's a fee.

In the Area: Gamla Uppsala

The old city of Uppsala extends 2½ miles north of the present city. The bus leaves from Gamla Torget or the train from the Central Station. This was an important political, adminstrative, and commercial center from the very first centuries. You can still see the three large royal burial mounds near the church. Having said this, even if these personalities were historically important in Sweden, we must admit that the interest is limited. The church contains some handsome wooden sculptures, a retable, and some frescos on the ceiling that have fresh, well-preserved colors.

Nearby is the *Odinsborg* restaurant, which claims to be the birthplace of Swedish democracy. The delegates of the people gather here each year. The decor inside includes souvenirs from the Viking era. The great specialty is mead drunk from horns. Very expensive for what it is. Satisfy yourself with a sandwich that is affordable.

GÄVLE

North of Uppsala, on the road from Sundsvall. A city of medium importance. Rather airy.

Where to Sleep

—*Vandrahmen* (youth hostel): Rädmansgatan. In the loveliest area of the city, and the oldest. Ask for the *Reservatet,* south of the center of town. This block of homes is impeccably preserved by the city. The youth hostel consists of several wooden houses around a pleasant little patio. It's a 5-minute walk from the center.

—*Camping:* 7½ miles north of the city on E4, then turn right.

To See

—*Reservatet:* Behind the youth hostel (see above).

—*Järnvägs Museum* (Railway Museum): South of the city, on the road from Stockholm. Note: Open only from 1 P.M. to 4 P.M. Half price for students. This no-longer used railroad yard has one of the most beautiful museums of its kind. The locomotives are exhibited in chronological order. Don't miss the incredible royal wagons and those of prisoners. The museum also has an automobile converted to roll on rails. Very pretty steam locomotive and a superb model at ¹⁄₁₀ scale. From Rådhuset, bus #6.

—*Sylvanum:* 32 Kungsbäcksvägen. Open from 10 A.M. to 4 P.M. A museum with a very modern idea that will interest only those who are into wood—its uses and results.

—The statue in front of the station, because of its particularly huge dimensions.

In the Area

—Numerous lakes where you can rent a canoe (50 Kr a day for two). It's a great experience to go away for 2 or 3 days with a canoe and a tent. Information and itineraries are available at the Tourist Office.

SUNDSVALL

Approximately 272 miles north of Stockholm. A small, gloomy city, but pleasant. Located between 2 hills that offer a beautiful view of the city and the Gulf of Bothnia

Where to Sleep, Where to Eat

—*Vandrarhem* (youth hostel): In the Stadsberget area, 1 mile north of the city. On one of the hills of Sundsvall. You stay in a small bungalow surrounded by a pine forest. Bus #2 from the bus station, then a 35-yard walk.
—*Flasian Campgrounds:* 2 miles south of the city on the road from Stockholm. In a pine grove by the sea. Sandy beach with a small peninsula.
—*City Konditorei:* Kirkogatan. From 7 in the morning, coffee and good pastries for 15 Kr.

Where to Cut a Rug

—*Strand Hotel:* 10 Strandgatan. This chic hotel boasts a nightclub with the advantage of being free. Dress to kill.
—*Bon Appétit:* On the pedestrian street, 50 yards west of the main place. Appeals to a younger crowd, has more rock music, and you have to pay to play.

KIRUNA

An industrial city, pleasant to visit, but that's it. Many hitchhikers. Notice that as in all Swedish cities, the young people ceaselessly cruise the city in their big fat American cars. It's the big fashion over here.
—*Tourist Office:* 42 Hjalmar Lundbomsvagen. Across from City Hall.

Where to Sleep

—There is a youth hostel, but it is often full, alas! The best thing to do is go camping. The city was built on a hill. Descend on the station side and follow the railroad tracks. About after ½ mile, you come upon some barracks. That's the inn. It's closed from 10 A.M. to 4 P.M..
—Camping is a bit expensive, but well laid out (particularly the cooking stoves, which are free). You have to pay for the sauna. Many mosquitoes and very cold nights. Go down to the ski trail by the lake.

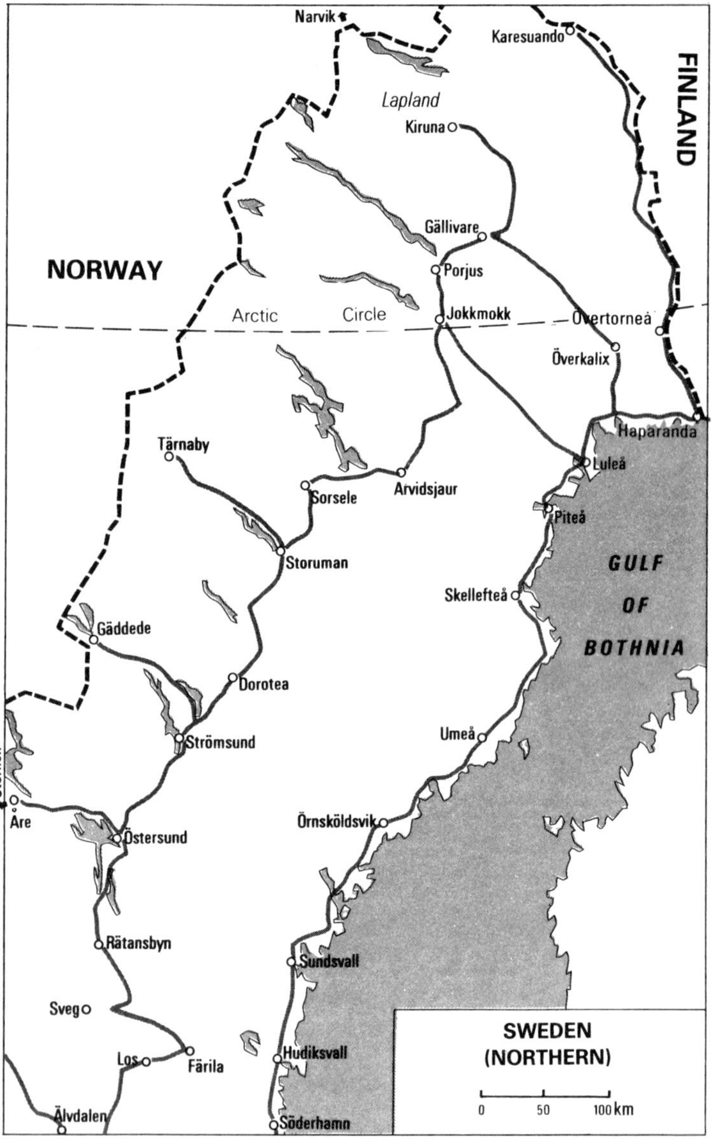
Narvik
Karesuando
FINLAND
Lapland
Kiruna
Gällivare
NORWAY
Porjus
Arctic Circle
Jokkmokk
Övertorneå
Överkalix
Haparanda
Tärnaby
Luleå
Sorsele
Arvidsjaur
Piteå
Storuman
GULF OF BOTHNIA
Skellefteå
Gäddede
Dorotea
Umeå
Strömsund
Storlien
Åre
Örnsköldsvik
Östersund
Rätansbyn
Sundsvall
Sveg
SWEDEN (NORTHERN)
Los
Färila
Hudiksvall
0
50
100 km
Älvdalen
Söderhamn

A superb site. The cafeteria offers a gigantic breakfast for 25 Kr that will hold you for the day.

—The locker room at the station is less expensive than the automatic lockers. The station closes at night.

Where to Eat

—Shopping at Domus and Tempo stores.

—You can eat cheap at the self-service eatery in ICA, the big department store, as well as at the kiosk at the bus station (until 11 P.M.).

—Next to the tourist office there's a self-service place, probably the cheapest in Kiruna. Open very late.

To See

You can visit City Hall (guided tours in English) and (additionally) the famous iron mines (closed August 15). For the mines, make reservations at the tourist bureau. Interesting tour.

Don't forget to see the church in the form of a Lapp tent. It's next to the firehouse and it's red. Closed after August 15.

Inexpensive sauna (5 Kr) at the municipal swimming pool.

—*Lapp Village* (Jukkastärvi) . . . interesting. By bus, the trip is picturesque. It's 6 miles from Kiruna. There's a family inn where Lapp specialties are served, including reindeer and Arctic blueberries. Campground and interesting Lapp museum.

KEBNEKASJE

From Kiruna you can take nice little walks. Leave the city by car or bus (there's one a day to Nikkaluokta).

In Nikkaluokta, don't camp next to the inn (always full) because they ask you to pay 5 Kr to use poor facilities.

From there, take a walk around Kebnekasje. From Nikkaluokta, after 3 miles, you come to a lake with a small shelter, where you can eat. Then, either take the small ferry to cross the lake (20 Kr), or walk around it (3 miles).

From the wharf you still have 2 hours of walking to get to Kebnekasje Station, a small, very touristy village with a superb inn (but it costs 58 Kr each in the dormitory!). It's 12 miles from Nikkaluokta to Kebnekasje Station.

From there you can climb to the summit of Kebnekasje, the highest mountain in Sweden (6880 feet). There are two routes: The western path is easy because there's no scaling, but it's long (4–5 hours) and not very pleasant (scree). The eastern path is shorter (2–3 hours) but impressive because you have to cross a snow bridge. After the bridge you'll have to scale a bit, but you will find ropes everywhere. You'd better wear hiking boots. At the peak there is a free, small shelter that fits 8 people. You must bring your own grub and a good map. A good steam bath will relax you instantly. The day after, continue walking . . . and you'll find Lapland huts, reindeer, as well as some rather rare animals like wild cocks.

Before beginning your venture, inquire about equipment.

ABISKO NATIONAL PARK

From Kiruna take the train toward Narvik and stop at *Abisko Turistation*. Superb landscape. A nature lover's delight. Don't forget to pack some grub, for stores are few and far between. Note: there are 2 stations, Turistation and Abisko Östra.

The Abisko tourist station is overpriced. But they do have bungalows with beds. Camping is also available in the area (very cold at night). The hotel at Abisko Östra costs 45 Kr per night plus 10 Kr for breakfast. Friendly.

Behind the station, in the forest, there's a Lapp encampment and an open-air museum.

A tip for those who can't afford the Abisko tourist station: If you're coming from Norway, stop at the station just before the one at Abisko. Go to the home of Mr. Kvist, a very nice man who will put you up; and you can cook. There's almost always room, even when there isn't any. Locally, he's very well known, and you can ask at the hotel where to find him. Or if you're adventurous, cross the train tracks and turn right; take the road to the telephone transformer, then make a left and an immediate right. The house is at the end.

For lazybones, it's only about 1 mile from Östra to the tourist station, on a barely used road.

The village is quite pretty, with its wooden homes, and you can go down to the lake (the water's cold). Only one hotel. Small and often full, but very pleasant.

Wilderness camping is prohibited because it's a reservation.

Be aware that the humidity is absolutely incredible, requiring special camping equipment, even for those not susceptible to rheumatism.

While it might be a little too tame for tourists, the park is really delightful. Campers prefer the "royal trail" to the campgrounds at the station. Camping areas are well arranged all along this trail. All the comforts are available, and you can make a campfire Not only that, it's all quiet and free!

There is no road through the National Park. Too bad for the hot-rod polluters!

If you are crazy about hiking, don't miss the *Kungslede* (royal trail) to Nikkaluokta. Takes 5 to 6 days at a rate of 12 miles a day. Maps of Abisko National Park are on sale at Kiruna as well as at Narvik (see Turistinform). You should know that it's chilly in the evening and that the mosquitoes are voracious. The sun shines 24 hours a day at Abisko, from June 13 to July 4.

Here and There

—When going up the Gulf of Bothnia toward the North Cape, you should know that at Luleå, about 63 miles from the border of Finland, there is a Citroën garage (that might come in handy). There's even a guy who manages some English.

—If you have time, take a trip to Gotland Island, to the southeast. Rather unusual scenery.

SOUTHERN LAPLAND

—*Jokknok:* Rather important city in Lapland and very pleasant. The main attraction is a Lapp art museum. Campgrounds are 2 miles from the center, on Route 97. Free swimming pool and sauna.
—*Arvidsjaur:* A village with a large Lapp camp that is not inhabited but gives an idea of Lapp life.
—*Arjeplog:* A large village built on the islands of Lake Hornavan. Follow the "silver road" that leads to a silent world. Kraja Campgrounds are well equipped and not expensive. Visit the Silver Museum which has silver and Lapp objects. You can eat reindeer in a variety of ways at Silverhatten Restaurant. And it is located on a hill, which doesn't ruin anything.

ALAND ISLANDS

The Aland Islands, located between Stockholm and Turku, are dependents of Finland. The ferry stops at the main town; Mariehamn. Finnish currency, but they speak Swedish. Several inexpensive campgrounds. Buses cross the island starting from Mariehamn. For more complete information, go to the Tourist Office in the port. For those who prefer nature to flocks of tourists.

A somewhat costly trip by Inter-Rail, since there's no discount between the mainland and the islands. But It's very beautiful, with scenery unknown on the mainland and windmills. However, there is a discount between Finland and the islands.

TOWARD OSLO

GÖTEBORG

The primary port and the second most populated city in Sweden. For centuries the city has made its fortune by maritime commerce.

Useful Addresses

—*Tourist Office:* Östra Nordstan. Telephone 19-07-31. It's not the main office (which is at 2 Parkgatan), but it is the most practical because it's located in a shopping mall in front of the station. They'll give a map of the city with transportation indicated and make reservations in hotels and inns (5 Kr commission). And they're very nice.
—*Ferry for Denmark:* 2 companies, Stena and Sessan. They offer a 50 percent discount with Inter-Rail and free with U-Rail. It is better to go directly to the terminals of these 2 companies rather than to their offices if you're rushed. Addresses of the terminals:
• Stena Line: Mast Huggskajen. Telephone 42-09-40.
• Sessan Line: Majnabbe. Telephone 12-49-80.
—*Bus Station:* Heden (near Sodra Vagen).
—*International Newspapers:* The kiosk at Kungsportsplatsen.
—*Exchange:* At the railway station.

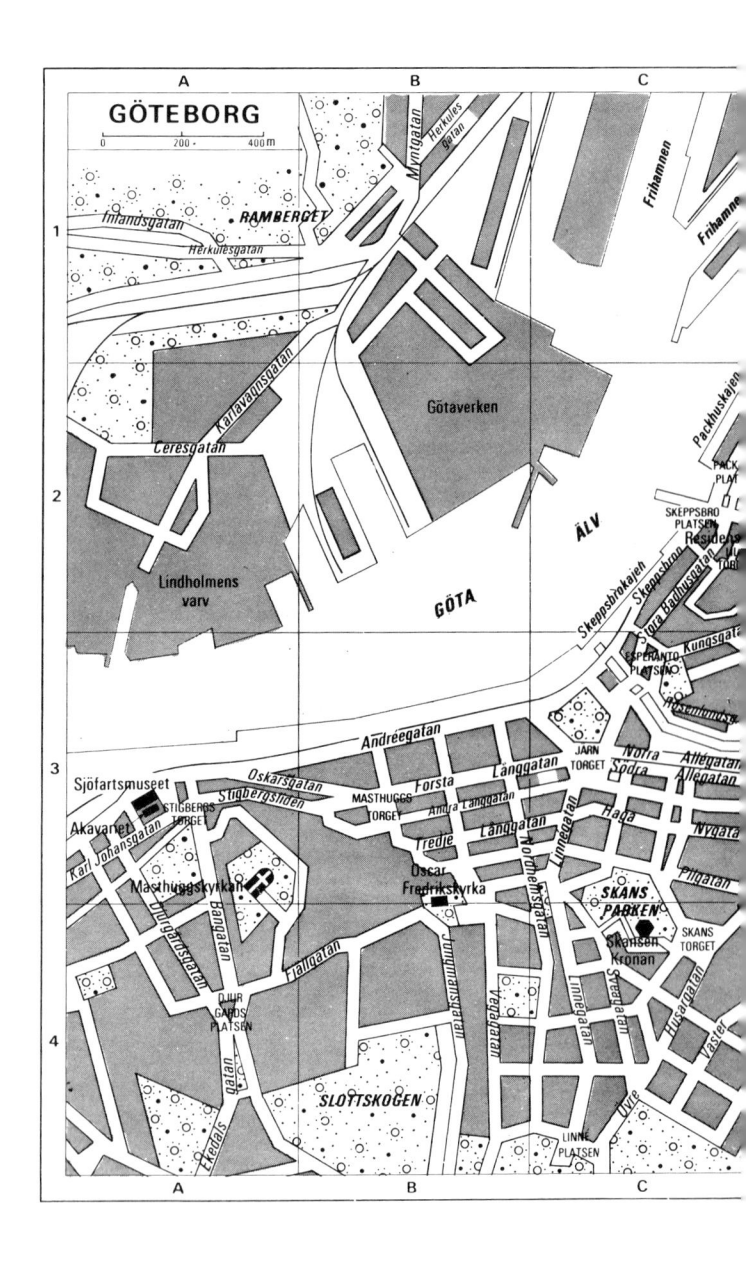

GÖTEBORG

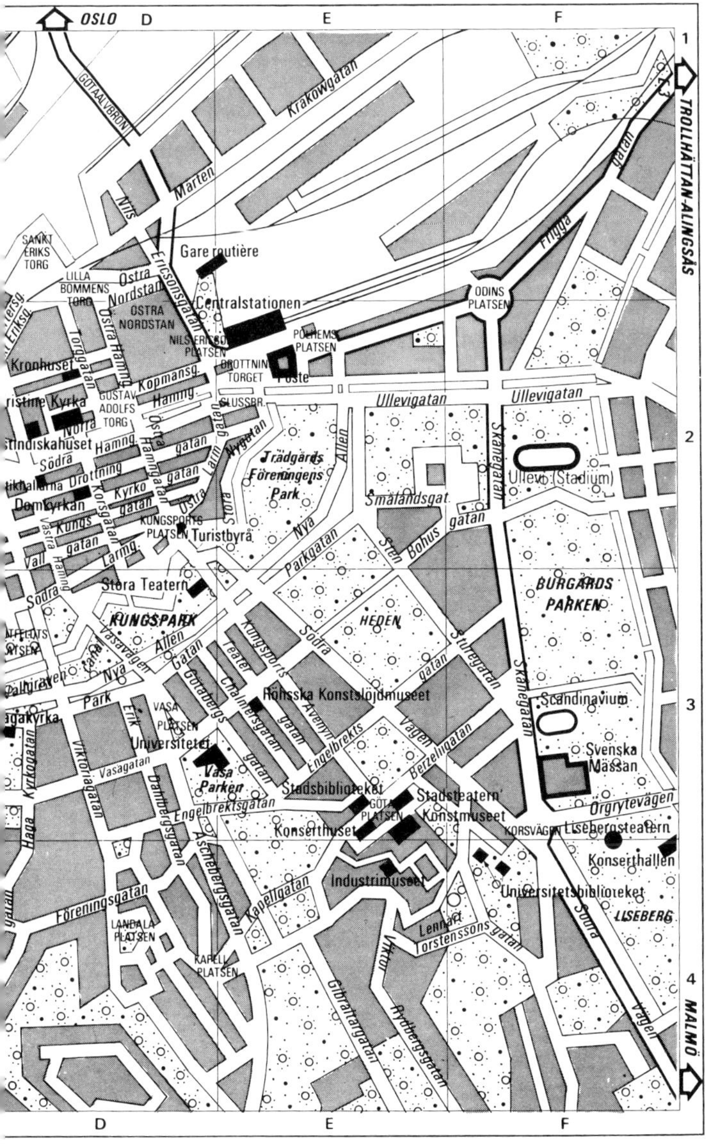
OSLO
D
E
F
1
2
3
4
TROLLHÄTTAN-ALINGSÅS
MALMÖ
GÖTAÄLVBRON
Krakowgatan
Nils
Marten
SANKT ERIKS TORG
Gare routière
LILLA BOMMENS TORG
Östra Nordstan
ÖSTRA NORDSTAN
Centralstationen
NILS ERICSONS PLATSEN
POLHEMS PLATSEN
ODINS PLATSEN
Frigga
gatan
Kronhuset
Torggatan
Kristine Kyrka
GUSTAV ADOLFS TORG
BROTTNING TORGET
Post
Köpmansg.
SLUSSBR.
Ullevigatan
Ullevigatan
Ostindiskahuset
Norra Hamng.
Södra
Trädgårds Föreningens Park
Allén
Skånegatan
Ullevi (Stadium)
Domkyrkan
Drottning
Kyrko gatan
Kungs gatan
Korsgatan
Smålandsgat.
KUNGSPORTS PLATSEN
Turistbyrå
Nya
Parkgatan
Sten Bohus gatan
Vall gatan
Larmg.
Stora Teatern
BURGÅRDS PARKEN
KUNGSPARK
HEDEN
Södra
Vasavägen
Allén
Kungsports
Teater
Avenyn
Sturegatan
Skånegatan
Röhsska Konstslöjdmuseet
Scandinavium
Hagakyrka
Park
VASA PLATSEN
Erik
Universitetet
Engelbrekts
Vägen
Berzeliigatan
Svenska Mässan
Kyrkogatan
Viktoriagatan
Vasagatan
Vasa Parken
Stadsbiblioteket
Stadsteatern
Örgrytevägen
Engelbrektsgatan
GÖTA PLATSEN
Konstmuseet
KORSVÄGEN
Lisebergsteatern
Haga
Dahlbergsgatan
Konserthuset
Aschebergsgatan
Konserthallen
Industrimuseet
Universitetsbiblioteket
Föreningsgatan
Kapellgatan
LISEBERG
LANDALA PLATSEN
Lennart Torstenssons gatan
Södra Vägen
KAPELL PLATSEN
Gibraltargatan
Viktor Rydbergsgatan
D
E
F

Where to Sleep

—*Vandrarhem Ostkupan:* 2 Mejerigatan. Telephone 40-10-50.

—A youth hostel south of the city. Those who arrive by car or hitchhiking have an advantage. From route E6, don't go to the center of the city but exit at the roadsign *Jonkoping Göteborg C.* A large, modern, white building, 200 yards from the exit, toward the right. A setting with no charm but with bathrooms, TV, washing machines, Ping-Pong, sauna, and kitchen. Rooms for 2 or 3. For meals, the cafeteria of the ICA supermarket is affordable. To get there from the center of the city, take tram #5 to Brunnsparken (across from the station) to Sigfridsplan station, then bus #62 toward Källeback to Grädgatan. Closed from 10 A.M. to 4 P.M.. This youth hostel has the advantage of being not too far from Liseberg. Slightly more expensive for non-hostel members. Breakfast, if you wish.

—*Hotel Ömen:* 6 Lorenbergsgatan. Telephone 81-07-30. In the center of town, not far from Eden Park. Atmosphere of a family inn for young people. You can use the kitchen.

—*Torrekula Turistation Youth Hostel:* Open all year. Telephone 75-14-95. Located 8 miles south of the city. Get there by the blue bus *Kallered,* which leaves from the Heden market.

—*Masthugghotellet:* 5 Masthuggstorget. Reserved for bums, Scandinavian drunks, and various down and outers. It's run by the cops. The average tourist is not welcome. Therefore, pointless to ask the Tourist Office to make a reservation. For emergency use only, of course.

• *Campgrounds*

—*Karralund:* 2½ miles east of the city in a residential neighborhood surrounded by greenery. Telephone 25-27-61. To get there, take tram #5 (across from the station) to Brunnsparken and get off at Velandersgatan. Along the river. Fairly well equipped, but you pay for showers.

—*Askim:* 6 miles south. Near the sea. Telephone 28-62-61. Open in the summer. These 2 campgrounds offer discounts. You don't pay separately for a tent, a person, and a car, but a package deal. Good deal. Tram #1 or #2 at Linneplatsen, then bus #82.

—*Lilleby:* 12 miles to the southwest. Near a not-too-clean sea. Telephone 56-08-67. Trams #2, #5, or #6, then bus #20, and get off at Vagmastareplatsen.

Where to Eat

—The cafeteria at the station isn't bad but a little expensive. Inside the station there's a supermarket open until midnight.

—There's another cafeteria in the underground passage that leads to the station.

—*Clock Hamburgerrastaurang:* 20 Nova Hanugatan. 200 yards from the station. Closes at 11 P.M.

—*Kopmännens Hus:* 52 Vasagatan. If you want, you can eat only a salad. The food in general is good. The bread that they bake themselves is delicious. Open from noon to 2 P.M.

—*Gyllele Prag:* 25 Sveagatan. A Czech restaurant. Not expensive. Near Linneplatsen in the southwest. Closed Saturday and Sunday.

—*Weise:* 23 Drottningatan. The oldest restaurant in the city. Affordable typical Swedish dishes. Closed Sunday.

Where to Down a Few

—*Rotary Pub:* 2 Richertsgatan. The best priced pub in the city, for its goal is not profit. Run by students. Next to the University of Chalmers. The most expensive dish is a steak. Open from 7:30 to midnight on Sunday, Tuesday, and Thursday.

—*Pub:* Dojan. Open every day from 7 P.M. Don't get there late unless you like standing in line. The fish is reasonably priced and copiously served. And for fans of new recipes . . . a great Camembert fried with jam (we're already licking our lips).

To See

—*Liseberg Park:* You buy your tickets at the entrance to go on the rides. In our opinion, these rides are more interesting than those of Tivoli in Copenhagen. Make acquaintances. Excessive drinking at the bar in the evening creates a rather raunchy atmosphere. The restaurants are fairly expensive, but you can get away with hotdogs or hamburgers. Dance floor a bit old-fashioned but nice. To get there, take bus #5 at the exit of the shopping mall across from the station.

—*House of the India Company* (Östindiska Kompaniets Hus): 12 Norra Hamnagatan, along the canal (Map D2). Open from 11 A.M. to 4 P.M., on Sunday from noon to 4 P.M. Closed Monday. There's a museum; in fact, 3 museums in 1. It isn't surprising that it's an indescribable mess, with the most interesting objects next to banalities. The curator would do well to put things in order.

• *Ethnographic department:* Many souvenirs carried back by sailors from far away places: jewels, totems, fetish dolls, thrones from Africa, North America, and Latin America. The Aztec room is particularly remarkable for funerary urns and incredibly fine textiles.

• *Historical department of Göteborg:* Interiors of peasant, worker, middle-class, and aristocratic homes. Interesting room devoted to ropemaking. Some of the documents trace the development and importance of the India Company. Models of India Company boats.

• *Museum of Archaeology:* Results of scavenging in the area. Viking jewelry and antique money.

—*Maritime Museum:* A 5-minute walk from the Museum of the India Company, at the end of Östra Hamnagatan, along the quay. 3 sailing vessels with 4 gigantic masts. Tours at 10 A.M. and 4 P.M.

—*Haga:* Very old area, near the port; slightly seedy occupants. Super wooden houses that will remind you of the Victorian houses of San Francisco. Tram #3 or #4 toward Jarntorget.

—*Museum of Fine Arts* (Konstmuseet): Gotaplatsen (Map E3). Open from 11 A.M. to 4 P.M. Closed Monday. The works of Carl Milles, the most famous Swedish sculptor, are in the large hall. Founded mostly with donations, the collection is rather eclectic. See the Venetian painters in room 7, the Rembrandt in room 8, and especially the Impressionist and Postimpressionist masterpieces in room 27. Several Picassos in room 29.

—For the beach, tram #4. Crowded on weekends.

—Canoe rides for 1 hour for 22 Kr. Fairly interesting with an English guide. In front of the Kiosk, Paddam Kungsportsplatsen.

Boat Rides

—*Göta Canal:* The prettiest waterway in Sweden. In principle, from Göteborg to Stockholm, but there are shorter routes on less luxurious boats for lower prices. Decent food. Those who are tired of canals can rent bikes and follow paths along the canal.

The voyage from Göteborg to Stockholm lasts 3 days. The highest point of the canal is 297 feet above sea level. For information: *Rederiaktiebolaget Göta Kanal:*

—In Göteborg: Bp 272, 2 Hotellplatsen. Telephone 031-17-76-15.
—In Stockholm: S-103 16. BP 2253, 20 Skepsbron. Telephone 08-24-04-79.

Boats for Denmark

The Friday evening crossing by the Stena Sessan is very pleasant (leaves at 6:30 P.M.). Most of the passengers go for the round trip just for the fun of it. Good atmosphere.

TOWARD THE NORTH

The northern coast of Göteborg, which leads to the Norwegian border, crosses one of the most unusual regions of the country. There are broken-up landscapes where blocks of granite alternate with stretches of moors. In the entire coastal region you'll find beautiful little ports.

LYSEKIL

Charming seaside resort on a very beautiful site, frequented by artists, sculptors, and fans of life in the great outdoors and nautical sports. The small city, asleep in the winter, doubles its population in the summer, thanks to vacationers.

Where to Sleep

—*Camping in Sivik:* 2 miles before Lysekil. A small rocky gulf by the sea.
—*Youth Hostel at Fiskebackskil:* On the other side of the fjord. Frequent ferries from Lysekil.
—*Rooms with residents:* Reservations at the Tourist Office located at the large plaza.
—*Hotel Fridhem:* At the end of the village, behind the tennis courts. Pretty wooden houses painted red. Smokers pay extra.

NORWAY

If you are going to Scandinavia to admire beautiful countryside, you won't be disappointed by Norway. Here, nature is queen and the people live in complete harmony with her. They've learned how to recognize and respect her.

The state of mind of Norwegians is different from other Scandinavians. They are individualists, and despite the discovery of great oil deposits in 1968, they refuse an unrestrained course of growth. They don't want to destroy their way of life but instead exploit these new natural resources with prudence and wise caution. The Norwegians have decided not to stray from the good path, which leads to happiness.

Useful Addresses in New York

—*National Norwegian Tourist Office:* 75 Rockefeller Plaza, New York, NY 10019. Telephone (212) 582-2802.

—*Norwegian Consulate General:* 825 Third Avenue, New York, NY 10022. Telephone (212) 421-7333.

By Train

Norwegian trains are well heated (travel in a T-shirt even in the winter). Reclining seats for sleeping. Sleeping berths are expensive. There are no discounts for foreign students in Norway. In the morning, around 8, in the dining car, you can have seconds of coffee, bread and butter for the same price, on the condition that you smile and act nice. There are often drinking water and cups at the end of each car.

You should make reservations for long trips. The trains are often full.

Ask for a train schedule *(lomme ruter)* in any station.

Fares depend on the distance.

• *A Small Inter-Rail Dictionary*
—*Yrkedagar:* Weekends only.
—*Helgedar:* Vacations.
—*Ikkje Fredagar:* Not on Friday.
—*Tog Fra:* Train coming from.
—*Tog Til:* Train going to.
—*Berre Mandagar:* Monday only.

By Boat

You take them often, particularly the ferries that cross the fjords. Free or very affordable crossings. Of course, great views of the fjords. There is a "Coast Express" that links Bergen to Kirkenes along the coast, servicing the ports every day. Count on a week to get up north. Interesting deal for returning from the North Cape, but quite expensive. You can obviously enjoy shorter trips. We strongly recommend that you obtain the complete schedules from the Tourist

Office for the buses, planes, boats, and ferries of Norway. Very manageable.

By Car

The road that goes to North Cape is almost completely blacktop except after Alta, around 37 miles. Off the main roads, the roads are quite bad (watch out for potholes!), but enormous efforts are under way to improve them. It is not unusual to encounter cows, sheep, and goats. Note: Many gas stations are closed on Sunday; therefore, you have to use the few automatic pumps that take only 10 Kr bills.

Road Maps

Obtain a very detailed map if you plan on leaving the main highways. The directions are often marked by the number of the road and the following city is not mentioned (ideal for getting lost!).

Lodgings

—*Campgrounds* are less expensive than youth hostels, and most of them are equipped with a collective kitchen. Take warm clothes because, even in August, the weather is very cool. There is a new mosquito repellent for those who have already tried everything: Cut an onion in half and rub on the exposed parts of the body. It's a trick used by Norwegian forest rangers. Of course, they don't mind the smell because they don't go out dancing at night.

—In every campground you also find some *hytters*. They are little cabins, more or less equipped, but you can always get a heater, electric stove, fridge, and beds for 2 to 6 people. Sometimes a shower and toilets are available. Prices range from $8 to $10 for a double bed.

—*Wilderness camping:* If you decide to camp in the Norwegian countryside near farms, you shouldn't forget to ask permission of the farmers. You'll discover that Norwegian hospitality does not stop at the city gates.

—*Youth hostels* (Ungdomsherberger): They are probably the most expensive of all Europe—you can pay 45 Kr per night. They are open to everybody, with no age limit. You will have to buy a membership card. You should seriously think of camping instead of using them. Save them for rainy days.

—*Lodging* in the homes of residents is a pleasant system, hardly more expensive than a youth hostel. You will soon understand Scandinavian cleanliness. This mode of lodging works throughout Norway. In large cities, the Tourist Offices make reservations for a few Kr. In the countryside and in the villages, rooms in people's homes are marked by a sign *Rom*.

Distances Between Norwegian Cities (in Miles)

	Bergen	Charlottenberg	Fagernes	Hamar	Hammerfest	Kristiansand	Kristiansund	Lillehammer	Narvik	Oslo	Stavanger	Tromsø
Charlottenberg	399											
Fagernes	218	206										
Hamar	303	174	98									
Hammerfest	1383	1271	1268	1201								
Kristiansand	253	316	323	308	1481							
Kristiansund	319	345	267	238	1101	496						
Lillehammer	278	148	78	40	1199	331	198					
Narvik	988	875	872	806	396	1123	704	803				
Oslo	308	86	120	77	1252	229	373	116	894			
Stavanger	93	486	315	326	1429	171	378	330	1033	365		
Tromsø	1138	1025	1021	956	336	1272	853	951	151	1043	1182	
Trondheim	429	316	297	248	971	549	129	228	575	320	458	724

Food

The cost of living is rather high. You can buy fish, however, at reasonable prices. Fresh meat is not affordable.

Note that often in the cafeterias you can have several cups of coffee or tea for the same price.

Finally, you should know that milk products are fairly priced (butter, milk, yogurt). The thrifty who travel by car can fill their trunk.

Those who want to fish for salmon must get a permit at the post office. In addition to the permit, you often have to buy a local license, for many rivers and lakes (especially in the south) are individually or communally owned. Always inquire locally and acquire local fishing rights. Fees by the day or week. Sea fishing in the fjords is free.

The Norwegians dine early in the evening, generally between 6 and 7 o'clock. For canisters of camping gas, you will usually find the blue canisters everywhere, but the 1, 2, and 3 kilogram bottles are much more difficult to find. There are scarcely any except at Oslo, Bergen, and Stavangel at "Pro-Gas" distributors.

Akvavit

Akvavit, or the art of recovering your strength after skiing all day. Do you know the secret of this miraculous liquor that makes all your aches and pains from skiing disappear?

True *akvavit,* the sublime Norwegian drink, makes a voyage that few Norwegians will ever make in their lives. Upon leaving the still, it is stored in barrels that travel all the way to Australia! Baptism transforms the divine elixir into Norwegian *akvavit.*

Temporary Jobs

You can get around with English. They'll give you a job on a Norwegian farm. You share the life of the family, being fed and housed. You do everything: milk cows, cut trees, paint fences . . . not monotonous. Minimum 1 month; maximum 3 months. Write to: N.I.U., 5 Grev Wedels Plass, Oslo 1, Norway. Not well paid. You might also try to work in the north with the fishermen (Lofoten Islands, for example).

Wooden Churches

These "stave" churches *(Stavkirke)* are the most famous inherited artistic curiosity. The stave is the key element in the construction. The first churches date back to the beginning of the eleventh century. Entirely in wood, some are in a perfect state of preservation, for the wood was covered with tar to protect it from humidity. The often complex decorations and ornaments are also carved from wood. You find in some pine groves certain constructions of the same dragon heads that adorn the prows of ships.

Seen from the exterior, the Stavkirke has a strange and unique character. The many-layered roofs might remind you of pagodas.

Fjords

You go to Norway to see them, so don't worry, you won't be disappointed. The fjords are the result of a strong erosion exerted by enormous masses of ice on the narrow river beds of the valleys that the sea filled during the end of the ice age. The water furrowed deeply into the earth, up to 125 miles into the interior of the land, and attained a depth of 4,500 feet. But the narrowest and most landlocked fjords are the most spectacular (the Geirange fjord, for example). Dear readers, here again, no problem for you. We have selected some superb fjords to bring to your attention. The erosion has formed an archipelago of islands—more than 200,000—that border the present coast. There is no coast in the world that is more jagged, which is its charm.

Store hours

They close early. Often at 4 P.M., sometimes 3:30, more rarely at 5 P.M. And on Saturday, practically everything closes at 1 P.M. The unprepared shall be punished!

This and That

—*Exchange:* You can change your money anytime in the Tourist Office, even Saturday and Sunday, but be careful: 2 percent additional commission for various expenses. Try to manage not to change those greenbacks in stores for tourists. They take enormous commissions. It seems that *Norges Bank,* the state bank, charges the lowest commission.

—Note: May 17 is a national holiday; therefore, everything is closed. Everything!

—Cigarette prices are outrageous. Come supplied.

—Film is definitely more expensive.

How to Get to Norway from Denmark

There are 2 possibilities:

—The first, climb to Hirtshals-Kristiansand. Good for visiting southern Norway. The prices are fairly high, unless you can take advantage of the deal: "car + 5 passengers." Hitchhikers, unite!

—The second solution, less difficult and useful especially for Oslo, and in general for north of the 59th parallel, concerns going to Göteborg (Sweden). You can also cross from Grenä with a student discount in the off-season. At any rate, pay attention to the difference in fares in and out of season.

For Going Farther

To tour the world in a Norwegian shipping vessel, buy *Norges Handels og Sjøfartstidende,* a newspaper giving the *Skiplisten,* that is, the destination, port of embarkation, name of captain, and date of departure for all Norwegian boats.

Special Inter-Rail Itinerary

A good number of globetrotters get around by train. But Norway presents 2 particular problems; one part of the country is extremely stretched out in length, making distances much greater than you would suppose, and the railroad system leaves from Oslo in a spider web. There are no links for changing, except for routes that rely on the railroad. Which is why we are providing you with an itinerary that will enable you when leaving Oslo to cross the fjords region—in our opinion the most beautiful.

From Oslo, a train to Bergen with, on the way, a stop at Myrdal and Flåm. Travel in the day, of course. The landscapes are magnificent.

From Bergen, road or train to Voss.

From Voss, road to Vangsnes and ferry for Balestrand.

Then road via Stryn to Geiranger and its superb fjord.

Finally, the road via Valldal to Åndalsnes.

Those pressed for time will return to Oslo by train. The others can continue on the road via Sunndalsöra, then Oppdal. There you will find the road from the North Cape (E6) for Trondheim. Some may get off the train at Oslo, others may continue on the train to Fausk and then by car to Narvik.

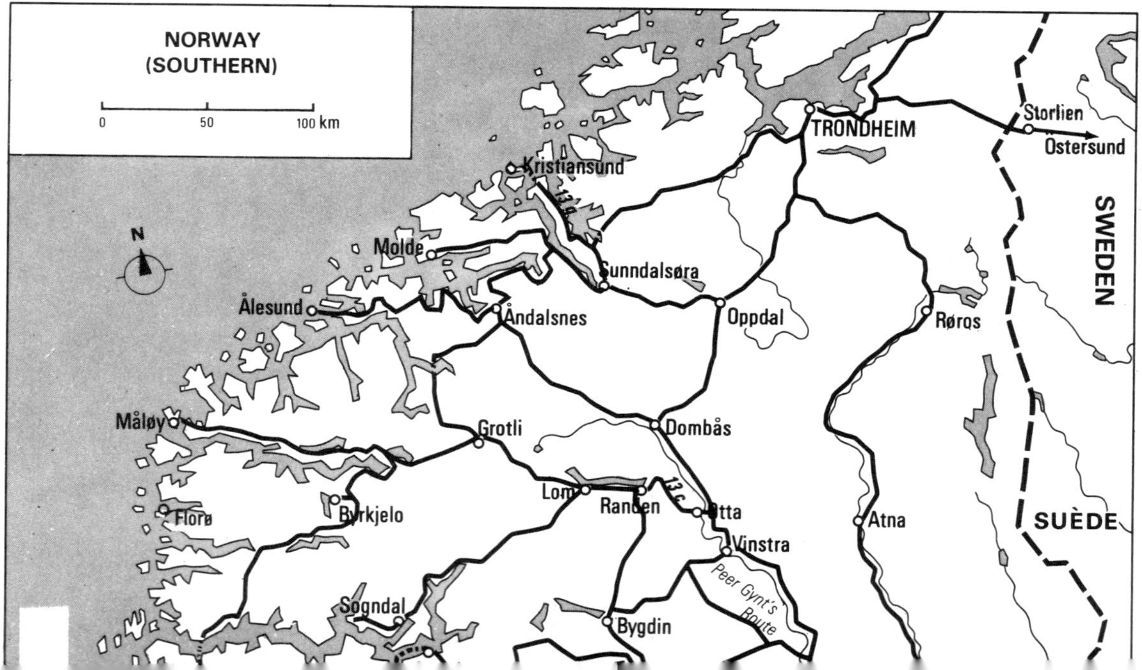
NORWAY
(SOUTHERN)
0
50
100 km
N
SWEDEN
SUÈDE
Storlien
Östersund
TRONDHEIM
Kristiansund
13 a
Molde
Ålesund
Sunndalsøra
Åndalsnes
Oppdal
Røros
Måløy
Grotli
Dombås
Lom
Randen
13 c
Otta
Vinstra
Atna
Florø
Byrkjelo
Sogndal
Bygdin
Peer Gynt's Route

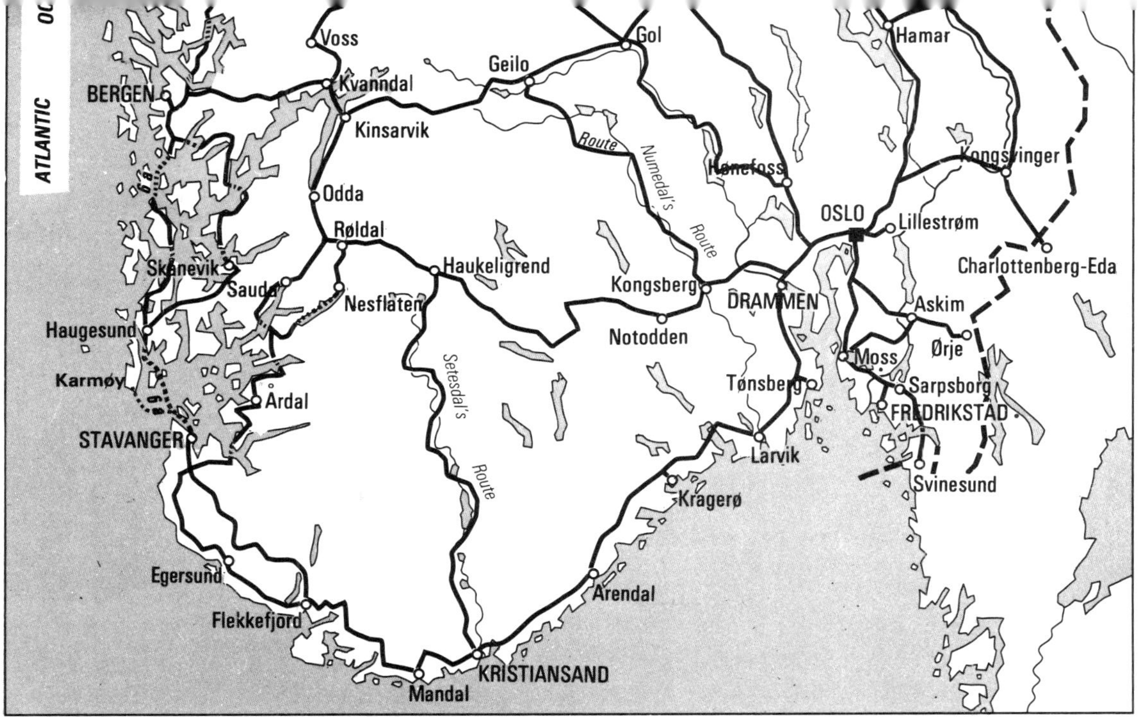
ATLANTIC
BERGEN
Voss
Kvanndal
Kinsarvik
Odda
Røldal
Skånevik
Sauda
Nesflaten
Haugesund
Karmøy
Årdal
STAVANGER
Egersund
Flekkefjord
Mandal
KRISTIANSAND
Arendal
Kragerø
Setesdal's Route
Haukeligrend
Geilo
Gol
Route
Numedal's Route
Hønefoss
Kongsberg
Notodden
DRAMMEN
Tønsberg
Larvik
OSLO
Lillestrøm
Hamar
Kongsvinger
Charlottenberg-Eda
Askim
Ørje
Moss
Sarpsborg
FREDRIKSTAD
Svinesund

Norwegian Vocabulary

yes	*ja*
no	*nei*
today	*i dag*
tomorrow	*i morgen*
yesterday	*i går*
where?	*hvor?*
how much (many)?	*hvor mye?*
when?	*når?*
to the right	*på høyre siden*
to the left	*på venstre siden*
(it's) too (expensive)	*(det er) for meget (dyrt)*
what time is it?	*hvor mye er klokka (hva er klokka)?*
good day (hello)	*godmorgen*
please	*voer så snill*
thank you	*takk*
pardon (excuse me)	*unnskyld* (pronounced *unsyld*)
I don't understand	*jeg forstår ikke*
tourist office	*turistkontor*
train station	*jernbanstasjon*
bank	*bank*
youth hostel (Y.H.)	*ungdomsherberger (U.H.)*
hotel	*hotell*
restaurant	*restaurant*
to drink	*drikke*
to eat	*spise*
to sleep	*sove*
sleeping bag	*sovepose*
room	*rom* or *voerelse*
may I have something (to eat)?	*kan jeg få noe (å spise)?*
do you have anything?	*har de noe?*
I want to buy	*jeg ville gjerne kjøpe*
water	*vann*
coffee	*kaffe*
milk	*mjelk*
beer	*øl*
bread	*brød*
anything you spread on bread	*pålegg*
cold	*kaldt*
hot	*warmt*
good	*god*
bad	*vond*
toilet	*toalett*

A few keys to pronunciation

ae	a		ø	e
å	o		e	ay
o	oo		y	ew

FREDRIKSTAD

This large, modern city, both industrial and commercial, is 25 miles from the Swedish border and 62 miles south of Oslo. Arriving from the east, when crossing the immense suspension bridge, the traveler discovers (Gamlebyen), one of the most beautiful fortified cities in Norway.

Founded in 1567 by Frederik II, this old city, remarkable for its right-angled streets, has preserved its wooden houses that bear the mark of the Nordic Renaissance. Inside the ramparts, the *Plusverkstedene* are shops and workshops of craftsmen who continue the work of yesteryear.

In addition, a group called *Plus* brings artists and craftspeople together. They organize walking tours of the different boutiques and explain the old methods of weavers, glass blowers, and so forth. The tours last an hour and are conducted between 9 A.M. and 2 P.M.

—*Fredrikstad Motel and Campground:* On leaving the old city by its main gate, go straight for 200 yards. Small bungalows *(hytters)* for those without a tent. Check if the youth hostel across the street is still closed.

—*Peppe's Pizza:* In the old city, on the street along the river. The interior consists of several vaulted rooms dating from the Middle Ages, all well laid out. Our favorite place for its ambiance.

—You can go to Oslo by train.

MOSS

Once you learn that this city has 300 industrial enterprises, you will understand why it doesn't have much to offer the visitor. And yet we advise a stop here for those who don't want to arrive at night in Oslo, where it's difficult to find a room. The following day you can reach the capital without any problem (1 hour by train).

The youth hostel *(Ungdomsherberger)* is one of the nicest. Located at the entrance to the city, ½ mile from the station, it was built by a lake in the middle of a vast park with bronze statues. A modern building. A very pleasant lobby with a fireplace, though some globetrotters may be upset by the portrait of Baden-Powell. You can cook, as long as you have plates, silverware, cups and so forth. Sheets are mandatory (down bags and comforters are forbidden) as in all other youth hostels. Nearby, there's a swimming pool and gymnasium.

OSLO

Norwegians love nature, which is perhaps why they have never built large cities. In Oslo, old architecture juxtaposes with modern constructions, all without much charm we must confess. And yet, Oslo is a lively city with a Latin side.

Arrival in Oslo

Note that there are two stations:
—*East Station* (Øslos): The main station. Terminal for trains com-

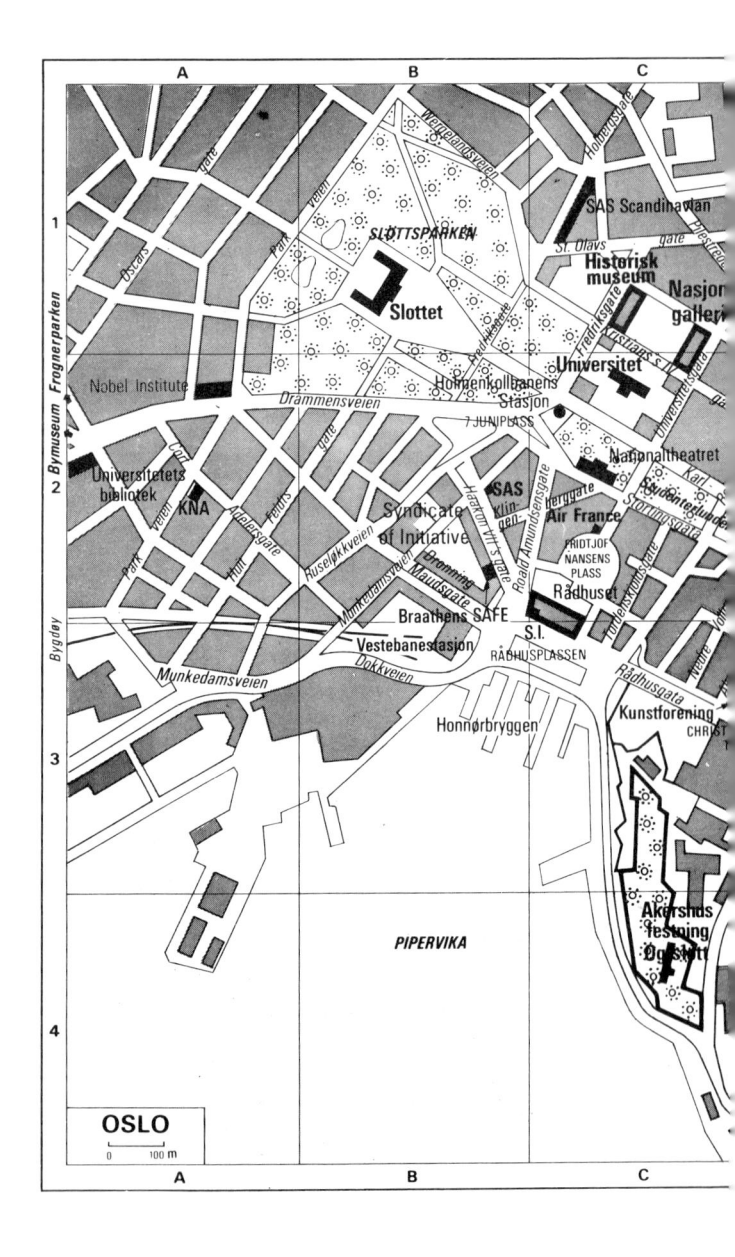

OSLO

0 100 m

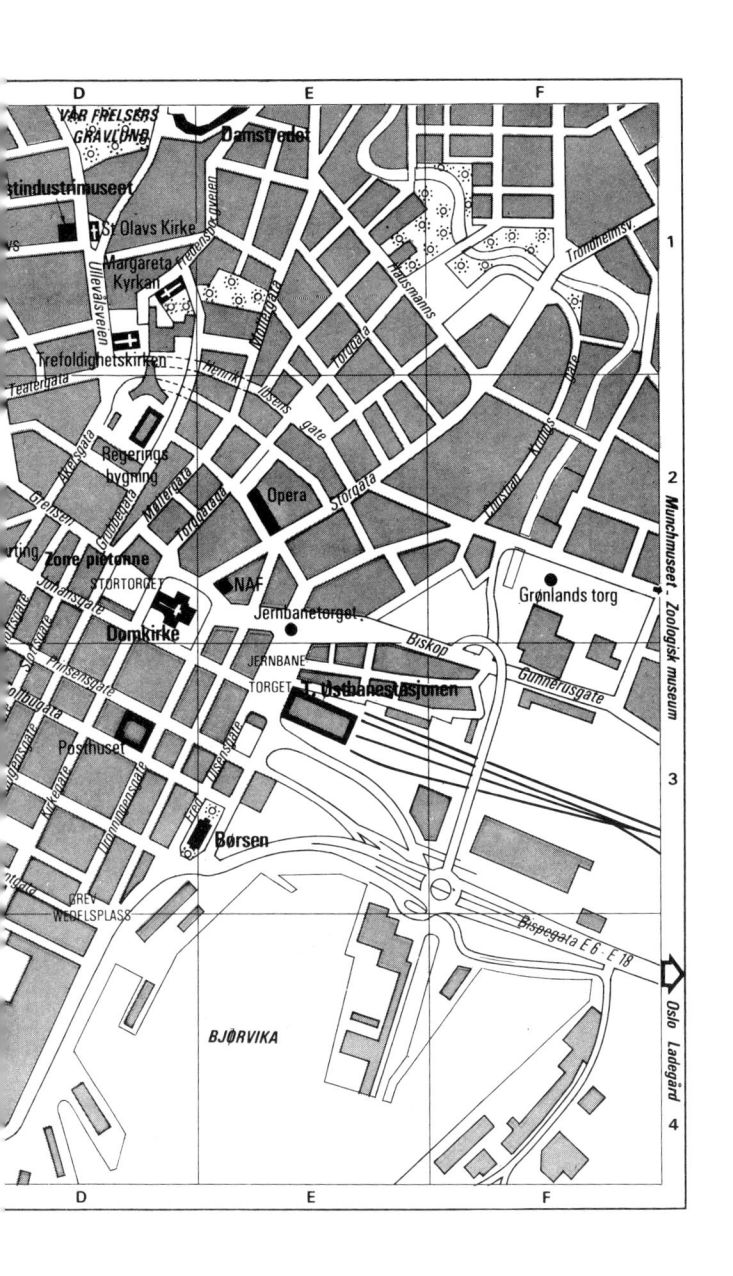

VÅR FRELSERS GRAVLUND
Damstredet
stindustrimuseet
St Olavs Kirke
Margareta Kyrkan
Ullevålsveien
Trefoldighetskirken
Teatergata
Henrik Ibsens gate
Torggata
Trondheimsv.
Regerings bygning
Møllergata
Torggata
Opera
Storgata
Akersgata
Grubbegata
Zone piétonne
STORTORGET
Johansgate
NAF
Jernbanetorget
Grønlands torg
Domkirke
Biskop Gunnerusgate
JERNBANE TORGET
Østbanestasjonen
Munchmuseet - Zoologisk museum
Posthuset
Børsen
GREV WEDELSPLASS
Bispegata E 6 - E 18
Oslo Ladegård
BJØRVIKA

ing from Sweden, Trondheim, and Bergen. Exchange open every day from 4 P.M. to 11 P.M. Lodging service (see below).

—*West Station* (Vestbanens): Smaller, it's the departure point for trains to Stavanger, Kristiansand, and Dramnen.

How to Get Around

You can use the subway, buses, and tramways with the same rather expensive, ticket. There's a small discount when you buy a book of them. A ticket remains valid up to 1 hour after its first use and entitles you to a transfer.

The Tourist Office offers a small guide that has maps of the different systems.

A 24-hour ticket for all public transportation (including the boat to Bygdøy and the museums on this peninsula) costs 30 Kr.

Useful Addresses

—*Turistinformasjon* (Map B2): Rådhusgate 19 (Town Hall). Full of useful documents, like the locations of youth hostels, tramway maps. Open from 9 A.M. to 3:30 P.M.; Saturday from 9 A.M. to 12:30 P.M.; Sunday from 9 A.M. to noon.

—*Main Post Office* (Map D3): 15 Dronningensgate (entrance at the corner of Prinsensgate). Open during the week from 8 A.M. to 8 P.M. and on Saturday from 9 A.M. to 5 P.M. Closed Sunday. *Poste Restante* at windows 37 to 41.

—*Sauna:* Tøyen Bad, 90 Helgesengate, near the Munch Museum. Open from 3 P.M. to 8 P.M., Saturday from 7:30 A.M. to 1 P.M., and Sunday from 10 A.M. to 5 P.M.

—*Medical Emergency:* 40 Storgate. Telephone 20-10-90. Open day and night.

—*24-hour Drugstore:* Jerbanetorget Apotek. Across from East Station.

—*Telephone, Telegraph:* Telebygningen, 21 Kongensgate. Open day and night.

—*American Express:* Winge and Co., 33 Karl Johans Gate. Telephone 20-50-50.

—*Norwegian Student Travel Bureau:* Universitetenes Reisebyra, Universitetessentret, Blindern, Oslo 3. Telephone 46-68-50.

—*Camping gas refills:* Sjursøva.

—*American Consulate General:* 18 Drannensveien, Oslo 1. Telephone (2) 56-68-80.

Where to Sleep

It's no piece of cake to stay in Oslo. And if you find some digs (even at the youth hostel or one of the campsites), the prices are very high. As a result, hitchhikers generally don't stay long in Oslo. It's a shame, since there's a rich diversity of museums.

The easiest way is to go to the Lodging Service *(Innkvartering)* at the East Station *(Øslos)* which will reserve rooms in hotels, inns, and homes of residents. Open from 8 A.M. to 11 P.M. Closed Sunday from noon to 6 P.M. It costs 7 Kr for the reservation.

• Youth Hostel

—*Haraldsheim Ungdomsherberger:* 4 Haraldsheimveien, Oslo 5. In the northeast suburb of the city. Telephone 21-83-59. Often jam-packed in the summer, so it's wise to telephone before arriving.

From East Station, take the pedestrian street right across from the main exit, then the second street on the left (Dronningensgate). From there, tram #1 to the last stop. This is a huge youth hostel among plenty of greenery, on a hill overlooking the city. Closed from 10 A.M. to 4 P.M. TV, washing machine, and even a fireplace. You can do your own cooking. Very expensive even if a large breakfast is included.

• Reasonable Lodgings

—*Bjerke Studentheim:* 271 Trondheimsveien. Telephone 21-19-34 or 22-19-71. This university house is open to travelers from June 20 to August 20. Bus #31 to Bjerke Travbane. Rooms for 2 or 3. One of the most affordable places. Be aware that the reception desk doesn't open until 4 P.M.

—*Holtet:* 55 Micheletsvei, 1320 Stabbek. Telephone (02) 55-38-53. Open from June to the end of August. It's 15 minutes by bus—#32, #36, #37—from the center of Oslo; get off at Kveldroveien. At Strand, turn left and follow Micheletsvei.

• Campgrounds

—*Ekeberg Campground:* 2 miles south of the city. Telephone 19-85-68. Very well marked when you get to Oslo by E6. Bus #24 across from the East Station. The campsite is perched on the summit of a hill overlooking Oslo. Very beautiful sunsets in clear weather. Very well equipped: showers, post office, bank, and supermarket. Truly great. It's 30 Kr a night and per tent. Rather crowded in the summer. Camping gas on sale.

—*Bogstad:* About 6 miles northwest of Oslo. Telephone 24-76-19. Bus #41 Sørkedalen from the Nationalteatret (½-hour trip). After a while you will see the campground on the right, at the foot of the mountain, bordered on the other side by a lake. You can swim there. Well equipped: bank, post office, grocery store, restaurant, washing machines. Camping gas for sale. Bungalows.

—*Stubljan:* About 6 miles south of Oslo, on the E6/E18 road. Telephone 28-62-35. Bus #75 from Central Station. Bank, washing machines, stores, kitchen, and near a beach. Open from June 1 to August 31.

Where to Eat

A preliminary remark: Food, when ordered in anything that resembles a restaurant, is simply not affordable.

—The best thing to do is go shopping in a supermarket. Speaking of which, pay attention to the particularly crazy hours of the stores; they mostly close at 5 P.M.

—*Friskporten:* 18 Grensen. A vegetarian restaurant that is not expensive but somewhat run of the mill. For the starving, because you can drink and eat as much as you want. From 10 A.M. to 8 P.M. Rustic interior decor with brick and wood. Right in the heart of things, on the street facing the cathedral.

—*Christina og Christian:* Stortoet. Cafeteria on the fourth floor of the department store. Hot dishes from 12:30 P.M. to 4:30 P.M.. No alcohol. Quite reasonable.

—*University Cafeteria:* A full dish for 19 Kr. We immediately felt sorry for the students.

—*The Scotsman:* 17 Kongensgate. On the pedestrian street, facing the station. Enormous pizzas. If you share, it's not too expensive. Beer and country music starting at 7:30 P.M.

—*Frognerpark:* Very pleasant park. In the corner, 2 large terraces, one of which has a trellis with flowers. One can drink a glass in the evening here, even late. Often very lively. The sunset in the park is memorable.

—Travelers who arrive on Saturday afternoon will be annoyed: It is IMPOSSIBLE to get supplies. All the stores are closed until Monday! Fortunately, in the Grønland subway station (near the West Station), there are a group of food shops. They really profit from the situation, since all their competitors are closed!

Where to down a Few

—*Guldfisken:* 2 Rådhusgate, not far from the East Station going toward the port. Decor and atmosphere like a bar for sailors. An immense room. Billiards. Jazz from Friday to Monday evenings. A good joint.

Nightclubs

—*Club 7:* 15 Munkedamsveien. Jazz club that, after some funding by the city, has become a kind of underground cultural center. Bar, restaurant, discothèque, TV, art gallery. Also, rock, folk, and jazz concerts. Open in the evening at 8. The schedule of concerts is in the newspaper or the Tourist Office.

To See

• In the Center

—*Karl-Johansgate:* The great artery of Oslo, particularly lively on summer evenings. Numerous cafés with terraces where guitar players try to strum some crowns from the strollers.

—*Cathedral* (Domkirke): Across from the East Station (Map D2). Tours from 9 A.M. to 3 P.M. (to noon on Saturday). Entirely restored in the nineteenth century. Famous for its retable which has the distinction of being decorated by characters in relief. The ceiling is decorated with modern frescos (4,600 square feet) inspired by the Old and New Testaments.

—*National Museum of Fine Arts* (Nasjonalgalleriet): 13 Universitetsgate (Map C1). Free admission. Open Monday to Friday from 10 A.M. to 4 P.M., Saturday from 10 A.M. to 3 P.M., and Sunday from noon to 3 P.M. There are important collections of Norwegian artists and also a magnificent collection of icons (room 32), the last self-portrait by Van Gogh and several Gauguins (room 39), some interesting abstract paintings from the Paris school (room 41), a famous El Greco (room 38), three rooms devoted to the fantastic Edvard Munch (rooms 24, 25, and 26), and a great number of works by Roger Bissière (room 42) which everybody makes fun of . . .

—*Munchmuseet* (Munch Museum): 53 Tøyengate. Open every day from 10 A.M. to 10 P.M. except Monday. Free admission. Bus #29 from Stortinsgate. Devoted entirely to this famous Norwegian artist. He was one of the precursors of the Expressionist movement that later developed in Germany and Scandinavia. Then its style evolved more toward French Fauvism with more vivid and pure colors. Munch's obsession with agony, death, decrepitude, and solitude are the themes constantly met in his work. Not until the last period of his life did his vision and feelings become more serene.

—*Norges Hjemmefrontmuseum* (Museum of the Resistance): In Slottet Castle (Map B1). While Sweden claimed neutrality during World War II, succeeding in amassing capital by selling iron to Germany, Norway was invaded by Nazi troops. This museum recalls the importance and breadth of the clandestine war against Nazism. There are photos, underground newspapers, tracts, homemade weapons, and so forth. You will discover the history of the attack at Rjukan, launched by Norwegian resistance in February 1944 and assisted by British paratroopers; it was known by the name Heavy Water Battle. Interesting, but most of the documents are written in Norwegian. Open from 10 A.M. to 4 P.M.

—*Frogner Parken:* Of the *Nationalteatret* (Map C2). Take the subway to Majorstuen. In this park you can freely admire the colossal statues of Vigeland, celebrated Norwegian artist. These huge works won't seduce everybody, but you may be impressed by the primitive force emanating from these men and women who evoke the gods and goddesses of Nordic mythology rather than mere mortals. Don't miss the monolith is composed of 121 entangled characters fighting to rise; it stands in an amphitheatre. You can visit the sculptor's studio (*Vigelandsmuseet:* 32 Nobelsgate); open from 1 P.M. to 7 P.M. except Monday. Free.

• **Museums of Bygdøy Peninsula**

The most interesting museums are located on this large peninsula to the west of the capital. Take bus #30 from Stortinsgate. Departs every half hour. In the summer it's so pleasant to take the boat that leaves from Utstikker C wharf, across from the Town Hall (Rådhuset).

—*Norsk Folkemuseum:* Open from 10 A.M. to 6 P.M., on Sunday from noon to 6 P.M. It's truly the museum of Norwegian folk culture. Approximately 150 cottages or wooden houses have been assembled in a vast park, to illustrate the modes of living in the different regions. In particular, don't miss the Stavkirke of Gol, one of the wooden "stave" churches that ranks among the most beautiful of the country. At the entrance to the museum, interiors of middle-class homes are reconstructed. You can see Ibsen's study. The "immigrant" home comes from North Dakota where thousands of Norwegians emigrated in the nineteenth century. Finally, a small Lapp ethnological museum: crafts, raising reindeer, hunting and fishing.

—*Vikingskpenemuseet:* This museum contains 3 Viking ships that were found basically intact. They strangely resemble the ships used in Egypt for the funerals of pharoahs. Their elegant forms and sometimes elaborate ornamentation are astonishing.

—*Fram Huset:* a building housing the polar vessel *Fram* that was used in 1910 by Amundsen for his expedition to the South Pole (when the North Pole was so near; what a waste!).

—*Kon–Tiki Museet:* next to the above. Astonishing raft on which, in 1947, Thor Heyerdahl and his 5 companions crossed the Pacific powered only by winds and currents, traveling 5,000 miles from Peru to Polynesia in 101 days. The ethnologist wanted to demonstrate that the first inhabitants of Polynesia had come from Peru and not from Asia. The balsa wood raft is a copy of the rafts used by the pre-Inca populations of this era. Besides the very interesting photographs taken during the voyage, don't miss the replica of the Easter Island statue, impressive for its size. Under the museum there's a reconstruction of a funerary cavern from the island.

An annex now contains Râ II, the balsa raft with which Heyerdahl crossed the Atlantic in 1970. Absolutely astonishing construction.

• Around and About

—For those who want to take a dip, the subway to Sognsvatn will bring you to a large park with a lake where everybody swims.

—*Holmenkollen:* Northwest of Oslo; from the Nationalteatret (map C 2), take the subway to Holmankollen. Those who are coming from Frogner Park can also take the subway to Holmenkollen. Known the world over, it's Norway's famous ski jump. Under the ski jump is the Ski Museum *(Skimuseet).* It exhibits skis from every country, from various periods, and in particular the famous Øvrebø skis, 2,500 years old, discovered in a swamp. Open every day from 10 A.M. to 6 P.M. (until 10 P.M. in June and July.

—*The Sonja Henie–Niels Onstad Center of Contemporary Art:* 7 miles west of the center of town, not far from route E18. Buses #32, #36, and #37 in front of the university. Get off at Høvikodden. Open every day from 9 A.M. to 10 P.M. This foundation results from the love of this rich connoisseur and his wife (the ice skating champion) for modern painting. The collection reflects the taste of its donors; thus, some masterpieces are hung next to some awful paintings. The museum will disappoint more than one, excepting fans of the Cobra group (Alechinsky, Corneille), the Abstracts (Bazaine, Nicolas de Stael, and of course Paul Klee), Cubism (Braque and Picasso), and Surrealism (Miró and Max Ernst).

—*Kalvøya Island:* Each year in the month of August on this island, located 8 miles from Oslo, a rock and reggae festival gets under way. At the same time, there's an art show, political and ecological stands . . . Full of people. To get there: go toward the airport to Sandvika. The island is just across a small bridge.

—*Tyrifjord:* A fjord located 2 hours by car from Oslo. Great for fishing and wilderness camping.

To Hitchhike Out of Oslo

—*Toward Bergen:* On Dokkveien, near West Station.

—*Toward Trondheim:* To get back on E6 (east of the city), take bus #66 from Arbeidersamfundets Platz, near East Station, at the intersection of Ulven. For easier hitching, take the train to Dal. There's a 2-way road there, not a highway.

—*Toward the south* (Göteborg or Stockholm): From the Nationalteatret, take bus #73 to Bekkelaget. Hitch from the service station.

By Train

—*To Bergen:* A reservation is mandatory.

Downhill Skiing

This paragraph is for those who love downhill skiing and especially those who come to Norway in the winter. No need to travel 3 hours looking for snow to ski, just go northwest of Oslo, near Holmenkollen. Take the train to Majorstua, where the subway stops on its way to Frognerseteren. It's a small, pleasant route that climbs the mountain and stops at about 15 stations before arriving at *Voksenkollen,* where those who have their skis with them can descend. A small rental shop is well supplied. From there, you can reach the top, the *Tryvannstårnet,* in a 10- or 15-minute walk. A large tower enables visitors to see a beautiful panorama of Oslo and the surrounding area, providing the weather is clear. The other side of the hill has an advanced level ski trail and the departure point for downhill trails.

The landscape is really worth the effort. You cross several frozen lakes where fishermen go fishing through holes they have made in the ice.

TELEMARK

This province west of Oslo is called "the miniature Norway" by its inhabitants because it contains the various landscapes of the country. It's a vast mountainous district covered with forest intersected by valleys that are often green, but sometimes it is also very boxed-in and forbidding. You'll find cottages, not with thatched roofs but covered with a thick layer of earth and high grass.

• *Kongsberg:* Silver mine on E76 between Drammen and Nottoden, in the middle of the countryside. You take a miner's old wire-meshed train to go all the way down the length of a tunnel hugging the walls, and you arrive at least 3,000 feet below in a heated and lit room. You find old machines, often steam-powered, used for extracting the mineral as well as for the rapid descent of the miners into the mine. Another world entirely.

• *Heddal:* 3 miles west of Nottoden. This important village boasts a wooden stave church *(Stavkirke)* that is very old yet well renovated. The sculpted portals are quite astonishing, along with the eighteenth-century furniture. Next door, a museum exhibits some typical homes of the region.

• *Dalen:* This little city is located in a former glacial valley, next to a lake surrounded by mountain peaks. You can camp near the lake (and there's canoeing). Nearby youth hostel. Take the cruise from Dalen and follow a network of lakes and rivers (one day to go, the next day to return). Departures 3 times a week. You cross marvelous landscapes. The boat passes through a series of astonishing flood gates.

—*Grimdalem Museum:* 3 miles from Dalen, on the road from Settesdal. Anne Grimdalem is a well-known sculptor whose works depict animals, people, or bas-reliefs. Next to the museum are nineteenth-century homes and stables.

—*Central Hydro-Electric Plant:* The most powerful in the country. Guided tours.

—3 miles from Dalen, on the Høydalsmo road, see the wooden church at Eidsborg. Nearby this church is a collection of art objects, utensils, and furniture.

• *Rjukan:* A small industrial city in the narrow valley of Vestfjord, famous for its powerful electric plant in Vemork. It was here, during the night of February 27, 1944, that the Norwegian Resistance sabotaged the plant in order to deprive the Germans of the "heavy water" needed for their experiments.

FROM OSLO TO STAVANGER

KRISTIANSAND

In southern Norway. Not to be confused with Kristiansund near Trondheim. An important port and industrial center. Also has a charming old quarter with all white wooden houses, especially near the cathedral. Even the streets of yesteryear were laid out with a view to urban planning, crisscrossing at right angles.

Where to Sleep

—*Roligheten Ungdomsherberger* (youth hostel): East of the city, 1 mile from the center, and not far from the sea.
—*Roligheten Campground:* Right across from the youth hostel. A small campground in the hills and rocks. Very pleasant.

Around and About

—*Setesdal Railway:* A steam locomotive dating from 1814 that leaves from Grovane, 12 miles north of Kristiansand. A 3-mile journey. Watch the days: only on Friday, Saturday, and Sunday. Information at the Tourist Office.

MANDAL

This southernmost city 26 miles west of Kristiansand is known for its twisty, narrow roads lined with low homes. A pleasant pit stop.

Where to Sleep

—*Ungdomsherberger* (youth hostel): A lovely youth hostel. Imagine a fisherman's home built in wood alongside a fjord, surrounded by greenery where you can picnic. Only 20 beds. Inside, the rooms are impeccable, with the intimacy of a cottage. East of the city. Take the street facing the Norol gas station and walk 300 yards to the right (not well marked).
—*Sjøsandem Campgrounds:* 1 mile west of the city, alongside an immense sandy beach.

FLEKKEFJORD

A small port squeezed between the sea and the mountain, owing its fortune to herrings. Don't miss the old quarter built by the Dutch

(Hollanderbyen) which has kept much of its original character, with narrow streets and fishermen's homes.
—*Ungdomsherberger* (youth hostel): east of the city. School rooms converted into dorms in the summer. You can camp behind it.

STAVANGER

The fourth city of Norway whose importance has grown in the last 12 years thanks to the discovery of oil in the North Sea. Different from Bergen, the city hasn't had a fire since the seventeenth century. Thus, its lovely wooden houses are well preserved.
—*Tourist Office:* Near the station. They make reservations in the residents' homes.
—*Camping gas refills:* 79 Lagårdsvn.

Where to Sleep

—*Moosvangen Campground:* Southeast of the city. Take bus #17 (hourly) in front of the Atlantic Hotel, on the left on leaving the station. Well arranged with a dozen bungalows. By the water.
—*Moosvangen Ungdomsherberger* (youth hostel): Right next to the campground. 160 beds. Closed from 10 A.M. to 4 P.M. Quite expensive: 62 Kr. but breakfast is included.

Where to Eat

—*Sjaluppen:* 14 Nedre Holmget, in the port. A restaurant in a large wooden warehouse painted red and magnificently restored. Somewhat expensive, but you can glom a hamburger at a decent price.
—*Supermarket:* Near Randaberg (where you take the boat). Open until 9 P.M., which is exceptional in this country.
—On the bridge, in the morning, you can buy fresh shrimp cooked in sea water.

To See

—*The old city:* This group of old wooden homes along sloping streets reminds some of San Francisco. The municipality is so proud that it has taken on the restoration of some of them itself. Upon descending to the port, some warehouses have been restored, the 2 loveliest being the local headquarters for Standard Oil and Mobil, which shows that one can have money and taste at the same time.
—*Cathedral* (Domkirke): Composed of 3 naves, it was originally constructed in the purest Romanesque style. After a huge fire in the thirteenth century, the choir loft was reconstructed in Gothic. The interior is decorated in baroque style. Given its diversity, there's still something to please everyone. Anyhow, altogether it's not ugly.
—*Stavangermuseum:* Don't follow the advice of tourist guides too carefully. It's not particularly interesting.
—Excursion on the *Lysefjord:* Several boats offer this journey. Take the one that goes to Prekestolen, that incredible 1900-foot-high rock cliff overlooking the waters of the fjord (more later).

Where to Knock 'em Back

—*Loftet Biljgarden:* 14-20 Nedre Holmget. An immense bar in a warehouse on the wharf. Open evenings only. Frequent rock bands.

—*Dickens:* Go down to the port from the cathedral. Our favorite bar is located along the wharf on the right. Pretty, rustic decor where sailors, oil engineers, and young people mingle.

FROM STAVANGER TO BERGEN

—*Prekestolen:* Pass by Sandnes, then take route 13. At Jøssang, 31 miles from Stavanger, make a right on the small road for 3–4 miles. There's a farm at the intersection where the road leads to Prekestolen. This astonishing rocky cliff overlooks the green waters of Lysefjord from 1,900 feet above. Unforgettable view. Count on 2 to 3 hours of walking in unspoiled nature. Rapturous! Another possibility for the athletic: Rent a bike at the Tourist Information Service at the Stavanger train station. Take the boat to Tau (short crossing and not expensive), and from there go about 6 miles along the fjord to Jøssang. Then comes the most irksome 4 miles. Leave the bike (locked) at a parking lot, and continue on foot. From Stavanger, the trip takes a day if you start early. If not, you can camp between Tau and Prekestolen.

—*Ardal Stavkirke:* An old wooden church from the sixteenth century. If it seems banal from the exterior, the frescos inside are exceptional.

—*Sand:* You can take the ferry for Ropeid from here, and then the road to Haugesund and Bergen. The others can continue by route 46 to discover beautiful landscapes with eternal snow.

—*Røidal:* A village in a pretty landscape, famous for its *stavkirke*. Dating from the thirteenth century, it has maintained its decorations in the choir and nave. Open from 9 A.M. to 5 P.M. Admission charge. 2 campgrounds nearby.

—*Odda:* 226 miles from Stavanger. Small industrial city without any charm but set in a pictoresque valley. Point of departure for the Folgefonno Glacier that you get to by a small road west of the city.

—*Øystese:* The village sprawls from the shore of the fjord. Just across, a view of the mountains eternally covered with snow.

Ungdomsherberger (youth hostel): In the center, along the main road. Self-service restaurant on the ground floor. Camping along the fjord with bungalows. Sauna in the hotel across from the youth hostel.

At Fossatun, 4 miles west of Øystese, on the road from Bergen, there are very beautiful water falls. You can walk under them without getting wet.

—*Kvamskogem:* A youth hostel right on the mountain, next to a stream. This wooden building faces a lake.

BERGEN

The second city and second port of Norway, Bergen is nestled into a hill. A large university lends a certain atmosphere to the city.

Useful Addresses

—*Tourist Office:* Torgalmenning. Open until 10 P.M. in the summer. Exchanges money when the banks are closed. Also makes arrangements to lodge tourists in the homes of natives. Reservations cost 7 Kr.

—*American Express:* Winge Travel, 4 Strandgate. Telephone 21-10-80.

—*Camping gas refills:* 17 Engen.

—*Central Post Office:* 10 Rådhusgate.

Where to Sleep

—*Montana Ungdomsherberger* (youth hostel): 3 miles from the center, on the road leading to Mount Ulriken. Bus #4 from the post office. Pretty view of the city. Expensive: 64 Kr with a decent breakfast. TV, showers with marble stalls . . . Luxurious. Telephone 29-29-00.

—*Berta Berge Halvorsen:* 60A Starefossvei. Telephone 31-12-16. In case the youth hostel is full. House maintained by a lady. It's the cheapest you'll find around here. Even when it's full, there's always a piece of carpet to rent. 50 Kr each.

—*Midttun:* Ugly. 7 miles south on E68.

—*Grimen Campground:* Next to a lake near a major highway. Bus #1 that you get behind the station. 10 miles from Hardangerveien. Unfortunately, very small and pebbly. Don't count on too much if you arrive late at night. Hot showers.

Where to Eat

—*Bors Café:* 12 Strandkaien wharf, near the marketplace. Reasonable restaurant considering the country. You can eat good fish and drink good beer.

—*Kaffistova BUL:* At Torget, across from the fish market. A buffet on the third floor, open from 2 to 8 P.M. Known for its smørgasbord where you can enjoy as much salmon, cold meats, cheeses and reindeer meat as you desire for 60 Kr. Expensive, but try it once. Self-service on the ground floor.

—*Kaffistora til Eryvingen:* 2 Strandkaien wharf, third floor. Decent meal at 30 Kr. Closes at 8:30 P.M.

To See

—The old wooden houses all along the Bryggen wharf. All pressed together, with high triangular gables, they were formerly merchants' warehouses. Today they are pretty but expensive stores.

—*Bergen Market:* In the port. Open until 3 pm. Despite its promotion to tourists by competitors' guides, we tend to think this fish market is utterly worthless. Fresh fish are rare. With a little luck you find some salmon all cut up and ready to be chewed for 10 Kr.

—*Rasmus Meyers Samlinger:* Rasmus Meyers Allé. A free museum where you can admire some works by Munch. Sometimes they hold piano recitals here.

—*Museum of Leprosy* (Lepramuseet): 59 Kong Oscarsgate. Open from mid-May to the end of August, from 11 A.M. to 3 P.M. only. In a

Map of Bergen

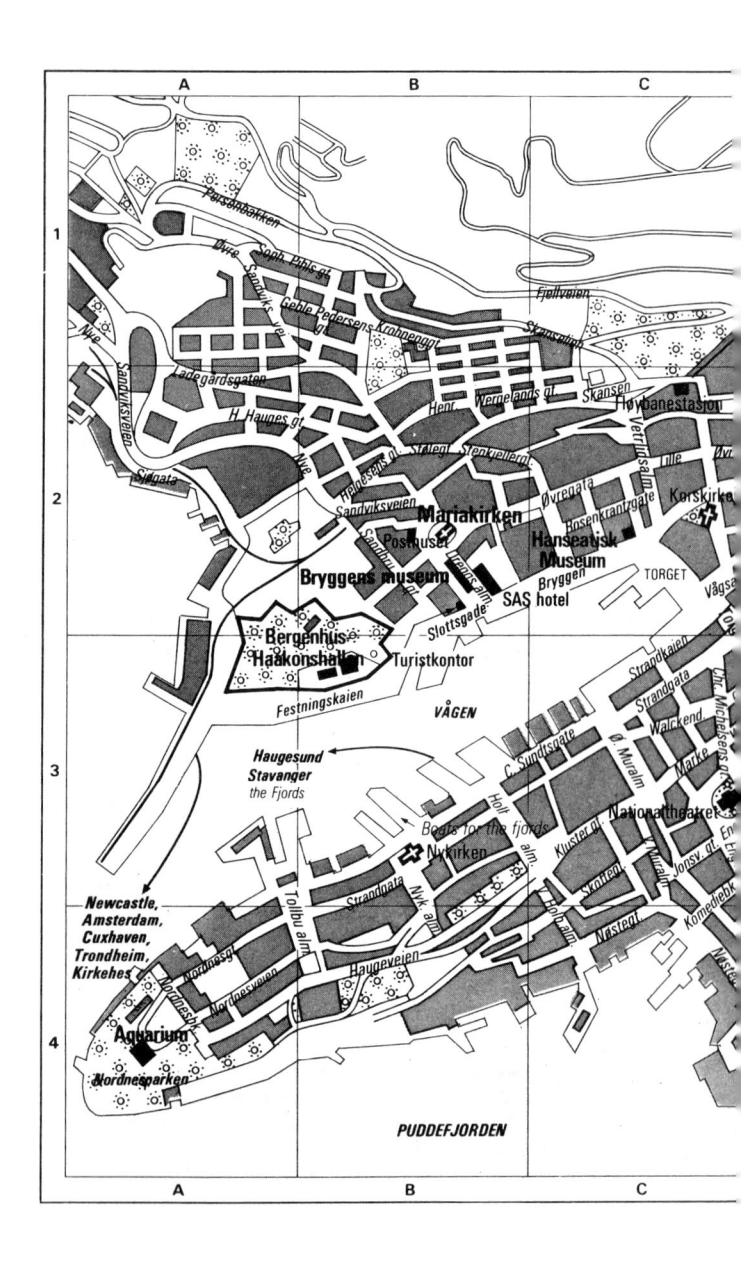

Grid references: A, B, C (columns) × 1, 2, 3, 4 (rows)

Streets and locations:

- Persenbakken
- Øvre Sogn. Enkl. gt.
- Stadsporten
- Gable Pedersens Krohnengg
- Fjellveien
- Strangehm
- Ladegardsgaten
- H. Hauges gt.
- Henr. Wergelands gt.
- Skansen
- Høybanestasjon
- Nye
- Sandviksveien
- Sidgate
- Hollendels gt.
- St. olen
- Steinkjelleren
- Øvregaten
- Vetrlidsalm
- Lille Øvr
- Sandviksveien
- Mariakirken
- Rosenkrantzgate
- Korskirke
- Posthuset
- Stadhm
- Mariasm
- Hanseatysk Museum
- Bryggens museum
- Bryggen
- SAS hotel
- TORGET
- Vågse
- Bergenhus
- Håkonshallen
- Slottsgade
- Turistkontor
- Strandkaien
- Festningskaien
- VÅGEN
- Strandata
- Walckend
- Marke
- Thr. Michelsens
- Haugesund
- Stavanger
- *the Fjords*
- C. Sundtsgate
- Ø. Muralm
- Holb
- Nationaltheatret
- Boats for the fjords
- Nykirken
- Kuster gt.
- Muralm
- Jonsv. gt.
- En
- Kornebp
- Newcastle,
- Amsterdam,
- Cuxhaven,
- Trondheim,
- Kirkehes
- Tollbu alm.
- Strandata
- Nyk. alm
- Skuten
- Nastegt
- Nordnesg
- Nordnesveien
- Haugeveien
- Aquarium
- Nordnesparken
- **PUDDEFJORDEN**

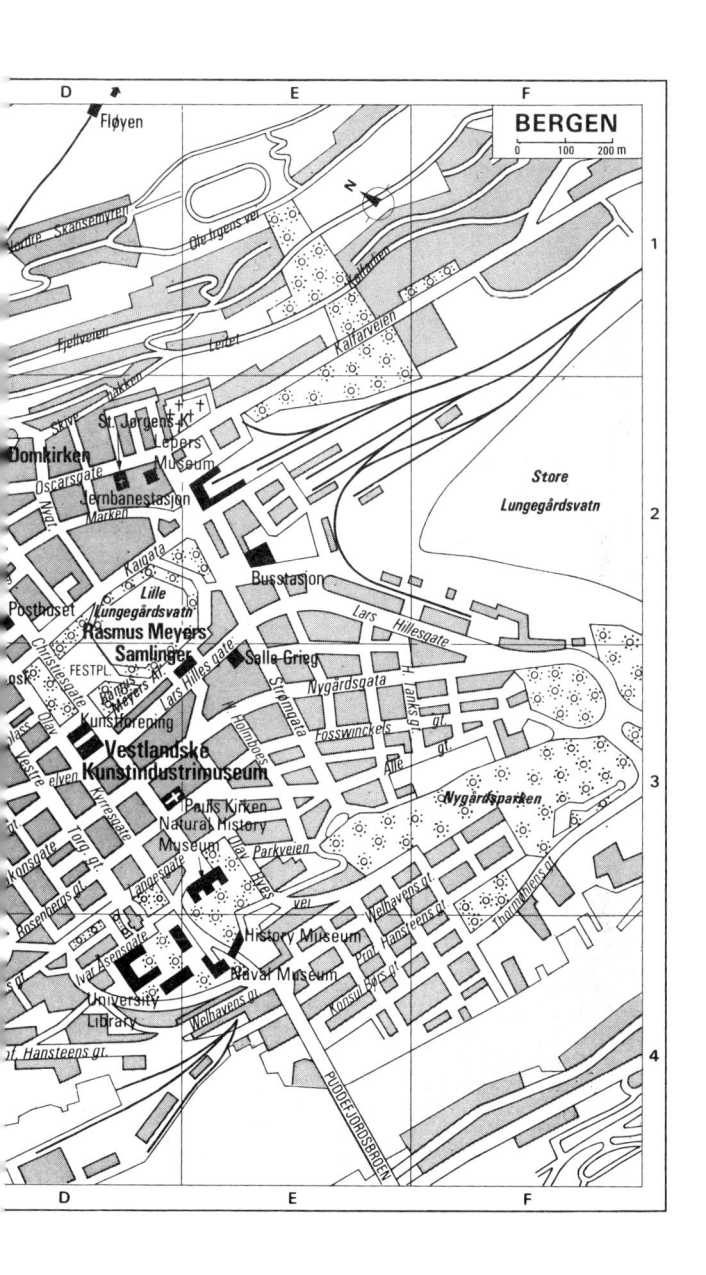

BERGEN

0 100 200 m

- Fløyen
- Ole Irgens vei
- Skansemyren
- Kalfarveien
- Fjellveien
- Lereí
- St. Jørgens kt
- Lepers Museum
- Domkirken
- Oscarsgate
- Jernbanestasjon
- Marken
- Kaigata
- Store Lungegårdsvatn
- Busstasjon
- Lille Lungegårdsvatn
- Posthuset
- Rasmus Meyers Samlinger
- Lars Hillesgate
- FESTPL.
- Lars Hilles gate
- Nygårdsgata
- Salle Grieg
- Strømgata
- Hanks gt.
- Kunstforening
- Fosswinckels gt.
- Vestlandske Kunstindustrimuseum
- Nygårdsparken
- Pauls Kirken
- Natural History Museum
- Parkveien
- Rosenbergs gt.
- Konsuls gt.
- Ivar Aasensgate
- History Museum
- Welhavens gt.
- Prof. Hansteens gt.
- Thor Møhlens gt.
- Naval Museum
- University Library
- Welhavens gt.
- Konsul Børs gt.
- Prof. Hansteens gt.
- PUDDEFJORDSBROEN

hospital building. To be perfectly frank, we didn't visit it. Besides, we're not convinced that it would interest the majority of our readers.

Where to Shake It

—*Hulen:* 47 Olav Ryesvei, along Nygardsparken park. A former shelter during the war, this discothèque is laid out in the caves under the hill of the university. It's the best place to listen to good music, drink beer, and mix. Live bands almost every evening. Student card required, but it generally suffices to say that you are a student to get in. Closed Monday.

Around and About

—*Fløyfjellet:* A hill overlooking the city that you get to by the funicular of Fløyen. Leaves from behind the fish market and climbs up 1,040 feet. From the summit, there's a great panorama of the city and the area. Hiking trips. Take only a one-way ride. Going down on foot is easy and pleasant.

—*Stavkirke of Fantoft:* 2½ miles from Bergen on E48. Bus from the terminal to Paradise. This stave church is remarkable for its roof, shaped like a *drakkar*. It was purchased in 1880 by a rich merchant who dismantled it in order to reconstruct it here. The interior is closed from 1 to 3 P.M.

—*Rope lift to Mount Ulriken:* Less interesting than Fløyfjellet.

—*Folklore evening in Fana* (a couple of miles from Bergen) is a real tourist trap. You go there to witness a supposed wedding ceremony like in the good old days, and you find yourself among batallions of tourists in an atmosphere decidedly lacking in naturalness and spontaneity. For 100 Kr there's really not much to eat besides the famous wedding porridge. Only the music and songs are worthwhile.

MYRDAL–FLÅM RAILWAY LINE

This is truly one of the most beautiful railway lines in Norway even if it is a bit of a tourist trap. Automobile drivers will cry because there's no road to get there. Myrdal is on the Oslo–Bergen train line. You can get there via other cities. But be aware that not all the trains leaving Oslo for Bergen stop at Myrdal. Likewise, not all the trains from Myrdal to Flåm stop at the waterfalls. From Myrdal, take the Flåmsbana line. The train leaves Myrdal at 5:20 P.M. and arrives at Flåm less than an hour later. It's not possible to return, so you must spend the night at Flåm. Extraordinary descent into the Flåm valley. An incredible number of cascades all along the way. The train stops at Kjosfonen, a great waterfall for the reason that it's a lake spilling over. Get off, then get back on the train.

You can also hike there—16 miles. Wonderful! In Flåm, there's camping next to a fjord, with *hytters* at 25 Kr, 100 yards from a small train station. You can also bed down at *Bekker Inn,* a 2-minute walk from the station. Hardly more expensive than the campground, but very small. *Svingen Pensjonat* is not bad either.

Don't forget that Flåm is the land of raspberries.

Avoid the cafeteria in Flåm station; it's not a bargain. On the other hand, there's a small supermarket in a wooden building behind the station.

From Flåm, all the way down, take the boat for Sognefjord, Vangsnes, or Balestrand. A great voyage. You cruise along the truly impressive cliffs.

FROM BERGEN TO BALESTRAND

—*Vangsnes:* A small village next to the fjord, from where the ferry to Balestrand leaves. There's a youth hostel at the southern exit whose rooms overlook the water. On the ground floor is a well supplied grocery store. A good place.

—*Vik:* 7½ miles south of Vangsnes, has a very charming *stavkirke* built in the twelfth century, but the exterior was redone in 1895. Massive columns inside support the roof. Each column has a capital in the shape of a bell. Few sculptures.

—*Balestrand:* Right next to Sognefjord, in an absolutely wonderful setting. The village is located at the point where several fjords meet. Balestrand was one of those romantic spots quite popular at the beginning of the century: the traveler wanted above all else to be in communion with the elements. The French went along the banks of the Rhine and hummed Wagnerian tunes. It was much more chic for the Germans to go elsewhere. Not surprising Kaiser Wilhelm spent long vacations here. The hotel where he stayed is still here. Hitchhikers will have to settle for a youth hostel ⅓ of a mile west of the center: an immense wooden house with its feet soaking in the edge of the fjord. Not far from the youth hostel is the *Sjotum* campground with several *hytters*. Otherwise, not much to see in the city itself, except for a wooden church, recent but pretty. Boat trips are available from Balestrand. Lost in nature and silence, you may be invited for lunch at a farm. In particular, don't refuse the surprising (very surprising!) caramelized goat cheese (yes!). They mix it with honey, but it's not to everybody's liking. It would truly be a shame if they realized how good it is. Keep smiling and you may get some of those famous pancakes.

The road from Vik to Voss is absolutely splendid for its view of Sognefjord. Then you cross a plateau on top of the mountain with small lakes, streams, farms, hamlets... Voss is a pretty little city. You can camp by the lake. Pretty Gothic church from 1270.

The youth hostel is expensive (70 Kr), but it has a sauna and stays open through October.

A train leaves from Voss at 7:30 A.M., and at 11:08 A.M. for Myrdal. From there, a train at 12:15 for Flåm.

FROM BALESTRAND TO ÅNDALSNES

One of the prettiest roads in Norway. We swear! The itinerary crosses a landscape of mountains and skirts along several views of the eternal snow:

—*Bergly:* Youth hostel 40 miles north of Balestrand and 18 miles from Moskog. Completely isolated at the edge of a mountain lake.

—*Loen:* 62 miles northeast of Moskog. From Loen, a small road climbs to the edge of Kjenndalsbreen, a large glacier.

—*Geiranger Fjord:* The most famous in Norway, and justly so. Approaching Geiranger from the south, you see one of the most famous panoramas of Norway, the *Geirangermotiv*. Below, the small village of Geiranger lies nestled among huge mountains and borders a superb narrow fjord. Truly grand. A spectacle to mark with a white cross, dear readers, for it takes your breath away.

In Geiranger proper, hotels are generally expensive but there are two pleasant campsites: one to the south, flanking the mountain and cut by an enormous cascade; the other along the fjord. In the village, a tourist office and a bank are open Monday to Friday.

Several trips are possible from Geiranger and are not indicated by the Tourist Information Office. You can, for example, go to the cascades at *Stornstenterfossen* where you can admire the *S*-curve of the fjord snaking through the mountains. Upon leaving the village on a winding road, stop at the last curve to walk on a small path leading to some houses built into the mountain. Very scenic view of the fjord. (Ah yes, again! But there's no sign to tell you to take a photograph!)

Those who have some dough can make a trip in a seaplane (110 Kr for 15 minutes). You must take the boat at Geiranger. Choose the ferry rather than the excursion boat for tourists. It's less expensive, you see more, and you have room to roam about since the boat is large. The ferry that crosses the fjord at Hellesylt takes more than an hour. An unforgettable journey. In a setting worthy of the gods, the seagulls follow the boat and are almost tame. If you extend your arm with some bread or potato chips at your fingertips, they will come nibble in their own inimitable fashion.

This fjord is dominated by an enormous rocky face with magnificent waterfalls, including "Seven Sisters" and "The Bride's Veil."

You land in Hellesylt and go up toward Stranda by a picturesque road that alternates between tunnels and views of the fjord. From Stranda, take the ferry to the east, via Valldal (youth hostel and campground with no charm). Or go west via Sykkyliven to get to Ålesund, the primary fishing port of Norway.

FLORØ

A small port between Bergen and Ålesund. To get there, take the coastal express. A magnificent journey, especially in good weather, with a view of the very jagged coast and the mouths of numerous fjords. There's a campground a bit far from the town, but it's worth it: It hugs the fjord; there are islands everywhere; rocks and coves; almost Mediterranean vegetation—pines, junipers, bushes. Above the campground on the hill, a breathtaking view of the entire region. Practically no tourists spoil your pleasure.

From Florø you can continue along the coast toward Måloy. You pass by the channels between the high rocky walls. So impressive!

ÅLESUND

Built on three islands, Ålesund is obviously centered around the sea. Due to its important port activities there is a flourishing industry, but its noise doesn't drown out the cries of the seagulls.

—Tourist Office: 15 Rasmus Rønnebergsgate. Telephone 21-202. The coastal ferry puts into port at Ålesund. The trip to Bergen is worth it (fjords, fjords . . .), although somewhat expensive.

To See

—*Sunnmøre Museum:* Open from 11 A.M. to 3 P.M. every day. Interesting collection of fishing boats similar in shape to the Viking *drakkars.* Nevertheless, the boat most admired by the local population is the kayak used by Norwegian Resistance fighters to blow up a German boat.

—*Runde Island:* West of the city, this rocky peak attracts tens of thousands of birds. From June 1 to August 1, the Tourist Office organizes 4-hour excursions (rather expensive) when the weather permits.

—*The funicular of Spjelkavik:* Runs on Sunday. Gives you a superb view of the entire region.

ÅNDALSNES

A small industrial city, of several thousand inhabitants, at the base of a fjord and surrounded by high mountains with eternal snow. Has no charm. It suffered terribly from German bombings. Not much to see.

—*Tourist Office:* In the center. Bike rentals.

—*Setnes Ungdomsherberger* (youth hostel): Telephone 072/21-382. 1 mile from the city on the road from Ålesund. From the station, take the red bus (not very frequent) or hoof it. The building is of recent vintage, not far from the water. Run by farmers. 50 beds. Great breakfast—as much as you want of traditional dishes.

—*Mjelva Campground:* On E69. The least expensive. 50 *hytters.*

—*Åndalsnes Campground:* On E69. Telephone 072/21-629. Better equipped than Mjelva, but obviously more expensive.

—*Camping gas refills:* Mjelva.

Around and About

—*Trollstigheimen Cascades:* To the south, on the road to Valldal, about 12 miles. From the bottom of the valley, the road scales the cliff, passing the waterfalls before reaching the plateau. Rather fantastic. For those who want to continue their hike, a little steep near the end but not dangerous, there's the small village of Övstestöl, 5–6 miles after the waterfalls. Walk to the right, toward the hamlet, pass the bridge, and go back up the river by the little path. Climb to the left, just above the falls. You'll find an immense circle of mountains with a small lake in the middle and the beginning of an impressive glacier. Don't forget your camera.

MOLDE

Not much left of the old narrow streets that gave it its charm. The German bombs put an end to them. Molde is known throughout Norway for its roses.

—*Molde Ungdomsherberger* (youth hostel): Møre Og Romsdal.

Open only from June 11 to August 23. Telephone 072/54-330. Reservations are recommended. 232 beds.

—*Kviltorp Campground:* On route 62. Telephone 072/52-642. There are 15 *hytters*. Grocery store.

—*Camping gas refills:* Romsdal Fiskevegnfabrik.

To See

—*Fiskerimuseum:* A fishing museum established on the small island of Hjertøya. An old village restored with a school and a boat house. Take a taxi-boat to the wharf (Torgkaia) for the ferry that crosses to the island.

—*Molde International Jazz Festival:* Held every year the last week of July or the beginning of August. This festival is great and won't disappoint real jazz fans. Gets under way at the fjord's edge with concerts, theater, and cabaret . . . For the program and reservations, write to: Gallen Karyobin, Møre og Romsdal, Molde 6400.

—*Molde Church:* In the center of town. Built in 1957. Will interest fans of modern architecture for its stained glass windows and streamlined form. Free admission from 10 A.M. to 5 P.M.

—At Varden (a suitable road for cars), a panoramic view of the 87 peaks that overlook Molde and the archipelago.

RØROS

The type of city to see on the rebound from the North Cape, which allows you, on a Trondheim–Oslo itinerary, to discover a pretty, little-known, region: Østerdalen—located 92 miles southeast of Trondheim. Norway's only "mountain vallage," according to tourist brochures. Perched at 2,113 feet, it is an interesting pretty mining town with many old distinct houses, a pretty octagonal church from 1784, and an original mining museum. In the cemetery, the trade of the deceased is inscribed on the tombstone.

—*Tourist Information:* Bergmannsplassen. Telephone 11-165.

—A youth hostel and campground.

—The train from Trondheim arrives at 3:30 P.M., and another leaves for Oslo at 12:30 A.M.

SUNNDALSÖRA

The great aluminum city, which is enough to keep many wanderers away. You might stop for the youth hostel, a pretty wooden house overlooking the fjord, ½ mile from the center on the road from Åndalsnes. Salmon fishing nearby. Ask the youth hostel manager for a permit. Bike rentals. Camping right near the *hytters*.

TRONDHEIM

Third largest city in Norway. Trondheim is a place we like a lot. The whole center area is for pedestrians only, and the people stroll as soon as there is a speck of sun. A very pretty city, in our opinion, even niftier than Bergen.

Useful Addresses

—*Tourist Information:* 7 Kongensgate, on the large square (Torget). Money exhcange.
—*Post Office:* 10 Dronningensgate.
—*Telephone:* 8 Kongensgate.
—*Camping gas refills:* 11 Lade Allé.
—*Coastal Express* (Hurtigruten): Toward the south, wharf 15. Toward the north, wharf 16.

Where to Sleep

—*Trondheim Ungdomsherberger* (youth hostel): 41 Weidemannsvei. Telephone 075/30-490. Take bus #63 from Munkegate. Even if the very full breakfast is included, it's very expensive. Perched on top of a hill with a superb view of the city. Open all year; single and double rooms. It's smart to make reservations in the summer. Cafeteria.
—*Sandnoen Campground:* 6 miles south on E6. From Trondheim, take bus #44, then go under a large road (pedestrian tunnel), and then 500 yards on your right on E6. Supermarket, TV, washers and dryers, hot plates.
—*Vikhamarløkka Campground:* 9 miles northeast on E6, toward Storjdal. From Trondheim, bus from the bus station. Decent camping at reasonable prices. Don't confuse with *Vikhammer Campground,* highly rated, on a slope, and always crowded. When you arrive, it's all you see. Take the small road to the right with a road sign. Go under the railroad tracks. The tunnel is so narrow that caravans can't get through, which eliminates those jerks. You finally arrive at this small, nifty campground on the water, where they serve breakfast and have a pizzeria. You pay for showers. One problem: The trains make a bit of a racket.
—*Flakk Campgrounds:* About 6 miles to the west, near the ferry embarkment. Small, pebbly, and near the water. 28 Kr a night and by tent.

Where to Eat

—*Pizzeria Frati:* 25 Munkegate, in the town center. A congenial restaurant on the second floor, with lots of young people and a nice atmosphere. You can have a salad of raw vegetables, a rare thing in this country. Open from noon to 11 P.M.
—*Leutenhaven:* At the bus station. Very reasonable.
—*EPA Stores:* In the center. Very good for stocking up on food and camping gas.
—*The Cafeteria:* Inside the Prinsens Hotel, 30 Kongensgate. As the name indicates, a cafeteria. No charm, but it attracts the local youth.
—*Fish Market:* North of the city, a 5-minute walk from the center. You can buy shrimp and salmon. Unfortunately, more and more often it's frozen.
—*Bokkafé:* A bookstore run by militant leftists. They serve coffee, tea . . . Very cool. It's on the left after the old bridge as you're coming from the cathedral.

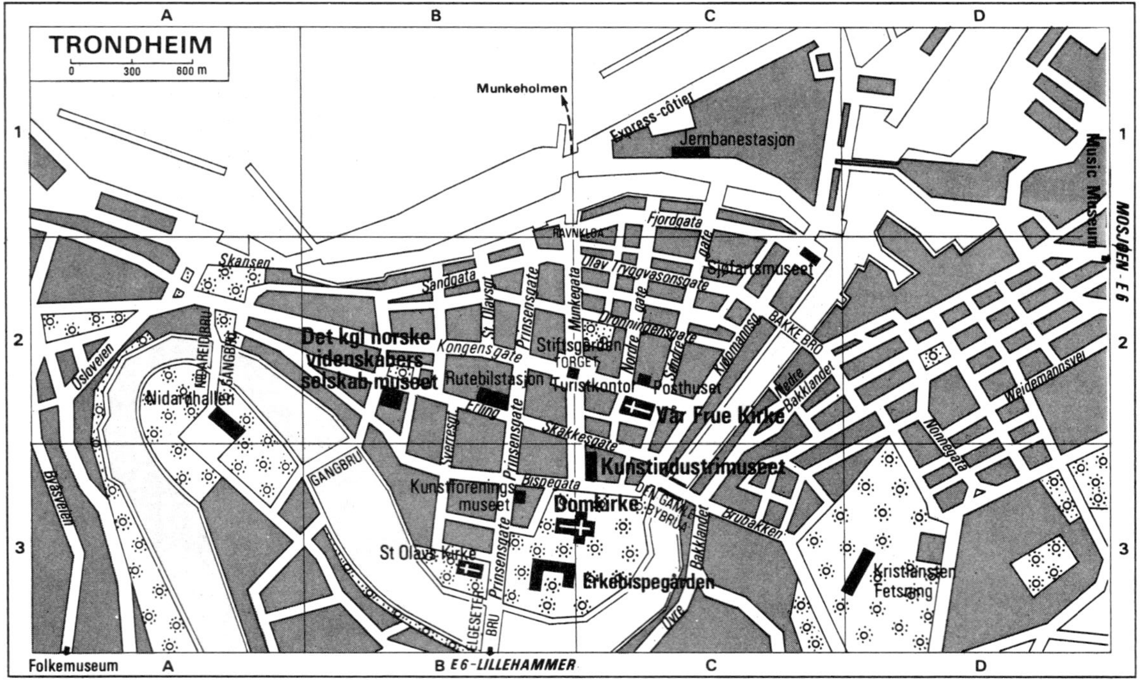
TRONDHEIM
0
300
600 m
Munkeholmen
Express-côtier
Jernbanestasjon
Music Museum
MOSJØEN - E 6
Fjordgata
RAVNKLOA
Sjøfartsmuseet
Olav Tryggvasonsgate
Skansen
Sandgata
St Olavsgt
Prinsensgate
Munkegata
Dronningensgate
Nordre gate
Søndre gate
Kjøpmannsgata
BAKKE BRO
Det kgl norske videnskabers selskab museet
Kongens gate
Stiftsgården
TORGET
Rutebilstasjon
Turistkontor
Posthuset
Vår Frue Kirke
Nedre Bakklandet
Weidemannsvei
Osloveien
NIDAREIDBRU
GANGBRU
Nidarøhallen
Erling
Sverresgt
Skakkesgate
Kunstindustrimuseet
Nonnegata
Bispegata
Kunstforenings museet
Domkirke
DEN GAMLE BYBRUA
Brubakken
Bakklandet
St Olavs Kirke
ELGESETER BRU
Erkebispegården
Kristiansten Festning
Øvre
Byåsveien
Folkemuseum
E6-LILLEHAMMER
A
B
C
D
1
2
3

To See

—*Kjøcmannsgate:* Along this street east of the city, a 5-minute stroll from the center, are enormous well-restored wooden warehouses, belonging to shipowners and merchants. Right next door is *Gamlebybru,* a famous seventeenth-century bridge. A must see.

—*Nidarosdomkirken:* The cathedral, in the center of town, is one of the most beautiful Gothic edifices in Norway. The facade is particularly large, with an impressive array of statues. Inside, superb stained glass windows, rather rare in Scandinavia. Organ recitals from June 15 to August 15 every day at 12:15 P.M.

—*Det Kunglige Norske Videnskabers Selskab Museet:* 47 Erling Skakkesgate. A museum renowned for its religious art collection, its minerals, and especially its treasures of the Viking era, discovered in boats and tombs.

—*Det Musikkhistorik Museet* (Music Museum): Located outside Trondheim and difficult to get to without a car, yet it is one of the most interesting museums in Norway. Classical music fans won't miss it. Bus #2 or #4 to the intersection of Lade Allé. Then take Lade Allé for a ½ mile. The museum is on the left. By car, it's 3 miles from the heart of the city: take route E6 north, then turn toward Ringve. Situated on the property of a rich family, this museum has assembled an exceptional collection of musical instruments: Chopin's piano, a harpsichord from the eighteenth century, an astonishing piano-harp, and a grand collection of instruments from the world over, notably Arabian and Indian. They've decorated a room in the corresponding style for each musical period.

Note: The hours are very strict. Guided tours (obligatory) at 11 A.M., noon, 1, 2, and 3 P.M. in Norwegian. Only 2 tours in English and German, at 10 A.M. and 2 P.M. Even if you don't understand any of the tour, it's worth it, since the guide, if in a good mood, will play compositions on the more interesting instruments.

The superb cafeteria is traditionally furnished. If it's nice out, stroll in the park where you can enjoy a pretty view of the fjord. Student discounts.

Nightlife

—*Strossa:* 1 Elgesterage, in the southern part of the city, just after the large bridge on the left. A 5-minute walk from the cathedral, in a large round building. Very hip music, with a student crowd.

—*Skansen:* Western part of the city in the port. A sailors' bar where youths go slumming. Nautical decor of doubtful taste. The waiters wear sailor suits, which would please Cocteau or Fassbinder. The music is good, with a penchant for hard rock.

Leaving Trondheim

—*By Hitching:* Toward North Cape, bus #2 or #4 from the bus station.

—*By train:* Toward Bodø. If you make the trip at night, we advise you to make reservations. Standing for 12 hours is a good conversation starter in the corridor, but it's long.

NORWAY (NORTHERN)

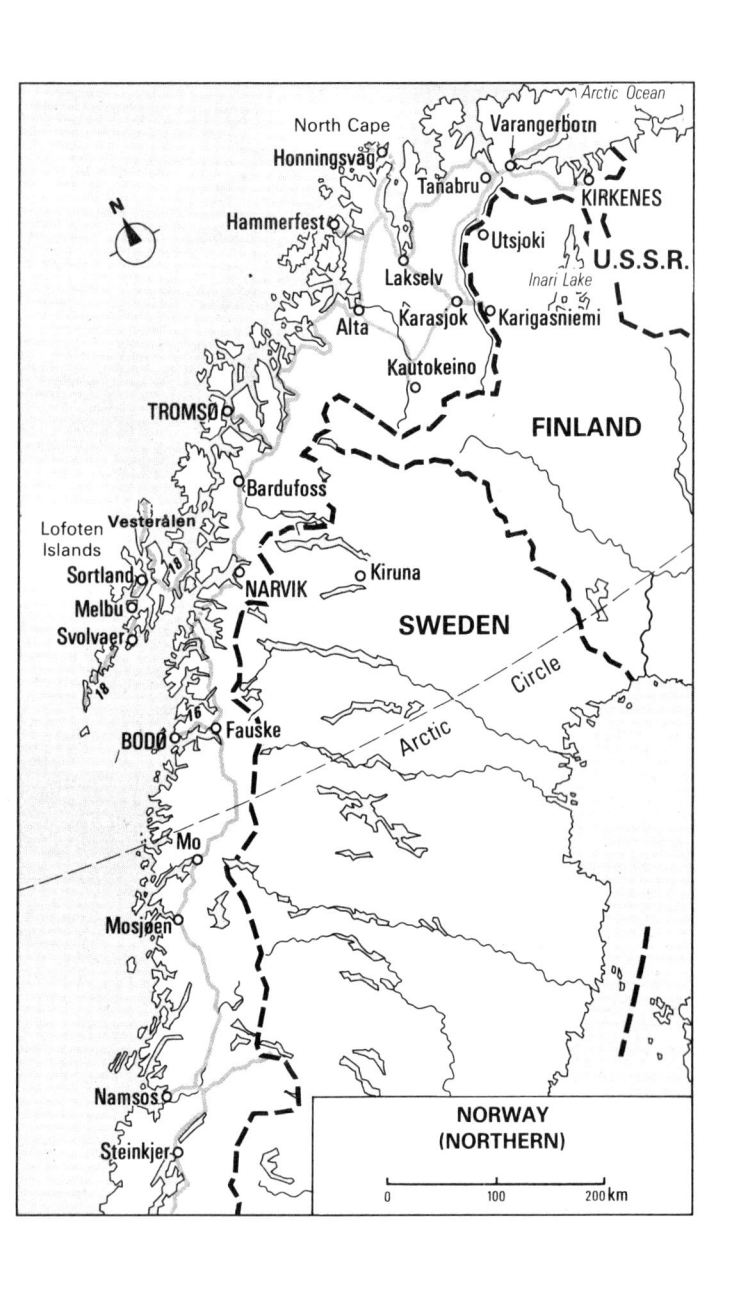

GRONG

A tranquil spot 125 miles north of Trondheim. Magnificent waterfalls and a lake.

MO I RANA

A small village 315 miles north of Trondheim. Not overly welcoming. The sunset on the fjord is pretty.
—*Camping gas refills:* 11 Nordahl Griegsgt.

Where to Sleep

—*Ungdomsherberger* (youth hostel): Toward the south, far from the center. Open from May to September. Quiet and comfortable. You can camp out back for half the price. There's a snack bar. You can cook, paying for it, as a rule.

—*Campground:* Below the factory and the extracting mine which operates day and night. It's really too much.

To See

—Salmon fishermen, west of the city, near the Ranafjord. The salmon are an impressive size.

—Upon leaving Mo i Rana toward Fausk by E6, turn left, about 8½ miles, and go to *Svartisen,* one of the largest Norwegian glaciers. The bus leaves from Mo i Rana at 10 A.M. It leaves the lake at Svartisen at 2 P.M. Take the boat at 1 A.M. No other bus. Otherwise, walk or hitch. The famous limestone grottos of Grønligrotten, next to Svartisen, aren't worth the time.

BODØ

Full of young people and soldiers. An infernal racket of fighter jets and bombers that take off every 5 minutes, only 2 miles from the center of town.

A small city (relatively large for the country), it has a very interesting fishing port. Stroll in the morning along the wharves; you can buy super-fresh fish for absurdly low prices.

The cafeteria in the train station closes at 8:45 P.M. except on Saturday.

—*Tourist Office:* 16 Storgatan. Open during the season until 8 P.M.

—*Camping gas refills:* 9 Tollbugt.

—*Bodøsjøen Campground:* Not too expensive. Bus #12.

—*Bafazzo:* On Storgatan. A nice little restaurant.

—If you stray from the city toward Kjerringøy in the south, you can go wilderness camping by the sea. Great.

—Just behind the Bodø youth hostel, you can climb the small mountain of Rønvik (20 minutes on foot) and discover a very beautiful panorama, especially at sunset.

The Fauske Campground is very comfortable. Located in a great spot on the road to Bodø, about 2 miles from the station.

Saltstraumen is 12 miles east of Bodø, an immense maelstrom (a watery whirlwind for the dopes). Take route 80. After Hoppen, go toward Straumen. Its exhibitions are episodic. Get information in advance (besides, the bus is very expensive).

From Bodø you can take the boat to the Lofoten Islands. Leaves every day at 3 P.M. This line services Stamsund (arrives at 7:30 P.M.; price: 130 Kr); Svolvaer (arrives at 9 P.M.; price: 139 Kr); Stokmarknes (arrives at 1 A.M.; price: 206 Kr); Sorland (arrives at 3 A.M.; price: 220 Kr); Harstad (arrives at 8:45 A.M.; price: 273 Kr); Tromsø (arrives at 3 P.M.; price: 401 Kr). Board the train near the taxi stand where you can buy tickets. A picturesque journey.

NARVIK

A rather curious elongated city but not very interesting. Almost nothing to see; perhaps the only things to photograph are the lake signs marking the distances between Narvik and major European cities. . . . We had to tell you. On the other hand, the outlying areas are superb.

French General Béthouart and his infantry landed in Narvik trying to combat the German invasion. The combat was so fierce that even though they were superior in number, the invaders had to retreat to Bjørnfjell. The city was seriously damaged, and several German torpedo boats and Allied ships were sunk in the Rombaksfjord. In clear weather, from on top of the peaks surrounding the city, you can distinguish the wrecks in the waters of the fjord.

—*Krigsmuseum* (War Museum) on Torg (the marketplace) is dedicated to military operations and the underground struggle during World War II. Maps, souvenirs, dioramas. If you saw these in Oslo, you can skip this.

Useful Addresses

—The *Tourist Office* exchanges currency. Not a rip-off as long as you change less than 100 Kr. Above that there's a tax of 10 Kr. Free maps of Sweden.

—Upon arriving at the station, a little before the youth hostel, mystics will find a church with a library, cafeteria, sauna, and shower. A great reception. Open after the closing of the stores, until at least 9 P.M. You could be helped out beyond your beliefs.

—Get a drink and forget your troubles at the hangout of students, among others: *Rallarin,* Kongensgate, near the bus station.

—*Camping gas refills* (blue) in the port and at 40 Kongensgate.

Where to Sleep

—If you come by boat, the youth hostel is found where the wharf begins. Often crowded and very expensive (58 Kr a night, but you can pay 39 Kr without breakfast). The manager closes the sanctum at 11 P.M. sharp. But the train from Stockholm (the last and the globetrotter's favorite) arrives at 11:15. We don't have to draw a picture—an inextricable situation. If by chance you do decide to take this train anyway, be sure your down sleeping bag is warm enough to let you sleep in the great outdoors. At the youth hostel taste the "champagne"—soda with the taste of bubble gum. Unique.

—Narvik isn't worth it. The campground is overpriced. It's better to walk another ½ mile. There are several interesting spots along the road, below and alongside the fjord. Great setting. Please don't leave any souvenirs like paper or tin cans.

—Sleep on the hill near the station. Sinks and toilets at the school (which serves the campground below). Nowadays you must pay for it. Notice that the young woman who collects the money makes her rounds about 11 P.M. To get there: go right on leaving the station, past the bridge. It is directly on the left. You can take advantage of the hot showers at the municipal swimming pool. Open from 8:30 A.M. to 3 P.M. The Tourist Office will give you the address.

Leaving Narvik

Toward the North
Very, very difficult to hitch to the North Cape from Narvik. It would be best to get to know some people at the campsite who plan to drive there.

—*Bus to the North Cape:* Leaving from Narvik, there's a 50 percent discount with the international student card, but not in July and August.

—*Plane:* Go to the airport at Evenes, about 31 miles (the bus is 40 Kr). Plane to Honnigsråg via Tromsø. A 50 percent discount for those under 21. For other student discounts check information.

Toward the South
—*Bus:* A 5½-hour trip to Fauske. Count on approximately $20 to $25. Truly wonderful landscape. No student discount. There is a card, valid for those under 26, students or not, which gives a 50 percent discount for one month.

—*Hitching:* Very difficult.

—*Boat:* Leaves from Narvik. From Monday to Friday at 3 P.M. to Svolvaer. Sunday at 1 P.M. Arrives about 4½ hours later.

LOFOTEN AND VESTERALEN ISLANDS

One of the most beautiful spots in Norway. Ideal for lovers of nature and vast landscapes. The further south you go, the fewer the people.

How to Get There

—Head north from Narvik. At Bjerkvik, branch off to the left. Then take route 19 for the Vesteralen and Lofoten Islands. The Vesteralen Islands are linked by toll bridges, and to get from one island to the other, you must take a ferry. It's expensive but worth it.

• Daily boat link between Bodø and Stamsund. Very expensive with a car (schedule and prices are in the Bodø section):
  —From Stamsund to Bodø: Leaves at 11 P.M.
  —From Bodø to Stamsund: Leaves at 3 P.M.
• From Sutvik, 75 miles south of Narvik, take the boat to Svolvaer.

To See

Midnight sun only on the northwest coast.

• *Svolvaer:* The city is not unique, and you can't actually see the sun at midnight. Information is given in costly brochures. A city to avoid despite a very comfortable though expensive (85 Kr), youth hostel. The breakfast is generous. It's in an actual hotel (double rooms with shower, cafeteria . . .).

Boat for Narvik from Monday to Saturday at 6:30 A.M., on Sunday at 7:30 P.M. About a 4½-hour voyage.

• *Hammarstad,* 6 miles from Svolvaer: Vaterfjord campground. Daily link with Svolvaer by bus. Lovely landscape. The owner lends bicycles for free. You can rent cottages for 75 Kr (3 people).

• Cross over the island of *Vestvagøy* to reach Stamsund, principal city of the fish industry. Wonderful and typical. The campground is 4 miles inland.

The youth hostel of Stamsund is less than 1 mile from the dock. This island truly deserves your lingering. A large fisherman's house on pilings. Truly great. The guy who runs it is adorable, and it is sufficiently comfortable. No strict hours of curfew or other stupid constraints. Located on a wharf in a small cove. Two fishing boats and some fishing lines are placed freely at your disposal so you can go fishing . . . and the fishing is miraculous. Compensates for the price of food. You can also rent bikes and even a tandem here.

On the west coast and a Vestvagøy there are marvelous white sand beaches, with coves along the blue sea . . . like the Mediterranean, with different colors ranging, depending on the depth, all the way to turquoise. At Vestvagøy, don't miss *Utakleiv,* a fine white sand beach with a great sea. A bit higher up there's a wide stretch of grass, as green as the sand is white. From this spot you can observe the phenomenon of the midnight sun. Wilderness camping is available, but do respect this blessing of nature. A few miles before Utakleiv there's a free campground with running water and sanitary facilities, but you can't see the midnight sun.

• Continue on your merry way by the island of *Flakstadøy,* and pass by Nusfjord (no youth hostel), where you can use your feet for some pretty treks. Then finish up at *Moskenesøy,* the southernmost of the Lofoten Islands.

• *Reine:* You can go here directly on Tuesday and Saturday from Bodø by the boat that goes to Røst and Vaerøy.

A must-see. No youth hostel, but you can camp at the southern edge of the city. Ah, to be truly lost at the end of the world. You can sleep in a fisherman's cabana, all laid out with a kitchen and shower, for 20 Kr a night. Check with Mrs. Sissel Johnsen. She lives in the yellow house across from the church.

The entire countryside is very interesting and populated by colonies of rare birds. Bird fans will go by boat to Røst and Vaerøy. They won't be disappointed (boats twice a week).

• In our opinion, the *Vesteralen Islands* are not as wonderful, but they're not bad. On the north of these islands, from Andenes, go to Bleik (5 miles). There, in the middle of the sea, there's a rocky peak covered with birds. It's crazy. It echos everywhere. You'll be surrounded by monk puffins.

TROMSØ

Former fishing and whaling capital. Nothing too frolicsome. No more whalers, and it's not bad. You must climb to the top of the city for the sunset, and if you are a bird lover, don't miss the photo safari organized by the birds' fans in the area There's camping with bungalows and a hotel in the city.

—*Geological and Zoological Museum:* On Lapland. Pretty reconstructions. On the other hand, the aquarium is pitiful.

—*The S.A.S. Hotel:* Exchanges money on Sunday, taking a mere 5 percent commission.

—*Camping gas refills:* 13 or 27 Sjøgt.

—A bus leaves Tromsø for Narvik at 9 A.M. From there you can take the coastal express to the North Cape. In the summer, there are some worthwhile discounts with an international student card.

Where to Sleep

—*A Iversens V.I.* (youth hostel): Telephone 829-91.

—*Folkeparken Campground:* Near the beach, on the southern part of the island.

—*Elvestrand Campground:* Near the river of Tromsdalen.

—*Schala Campground:* Near the dock of the ferry to Langnes.

—*Lodging in private homes:* See *Tourist Information,* 18 Parkgata.

NORWEGIAN LAPLAND

Deserted, yet overpopulated with mosquitoes. The Lapps are reserved and don't like tourists who consider them an underdeveloped minority, and you'd better know it now. Along the roads of the Lapp camps, you'll find reindeer hides and bones. For your outings, we advise not to go it alone, to be aware of the weather, and to be careful of dangerous swamps.

FINMARK

The most northern province of Norway, in the heart of Lapland. Stroll on the trails (not great for hitching). At the end of April or the beginning of May, the reindeer move to the islands where there are fewer mosquitoes. It's done by swimming or by Norwegian navy ships. Go to Kautokeino.

ALTA

It's the last large city before the North Cape and also the state capital. In addition, it has the biggest grouping of rock drawings in Europe; many of the rocks along the coast are drawn on. Get information at the Tourist Office at the edge of town as you head toward the North Cape.

HAMMERFEST

There are 8,000 inhabitants. It lies at 70°40′ N., 25°30′ E., the northernmost city in the world (says the guide). This wasteland has nothing special. It's like all the other northern cities in Norway, but there are some pretty mountains around and the road leading to it is lovely. The people are quite different and can teach you a few things. In the summer, there are at least 3,000 tourists, as many as there are reindeer and Lapps.

Don't forget to taste the catfish at Pomoren. For the rest, see the "North Cape" section.

The Midnight Sun

The goal for most people visiting northern Norway is the North Cape, where the sun shines at midnight from the middle of May to the end of July, as long as the fog doesn't prevent the tourist from admiring this reddening globe that seems to rise from the sea and ignite the entire unreal landscape. As it rises little by little into the sky, all of nature undergoes a metamorphosis: the distant horizons suddenly appear within an arm's reach, then everything that is near or familiar suddenly becomes distant and strange. A captivating and unforgettable spectacle.

FINLAND

As you know, the Finns are not overly fond of the Russians. It would be wise to tell them that their way of life is much more Swedish. Whoops, goofed again, for the Finns don't like the Swedes much either. Cornered between these two countries and culturally akin to neither, the Finn is proud of his independence and particularly does not seek the western way of life. Be careful about this when you speak with them (if they understand you, which is not always possible).

Note: Contrary to expectations, life is not much less expensive here than in other Scandinavian countries, except perhaps for cigarettes. Milk products are even more expensive.

Useful Addresses in New York

—*Finland National Tourist Office:* 75 Rockefeller Plaza, New York, NY 10019. Telephone (212) 582-2802.
—*Consulate General of Finland:* 540 Madison Avenue, New York, NY 10022. Telephone (212) 832-6550.

Language

It's worth taking a few days to learn a few words of Finnish. Otherwise, there's a good chance you won't be understood at all, especially by people over 30 who know only Finnish. Moreover, it's a language with astonishing sounds. It has no relation to any other European language (except that it sounds a bit like Hungarian). A good number of Finns speak Swedish (hope that helps), especially on the western coast and in the south (Hanko, for example). Most of the young people speak English, and many of the others know a few words.

For Finnish pronunciation, each letter is pronounced separately. Double letters are well marked.

y is pronounced *ew* (chew)
u is pronounced *oo* (boot)
e is pronounced *ay* (play)
ä is pronounced *a* (man)
ö is pronounced *u* (put)
j is pronounced *ye* (yes)

hello	*hyää paivää*
how are you?	*mitä kuuluu?*
I would like	*haluaisin*
I don't speak Finnish	*en osaa puhua suomea*
yes	*kyllä*
no	*ei*
I	*minä*
you	*sinä*
thank you	*kiitos*
pardon	*anteeksi*

Finland	*Suomi*
beer	*olut*
coffee	*kahvi*
bread	*leipä*
potato	*peruna*
bank	*pankki*
youth hostel	*retkeilymaja*
one	*yksi*
two	*kaksi*
three	*kolme*
four	*neljä*
five	*viisi*
six	*kuusi*
seven	*seitsemän*
eight	*kahdeksan*
nine	*ydeksan*
ten	*kymmenen*
one hundred	*sata*
one thousand	*tuhat.*

How to Get There

—The Viking Line Company (50 percent discount with Inter-Rail card and student card, but only for bridge class) links Stockholm with Helsinki. A comfortable boat with swimming pool, saunas, and duty-free cigarettes. In the evening, there's a discothèque.

In the restaurant on board you can eat as much as you want for 40 Kr: shrimp, smoked salmon, lox, various fish, reindeer, pâté, hot dishes (chicken, omelettes, and so forth), not to mention cheeses and desserts. Food is so expensive in Scandinavia that it's a real pleasure to make up for it and regain your health. Don't forget that you should make reservations for dining as soon as you get on board.

—Those who want to economize during the voyage and who have the time can cross from Stockholm to Turku, with a port call at the Aland Islands.

Food and Drink

The food is good (based on fish). In the center of each city there's a commercial center where you can eat decently. As in all of Scandinavia, food is expensive, even the self-service joints. Better to buy your grub in the supermarkets. Fresh fruits and vegetables are exorbitant.

Grocery stores close around 6 P.M. during the week. Watch the weekends: They close on Saturday at 2 P.M. and don't open until Monday morning. In an emergency, the *kioski* are open late in the evening and on weekends.

In the north, eat reindeer (called *poro*). Served smoked or with cranberry jam, it's very good. . . .

The bars *(barri)* don't serve much fish, but instead mashed sausage or oatmeal.

There are four types of beer, numbered 1 to 4. Number 1 is nonalcoholic and disgusting. Number 2 no longer exists, number 3 is like Kronenborg, and number 4 is excellent.

Don't forget to taste, (especially at Kuopio) *Kalakkuko,* a cumin bread stuffed with small fish.

During the tourist season several hundred restaurants serve a regional dinner called *Finland Menu,* ranging in price from $5 to $9.

Interior Transportation

—Hitchhiking: Even if it's poor, there's no other choice for a hitcher. The Finns generally drive slowly on their dirt roads so it's easy for them to stop regularly for hitchhikers. As flag on your backpack might help.

—By train: The Finnish railways offer a *Finnrail-Pass* which allows you to travel freely all over the 3,750 miles of railroad tracks in Finland. It is valid for 8, 15, or 22 days. Its price in 1983 was, respectively, $48, $69, and $95 for second class. The sleeping car is a good deal (about $7). It's interesting if you're crossing the country at night, and it's very comfortable.

Inter-Rail cards are always valid in Finland.

—By car: Fill up with gas before 6 P.M. or you'll pay an additional night tax, except in self-service gas stations.

Those who arrive in Helsinki and Turku and who wish to continue tirelessly to Lapland can take the auto-sleeper trains daily to Rovaniemi (562 miles) You have to buy a ticket for the car, for the driver, and for the sleeping car (448 Finnish marks), plus 179 marks per passenger.

—Lapland by Bicycle: An attractive way to discover the natural beauties of the extreme north of Finland: Lapp mountains, the tundra and its dwarf birches, as well as its numerous villages. Let's not forget the regional culinary specialties nor the traditional sauna every night!

A specialized agency organizes 5-day trips leaving from Helsinki. You can go from Helsinki to Ivalo by airplane. The itinerary, from Ivalo, passes by Inari (located on the largest and most beautiful lake of Lapland) where the reindeers roam even in the village and campground, by Kevo (national park renowned for its trees and plants, as well as for its varied species of birds), and by Utsjoki. It then continues along the Norwegian border and the banks of the Tend River (one of the best places for salmon fishing) and goes back down to Ivalo.

Thus in 5 days you can cover 250 miles. It requires good physical conditioning to average 45 to 75 miles a day. The longest haul is 82 miles between Utsjoki and Karigasniemi. But the physical effort won't be too exhausting because this ground is covered at night. A very bright night, since the Lapp summer skips night completely; the air is light and sweet, and the trip will be without pain or fatigue.

They depart every Friday, from June through the beginning of September, which gives you enough choice to discover Lapland: the end of spring in June, the midnight sun throughout July, and the exploding colors of autumn from the end of August to September. A diploma and a medal will be awarded to each participant at the end of the journey. Yes!

For information, contact Arctic Cycling, 19 A Hämeenkatu, 15110 LAHTI, or the Finland Tourist Office.

—By plane: A relatively good deal. There's a 25 percent discount for those under 26 with an international student card, and a 50 percent discount going and 25 percent returning for those under 21.

The *Finnair Holiday Ticket:* Allows travel on all interior air routes

on Finnair among the 20 Finnish airports within 15 days. No limitation of travel. It cost $240 in 1983.
—*By bus:* The busy system is well developed and less expensive than the train. You can buy a pass for 8 or 15 days without a mileage limitation.

Campgrounds

Campgrounds are generally well equipped with sauna, free cooking stoves, showers. You can make cooking fires. . . . Though some campsites are expensive, in general they're more reasonable than the youth hostels.

On the other hand, wilderness camping is not so readily available. Large tracts of land are swampy and mosquito infested. You absolutely must pack a good repellent. Other spots are occupied by farms (and the farmers don't speak much English) or by vacation homes where the people are justifiably attached to their tranquility.

Finnchecks

As in Sweden and Norway, there are hotel coupons (*Finnchecks*) worth 95 Finnish marks per person, good for lodging in a double room with breakfast. Valid in 145 hotels. Information can be obtained at the Finnish Tourist Office.

Cottages along the Water

In the middle of nature, the dream of many. And an attainable dream, thanks to a large choice of vacation homes placed at the disposal of tourists in Finland. These homes are residences that allow you to enjoy excellent roomy vacations. You rent them by the week (from Saturday to Saturday, generally). The prices vary depending on the house, the location, and the extras. On the average, a cottage for 2 to 3 people goes for $100–150 a week, not including transportation.

Geography

Finland is about two-thirds the size of France in surface area but has only 4,800,000 inhabitants. It's not a mountainous country (the highest point is 4,207 feet), but it's not exactly a flat terrain either. Glacial deposits created hills and moraines, creating a lovely palette of landscapes and lakes (60,000 in the last census).

A Little History

Finland has been inhabited since the Stone Age, but the Finns proper didn't arrive until the beginning of our era. They survived for many centuries under the domination of the Swedes, who prevented them from developing a cultural and social life of their own. After the war in 1809, Sweden left Finland to Russia. Finland became an autonomous grand-dukedom of the Russian Empire. Not until 1917, at the time of the Russian Revolution, did Finland become an independent country with a democratic parliamentary government.

The People

The Finns, especially in the east, are very warm and good natured. You may be invited to take a sauna with them. A great experience. They'll invite you to drink, eat, and sleep. You won't find it easy to give them money, so try to offer them presents, at least some cigarettes.

To understand Finland, you shouldn't hesitate to get off the main roads and plunge headlong into back roads to find the hidden lakes. Finland is forest from Borga-Porvoo to Karigasniemi, with thousands of hidden lakes behind the trees. So hidden, in fact, that we know someone who was furious because he crossed all of Finland from Tampere to Mikkeli without seeing a single little lake!

Hours

—Banks close at 4 P.M. After 4, it's still possible to exchange money in the large stores, where they often have their own exchange offices. The same is true for train stations and airports in large cities.

—Note: Everything closes from Saturday to Monday, including the post office.

Medical Care

Medical care in the hospitals is really not expensive.

Post Office and *Post Restante*

The post offices are open from 9 to 5, closed on Saturday and Sunday. You can buy stamps in the post office, libraries, stationers, and at the kiosks in the train stations.

To receive your mail *Poste Restante,* you must have it addressed in the following way: Mr., Ms., and so forth, *Poste Restante,* name of the place. The *Poste Restante* office is always at the main post office of the given city. This service is free.

Midnight Sun and Polar Night

The midnight sun is visible in Lapland, North Latitude:

Utsjoki, Kevo 69°52′	from May 17 to July 27
Ivalo 68°40′	from May 22 to July 21
Sodankylä 67°25′	from May 30 to July 14
Kemi 65°45′	from June 18 to June 25
Rovaniemi 66°30′	from June 6 to July 7
Kuusamo 65°59′	from June 12 to June 30

On the other hand, the sun disappears entirely in the extreme north from the end of November to the beginning of January—the polar night period.

Nightlife

Night owls can take advantage of Finland: discos have ridiculously low cover charges (you pay only for the coat check, in fact), and

FINLAND • 169

drinks are no more expensive than in the cafeterias. The music may not be the best, but meeting the locals is easy. The clubs close rather early, alas, at 12:30 A.M.

There is a checkroom at the entrance of most discos and cafeterias. It is not unusual to be "rejected" if you appear too slovenly.

TURKU

Our favorite city in Finland, with its parks, canals, observatory, the market in the big square, and particularly a very old open market (very unique atmosphere).

—*Folklore Museum* with crafts people at work. You can even learn to comb and card wool *(Luostarinmaki).* Really worth the detour. Get there early.

—*Museum of Fine Arts* and the *Waino Aaltonen Museum* are excellent.

—You must visit the *castle,* near the embarkment. You pass by it on your way to the youth hostel.

—Boutique *(kioski)* open Saturday and Sunday until 10 P.M. near the marketplace.

—*Turku-Stockholm crossing:* A 50 percent discount with the Inter-Rail Pass. The crossing in the daytime is rather long. The one at night is worth it, not for the disco (awful music and atmosphere) or for the view (obviously!), but for the feast you can eat for about $7. There are about 40 dishes (hot and cold) at your disposal—meats, fish, salads, cheeses, fruits . . . and all in a luxurious setting. This is a restaurant you will never forget. Exchange office on arrival, at customs.

Where to Sleep

—*Ruissalo Campgrounds:* 5 miles from the city (bus #8 from the center). Very large, and you can swim. Very well arranged, and everything is free except the sauna which you must reserve.

—*Youth Hostel:* At the intersection of Allegatan and Slottsgatan. A bit difficult to find. Ask for a map at one of the kiosks that sell food. The maps are free, and the youth hostel is marked. Bus #1.

Where to Eat

—*Hotel Maakunta:* 7H Humalistonkatu. An excellent restaurant on bus route #8. Large portions and not expensive between noon and 2 P.M. Afterwards, it's a normal and costly restaurant.

Just across, at 8 Humalistonkatu, is the Thrinase Restaurant. Less expensive and very pleasant. Between 11 A.M. and 3 P.M. it's a bargain.

—*Cafenoir:* 10A Erikinkatu, 50 yards from the marketplace. Very reasonable restaurant with generous portions.

—The university restaurant is very special. A must-see. Reception at the entrance and a game room. Upstairs, a restaurant with subdued lighting, music. . . . It opens late in the afternoon. Also a bar. Very full meals. Discount with a student I.D.

Nightclub

—*KY Club:* 5 Rehtorinpellontie (Turku University). A student hangout. Open Friday and Saturday. Very nice, but few people.

SALO

The campground is truly a wreck in the middle of nowhere, down by the sea. The area is very pretty. Not very well equipped. Not easily accessible, except by bus, but it is relatively easy to get picked up hitching. People don't drive fast on these dirt roads.

HELSINKI

A rather ordinary city. A 1-day visit is enough. Many great houses in the center of town, a police station that looks like a church, and a church that looks like a prison . . .

You will be struck by the harbor dominated by an all-white cathedral, by the enormous fish stands situated right on the sidewalk of the President's Palace (where there's a flag), and also by the sun that does not want to set.

Useful Addresses

—*Tourist Office:* 19 Pohjoisesplanadi. Telephone 169-37-57.

—*Main Post Office:* 11 Mannerheiminte. *Poste Restante* open from 8 A.M. to 10 P.M. during the week and from 9 A.M. to 10 P.M. on Sunday.

—*Exchange Office of the Central Station:* Open from 8:30 A.M. to 8 P.M. during the week and from 12:30 P.M. to 7 P.M. on Sunday.

—*Car Rentals* (Opiskelijain Autovuokraamo): 2 Apollonkatu, Helsinki 10. Telephone 447-143 and 446-429. A student association that rents cars to those over 18 at half the price of Hertz or Avis! Daily or weekly rentals.

—A daily pass for public transportation is 22 marks.

—Be aware that you must buy your ticket for the tramway before boarding. Or you can buy a pass good for 10 rides.

—*U. S. Consulate:* 14 Itainen Puistotie. Telephone 171-931.

Where to Sleep, Where to Eat

—*Youth Hostel of Retkailnaja:* Opens at 9:30 A.M. and closes between 11 A.M. and 4 P.M. The cost is 16 Finnish marks a night. You can cook. Bike rentals. It's a bit of a barracks.

There's another hostel, in Otaniemi, but it's much more expensive (bus #102 and #192).

—*Camping:* Take the *Östra Centrum* subway, then one of the following buses: #90, #90A, #96, or #98.

—There are 2 university restaurants in the center of town. Very good and not expensive. Open to everyone, but a student card entitles you to a discount. For shopping, some supermarkets open late, from 10 A.M. to 10 P.M., are in the brand new subway passages (access from inside the train station or from the sidewalk).

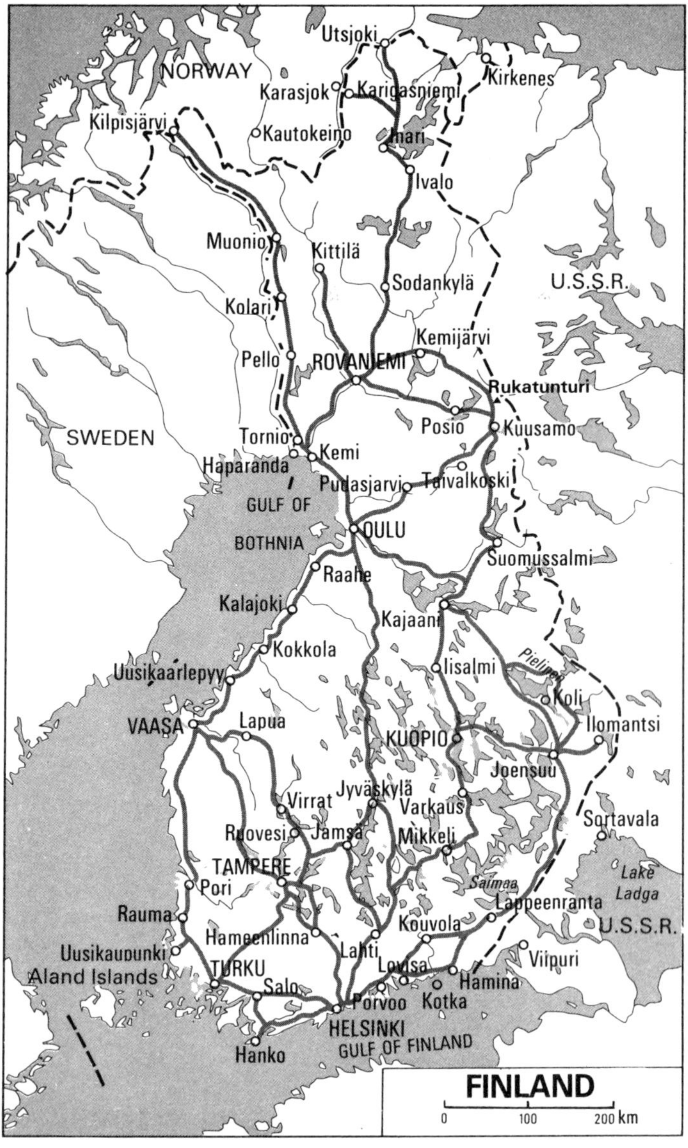
NORWAY
Utsjoki
Karasjok
Karigasniemi
Kirkenes
Kilpisjärvi
Kautokeino
Inari
Ivalo
Muonio
Kittilä
Sodankylä
U.S.S.R.
Kolari
Kemijärvi
Pello
ROVANIEMI
Rukatunturi
Posio
Kuusamo
SWEDEN
Tornio
Kemi
Haparanda
Pudasjarvi
Taivalkoski
GULF OF
BOTHNIA
OULU
Suomussalmi
Raahe
Kalajoki
Kajaani
Kokkola
Pielinen
Iisalmi
Uusikaarlepyy
Koli
VAASA
Lapua
KUOPIO
Ilomantsi
Joensuu
Virrat
Jyväskylä
Varkaus
Sortavala
Ruovesi
Jamsä
Mikkeli
TAMPERE
Lake
Ladga
Saimaa
Pori
Lappeenranta
Rauma
U.S.S.R.
Kouvola
Hameenlinna
Lahti
Viipuri
Uusikaupunki
Lovisa
TURKU
Aland Islands
Hamina
Salo
Porvoo
Kotka
HELSINKI
GULF OF FINLAND
Hanko
FINLAND
0
100
200 km

To See

If the city as a whole is not sensational, there are some very pretty things to see.

—*Strawberry market* in July. Very interesting. On the port.

—*Island of Suomenlinna.* To get there, take a boat from the port.

—The church built into the rocks *(Tempellinaukion Kirkko),* near the town center.

—*The white cathedral.*

—*Finlandiatalo:* The civic center. Very modern architecture. Built by Aalto, a top Finnish architect.

—Helsinki has some very beautiful museums, in particular the *National Museum* (prehistoric, historic, and folkloric sections) and the *Atheneum.* The outdoor museum is also very interesting.

—*Sibelius Monument,* in Sibelius Park *(Sibeluiksenpuisto).*

—*Luna Park.*

—*Taivalkoski Church* and the *Island of Seurasaari* where they reconstructed an ancient village of Finland. The squirrels come to eat out of your hand. *Museum of Animals.*

—Shaded paths with little fountains.

—*Fish market.*

Around and About

You must see the wonders of modern architecture, for Finland is a very avant-garde nation, particularly on the *Otaniemi Peninsula,* which is located east of Helsinki. There are three buildings to see:

—*Institute of Technology* which was created by Alvar Aalto. In particular, you should see the interior and the exterior of the amphitheatre, *Aula Magna.*

—*Dipoli* (university residence). The architect Reima Pietila built this structure so that it is totally integrated with the surrounding landscape. The interior is the continuation of the exterior. A truly unique building. Rather expensive to visit, however.

—The chapel designed by Heikki Siren. Here also there's a marvelous integration with the surrounding landscape. The forest serves as the retable, and the inside is all wood.

—The city garden of Tapiola located near Otaniemi. To get to Otaniemi, take bus #102 or #192 at the bus station, 300 yards from the train station; 10–15 minute ride.

—Also at Otaniemi, at the bus station, there's a very pretty youth hostel (also called *Dipoli*), much better than the one at the Olympic stadium and much less crowded. From Helsinki, take bus #102 or #192. The youth hostel is truly very comfortable; the rooms have 2 beds and complete bath! Moreover, a radio and kitchens.

Next to this youth hostel is swimming pool and also a nighclub, which is frequented by students. All of Otaniemi is magnificent.

TAMPERE

The second largest city in Finland. An enormous amount of young people. The most industrial city in the country, but there's little of interest.

—*Tourist Information:* 14B Alexsis Kivenkaty. Not far from the station. Exchange money on Saturdays in emergency from 9 A.M. to noon.

Where to Sleep

There are 2 youth hostels open all year:
—*Uimakallin Maja:* 10-12 Pirkankatu. About 30 marks a night.
—*NNKY,* 12A Tuomiokiakontako. 5 minutes from the train station.
—*Härmälä Campgrounds:* 3 miles from the center of the town. To get there, take bus #1 (the last one is at midnight).
—*Ekeberg Campgrounds:* Great, but far from the center. Take bus #24.
—*Maisansalo:* 22 miles from the center of Tampere, in Teisko. 20 marks a night.

To See

—*Cathedral.*
—*Belvedere of Nasinneula:* Located in the community center of Sarkanniemi. The highest observation tower in Finland. Also, go to the aquarium, which has nearly 200 species.
—*Museum of Modern Art* (Nykytaiteen Museo): 23 Palomäentie. Open from 11 A.M. to 7 P.M. every day. Admission is 5 marks, but only 1 mark for students. To get there, go to Satamakatu, then take Laiskolankuja to the end. In Palomäentie observe the strange pavement of round gray and pink shingles.
—*Doll Museum of Kaukajarvi* (Nukke Museo): Bus #24 from the bus station (near the Tourist Office) and get off at the last stop. Magnificent Japanese dolls.
—*Kesateatteri Pyynikin:* Outdoor theater in the Pyyniki Park in the summer. Everything is sold out weeks in advance, but it's possible to get stand room for 30 marks. Performance at 7 P.M. every day. In the same area, a great spot for swimming.

JÄMSÄ

In the very heart of Finland, with a landscape of forests, lakes, and rivers. Several types of excursions are offered to nature lovers. In fact, the riding school of Jämsä organizes outings on horseback, with carriages, or with vans. These trips last 6 days, from Saturday to Thursday, from June 7 to August 15.
—The vans are equipped with 4 bunk beds and a complete kitchen. Detailed maps are given to the participants, and the itineraries are marked with red and white ribbons. The stops at night are in farmyards.
—The carriage outings are advantageous for those who want to discover the region in daily trips. Lodging is at horse relay stations in Jämsä. Only one night is spent on a farm. Price (according to the number of people, maximum three) includes lodging, horse, and carriage.
—The horse outings cover 20 miles or so per day. Lodging and meals during the trip are at farms. A basic training is required. Information can be obtained at the Finland National Tourist Office.

LAKE SAIMAA

An immense lake scattered with little islands. You can swim here since the water isn't too cold. You can always find a farmer who will rent you his fishing boat for a modest sum.

Don't bother going to Lappeenranta. It's an overcrowded and expensive campground, not particularly well located and packed with tourists.

On the other hand there's Parikkala, a down-and-out country spot known for its wooden church; camping is not so costly, and it's well placed in nature). To get to the campground, Inter-Rail travelers should get off at Simpele (which is 4 miles from the campground, instead of the 8 miles if you get off at Parikkala). The youth hostel is 2 miles from Parikkala, located in a forest by a lake. Sauna and swimming pool. Bus on Monday and Friday at 11:25 A.M., noon sharp, and 2:05 P.M., on Wednesday at 11:25 A.M. and 2:05 P.M.

Be aware that of all the buses that connect Simpele to Parikkala, only 4 stop at the campground. The sauna is heated with firewood, and there's no electricity, as in most campgrounds. A well-stocked kitchen but insufficient sanitary facilities. It's 2 miles from the Russian border, and you can even see a guard tower. . . . Don't miss the crossing from Punkaharju at sunset.

SAVONLINNA

The first station as the train comes from Parikkala. If you are not in a hurry, you can stop for the fun of it, for it borders a lake scattered with little islands that you get to by pretty wooden bridges. From the other side of the station, toward the center, there's a restaurant-bar on a barge with a rather pleasant atmosphere.

See the fort on the rocky little island, which is quite rare in Finland. Numerous small ferries enable you to cross the lakes, and they're free.

—*Kironniemi Campground:* Take bus #2 across from the bus station. It's ¼ mile from the railroad station, somewhat expensive, and not well equipped.

IMATRA

For motorcycle fans. World renowned motocross racetrack.

On Lappeenranta there's a pub where, if you play piano, they pay for your drinks. This advice is for alcoholic globetrotters who studied at the conservatory.

The waterfalls at Imatra are worth seeing. They can be visited on Sunday at 2:30 P.M.

KUOPIO

A wonderful city. *Kalakukko* is the specialty of the city: small fish eaten with cumin bread.

To See

—Famous *Orthodox Museum:* Icons, crucifixes, chalices. Allows you to realize the wealth amassed by the Church. Of course, compared to the treasures of the Vatican, it's cat pee.

—The *market,* with its fruits and vegetables, its vendors of fritters (with rice or mashed potatoes) and *kalakukko.* Not expensive at all.

—*Tarzan:* 39 Kauppakatu, right near Kauppatori. All the Finns will tell you that it's the best club in the city.

Where to Sleep, Where to Eat

—*Taivalharju Campground* (3 miles from the city): Take bus #15 in front of the bus station. Ask the driver where to get off, for it's not well marked, and he will drop you off right in front of the campground. Boats, sauna, volleyball . . . Closes on August 31.

—*Rauhalathi Campground:* 2½ miles from the center. Bus #20 in front of the Sokos store on the big square. Very well equipped: sauna, golf, restaurant, boat, bikes, canoes, and so forth. Reasonably priced.

—*Self-service restaurant:* At the marketplace, under the Sokos store. Good, filling, and a good deal (20 marks).

LIEKSA

A city situated east of the lake region, by a lake, of course. Visit the *Folklore Museum* in a school and an outdoor museum of Pierlinen at *Pappi-Panniemi,* regrouping of characteristic houses from the region. There's a brand new cathedral with a rather crazy modern architecture and an all-white exterior.

Youth hostel. Very pleasant camping: lost in the trees, by a lake; with, of course, all the comforts including a grocery store and a sauna.

A boat links Koli, one of the most important tourist places in Finland. Very pretty with its forests, its heaps of rocks, and its ravines.

VUONISLATHI

A beautiful spot 18 miles south of Lieksa. The train stops here. A youth hostel lies 500 yards from the station, a veritable haven of peace.

FINNISH LAPLAND

There is no real difference in the physical characteristics of Lapland and the southern regions; from north to south there's a scarcity of vegetation and population. It's only north of Inari Lake that a landscape of sparse birch groves begins. A certain prudence imposes itself when you visit this region: the directions given on the maps are sometimes too optimistic, and what seems to be a city turns out to be a group of 3 or 4 homes, where you'll have trouble getting supplies. Note also the enormous distances separating these inhabited sectors. Finally, be careful of the forests with boggy soil, in spite of a layer of humus. Each year these forests swallow up their ration of tourists. Don't panic, though. With some precautions you can enjoy the beautiful landscapes.

Generalities

—*Finnish sauna:* In addition to the hot room and the shock of the cold shower, you may enjoy being whipped with birch branches.

—Myth of the "old American car" among the youth. In the evening, in some cities, there's an "American Graffiti" atmosphere complete with hot rods and pickups (not trucks).

—By going along the railroad tracks, you'll find woods with reindeer and moose.

—Hitching is much more difficult here than in Norway.

—Postal buses are a very good means of getting around in Lapland. They go everywhere and are quite reasonable.

—"Dancing" means a place where you drink alcohol and meet friends. It's not the greatest for dancing, but for meeting people, it's interesting.

ROVANIEMI

The capital of Finnish Lapland is unfortunately too Americanized. There's very little of interest. If possible, go out at night. Everybody is outdoors. The sun disappears for hardly more than an hour, just enough time to get a drink.

It's an expensive city, too modern for our taste, excessively touristy and has too many boot camp soldiers. Rovaniemi is serviced by direct trains from Helsinki (10–12-hour trip).

Where to Sleep

—*Camping* is available on the other side of the river. Barbecue with available wood to cook the fish that you can catch in the river.

—*New Youth Hostel:* 16 Hallitwkatu. 200 yards below and to the left when you leave the bus station. Not very expensive.

—*Youth Hostel* at the edge of the city, about ½ mile away from the train station. Situated in a school. Double rooms for couples. Take bus #5 or #6 from on top of the slope that overlooks the station. Stop at Valtatie (the driver systematically stops there for backpackers). Open only from June 5 to August 8. You can cook (great kitchen and fridge).

—*Domus Artica Youth Hostel:* 8 Ratak. Telephone 991-2981. Very luxurious and therefore expensive.

Where to Eat

Don't miss the good local specialties: smoked leg of reindeer, roasted reindeer with cranberries, ice cream from marsh blackberries, and so forth.

—*Ravintola:* 200 yards to the left as you leave the bus station and 100 yards behind the Shell station, at the foot of 2 small buildings. Scandinavian lunches at rock-bottom prices. Moreover, this Shell station is the only place in the city that sells camping gas refills.

—*Cafeteria Supermarket:* Across from the bus station. Daily special served from 10 A.M. to 2 P.M. Filling for those who are very hungry.

Purchases

Reindeer and fox hides, Finnish knives, and smoked legs of reindeer can be bought leaving the city by the road parallel to the river, behind the campground.

Be careful of the inferior quality skins coming from the U.S.S.R. You can recognize them by a cylindrical stamp on the back. You can't just shake the skins and pull the fur, you also have to check to make sure there are no moths! Approximate prices: 110–150 marks, according to size.

To See

—*Forest Museum of Salmijärvi* (2 miles from the center).

—*House of the Polar Circle,* 6 miles from the center on the road from Ivalo. Take the road alongside the campgrounds, past the base of the ski jump, and again past the river. A tourist trap.

—*Municipal library* on a long rainy afternoon. You can listen to records (jazz, jazz-rock, rock) for free. Nice atmosphere.

—Upon leaving Rovaniemi, you have a wide choice of private and postal buses. Ask at the bus station for a tourist's fare (an appreciable discount). No proof needed. Hitching isn't too good, since cars are so expensive and distances are so great . . .

KEMIJÄRVI

Between Rovaniemi and Kemijärvi, the countryside is lovely, with forests and marshes. The city is small and ordinary but has a lovely sandy beach on a lake, and all around is very pleasant. In addition, the lake water is about 68° F in the summer.

—*Tourist Office:* At the bus station. Telephone 992-11777. Open June 1 to August 31, from Monday to Friday, 8 A.M. to 8 P.M., and on Saturday and Sunday from 10 A.M. to 6 P.M. From September 1 to May 31, open from 8 A.M.to 4 P.M.

Where to Sleep

—*Youth Hostel Sepänsälli:* Take a right at the end of the road that comes from the train station. Brand new. Kitchen, showers, sauna, and cafeteria. A pleasant welcome, and not too many people in the summer.

To See

—*Ethnographic Museum:* 2 Sepänkatu. Next to the youth hostel. Telephone 992-12494. Open in the summer every day from 10 A.M. to 6 P.M. Admission is 2 marks. Installed in an eighteenth-century house. Tools, and so forth. Interesting.

Advice: In Kemijärvi, stock up on food and go into the forest for a few days (take survey maps). You can see so many animals (notably, elks). Don't forget a compass!

After looking far and wide in this village, we found women who make *poppanaliina*, a typical Finnish handmade fabric. You can purchase it inexpensively. Avoid buying it from the Tourist Office, where it is very expensive.

SÖDANKLYLA

Relatively important village located on the road from Ivalo. You can see the midnight sun.

VUOTSO

A small village, with its own post office, store, and service station. There's a campground with bungalows you can rent.

TANKAVAARA

This has become the place of meetings for all gold diggers. They meet here to determine the champion gold washer. The competition takes place at the beginning of August and is open to professionals and amateurs alike.

But gold goes with precious stones: A market with precious stones and minerals opens along with the competition. Anyone can exhibit, exchange, buy, or sell the stones of his/her choice.

Those who prefer to discover their own in the field can also come here, a region rich with various lodes: jasper, quartz, hematites, tourmalines, and many others. Week-long sojourns devoted to digging for precious stones are organized at the holiday resort in June, August, and September.

IVALO

A big village on the Ivalojoki River, less touristy than Inari. See the modern church. The hospital makes you want to be sick. Across from the hospital is a tiny orthodox church. The campground is located south of the village and to the right going toward Rovaniemi.

There are still some gold prospectors. A visit is recommended to the Museum of Gold Washing in Tankavaara.

INARI

This village is located by a lake which you can only barely see a part of. In the city itself, there's nothing to see. Otherwise, the surrounding region is interesting. If you go out on treks, be wary of the markings of inhabited zones on the survey maps. Tourist Information can be found in a hotel.

—The *campground* is across the village square, on the other side of the bay. (It is also an inn.) Cross the Lemmenjoki River and turn right. The campground includes several bungalows and opens late in the season (June 15–20). Otherwise, you can use it freely, since it is permanently open. Remember: This region is infested with mosquitoes. Bring along your repellent.

—*Retkeilymata Kukkuca Youth Hostel:* Telephone 997-51244. 500 yards from the bus station, following the road on the left. Small rooms in cottages. Very sweet. You can take canoes and kayaks out on the lake. Rather expensive.

—*Outdoor Lapp Museum:* Very interesting, if only for the bear traps and the prospecting displays. Of course, the Lapps in the souvenir shops get out of their jeans long enough to dupe the tourists.

For fishing and tranquility, it's an ideal spot. The cottages are expensive, and there's no heat. The rich can cruise the region in seaplanes, while the paupers have to hoof it.

To return to Rovaniemi, hitching isn't at all easy, but try the Shell station.

Observation: In the summer these regions are very dry. Watch out —don't start a forest fire. We made a fire one time that spread farther than we had planned. It's not at all amusing to be such dopes. Later we dispensed with a campfire.

KARIGASNIEMI

A small village located on the Norwegian border. Stores. Campgrounds well marked and very well fixed up along the river banks. Bungalows.

Karasjok, the neighboring Norwegian city, is 5 miles away. Be careful of this place, with its time changes, and don't miss your bus. The postal buses go to Karasjok. The rivers here are jumping with salmon.

ENONTEKIO

A small village on the Swedish border. There are several campgrounds spotted with bungalows. Also serviced by postal buses. A picturesque church. You absolutely must find an excuse for entering the bank, located near the church, in order to get an idea of what is real Finnish all-wooden architecture.

PALOJOENSUU

A store, a gas station, a post office. Don't hitch toward Karesuando, for each stop could be a long one.

KARESUANDO

A commercial village on the Swedish border. Sometimes there's a market. Spartan campgrounds at the edge of the city near Palojoensuu, to the left along the river. Just across the lake is the Swedish village of Karesuando. The ferry is free. Very important if you have a car. This ferry is the northernmost point of access to Sweden if you're coming from Finland or Norway. You can reach Kiruna only from the south, the east, and Karesuando. It's not possible to get there from Norway between Namsos and Narvik without making a long detour.

KILPISJÄRVI

Not exactly a village but a tourist complex with hotels and an immense campground that is very much in use. Bungalows, a store, and a cafeteria. The lake stays frozen very late into the season, and the area is cold. A bus that doesn't run every day links Kilpisjärvi with Skibotn and Tromsø. There's a time change at the Norwegian border. In good weather, go to the top of the sacred mountain of the Lapps.

In all of the cities and villages around here, you can find all sorts of food and supplies. Several major stores in the large towns sell everything (beautiful Lapp knives, fishing gear, cigarettes). Stock up on camping gas that you can refill along the way.

For smokers who plan to cross into Norway, stock up in Finland where it's cheaper.

KUUSAMO

The southern part of Lapland. It's a change from flat country, for here they've got what it takes for climbing: canyons, waterfalls, magnificent rapids. Get info at the Tourist Office. Beautiful hikes around here.

Oulanka Park, north of Kuusamo, has Kiutakongas Campgrounds, which is worth going out of your way for. Judge for yourself: an old woods, partly cleared so that you can pitch your tent. The parking lot is in the middle of the campground, from where you can use carts to reach the campsites where cars are not allowed. The sanitary facilities and kitchen-dining rooms are impeccable. Very lovely hikes all around.

NORTH CAPE

Via Norway

The most direct route to the North Cape, which has become a tourist spot in the last 10 years, is by route 6, Oslo–Kirkenes. You ride along the fjords; and to catch the ferry (there are fewer and fewer), cars and camping vans take the exact same course. That's nice, but it complicates things, for you must often wait hours before boarding. One trick, however, is to get to the dock early in the morning or late at night. Route 6 is good, in general, except after Alta (37 miles of trail). Hitchhikers have a lot of competition in their quest to go north, and traffic is not heavy.

In *Olderfjord,* you get off route 6 for route 95 to Kajfjord. There, you take the boat to Honningsvag. There's a youth hostel and campground four miles from there, as you go toward North Cape. You can rent cottages. Then take a bus the next 25 miles.

Hammerfest is a wonderful city in a grand setting. The campground near the youth hostel (which is often full) is very pleasant (free kitchens) and less expensive than those at the entrance to the city. Don't buy anything from the only store open on Sunday: It's worse than being pistol-whipped. If need be, do your shopping at the campground. You can see reindeer in the middle of town.

The bus to the North Cape is expensive, but it's worth the detour. Everyone camps in the wilderness, even though it's forbidden.

Globetrotters with dough can take the coastal express to Honningsvag. A superb crossing. If the weather is good, sleep on the deck. If not, the second-class smoking lounge can serve as your dormitory.

By car, an official will make you pay at the entrance to the parking lot. They gotta live! North Cape is a typical example of a tourist rip-off. Sandwiches and drinks are terribly expensive. They even issue diplomas decreeing that you've been there. And you have to pay for them! We even saw a tourist who was furious because there were no diplomas in his language. What isn't expensive is the telephone, so wake up your friends at midnight to announce that the sun is shining. There are a lot of people milling about at midnight on the North Cape. Other than that, the cape itself is quite ordinary, but the landscapes on the journey up are magnificent.

The place is fantastic at 5 in the morning when you can be alone with the landscape, but you can also choose to arrive at 10 P.M. and wait until 2 A.M. (in August). It becomes quite disappointing at 11 P.M. when 15 tourist buses arrive. Go hike on the island. Farther north, about 1 mile, on a strip of land jutting out there are fewer people (it's marked in the book on sale in Hammerfest).

You're not allowed to pitch a tent. On the island of the North Cape (its real name is *Magerøya*), the Honningsvag school is converted into a youth hostel in the summer, located toward the North Cape. Unfortunately, it has a mere 15 beds. You can camp, in spite of the law, if you wander away from the cape, but it's very cold. You can, of course, arrive on the North Cape at midday, leave with the last bus at

1 or 2 A.M., then take the ferry to Kafjord and sleep on the floor in a small waiting room at the dock in Kafjord. It's not ideal, but it's better than sleeping in the cold.

Note: The bus on the North Cape island is horribly expensive.

Observation: In Honningsvag you can work in the canning plant a few days (it's hard work but well paid). No special permission is required. Moreover, motorcycle fans receive a warm welcome from North Cape's Motorcycle Club (upon leaving the ferry, toward Honningsvag, 1 mile on the left). If you can repair motorcycles in their garage, you can sleep 1 or 2 nights in a dormitory they've set up.

Via Sweden and Finnish Lapland

It gets a bit complicated. From Stockholm, follow the Swedish coast to the border, Tornio, where you'll see a wooden church. It's a viable alternative for the hitchhiker because competition is weak. There's a charming youth hostel at Lövanger (between Umes and Skellefteas).

They accept Swedish currency in the grocery stores at Tornio. Free camping is available near the bridge at the border. The shuttle between Haparanda and Tornio has been shut down, so it's better to go directly to Tornio.

In Finland, a country of 62,000 lakes—undoubtedly true, judging by the number of mosquitoes that continually hassle you, especially in Lapland (don't forget that repellent)—there are two solutions:

—Go by Rovaniemi, Ivalo, Karigasniemi, back into Norway at Karasjok, back on route 6 at Lakselv (which means salmon river). From there, on route 6, figure out how to get to Repvag. It's easy by car.

—Or, go back up to Tornionjoki by Ylitornio to Palojoensuu, hoping, if you're hitching, that you will reach this route before the only car of the day passes. Go toward Enotekiö, back into Norway at Kautokeino, getting back on route 6 at Alta. Again, figure out how to get to Repvag.

The first itinerary is easier: Until Rovaniemi, the road is pleasant and relatively busy. (Blacktop roads the whole way.) Toward Ivalo, there are many lakes, not equipped for tourists. You can rent bungalows, but they're far from the city. Be careful of the good old boys in the bars at night, for they have a tendency to get drunk and violent.

A hint for those in a hurry: The road from Sweden and Finnish Lapland is faster than the road in Norway and also shorter (because of the fjords).

Via Finland

This becomes a sport but allows you to discover a country that resembles no other. From mid-August it's madness to even travel there. Bring sweaters. Even bivouac equipment can come in handy if you want to have all your cards ready to play when you're thumbing (stay patiently on the side of the road). But, in spite of everything, it's great.

Take the ferry to Travemünde (near Lübeck) for Helsinki. Cafeteria on board. Take route 5 which crosses Finland from south to north, passing by Mikkeli, Varkaus, Kuopio, Kajaani, Kuusamo, and reaches Kemijärvi. From there, go to Rovaniemi and continue by the itinerary we described above.

ICELAND

We often have illusions about Iceland. We expect to find a Nordic country in its pure state, deserted and totally natural. While that remains true for the countryside, the Icelandic cities are rather sad. So don't go to Iceland for these uninteresting cities. On the other hand, the countryside corresponds to what you expect: wild and untrampled.

Useful Addresses in New York

—*Icelandic Consulate General:* 370 Lexington Avenue, New York, NY. Telephone (212) 686-4100.
—*Icelandic National Tourist Office:* 75 Rockefeller Plaza, New York, NY. Telephone (212) 582-2802.
—*Icelandair:* 610 Fifth Avenue, New York, NY. Telephone (212) 757-8585.

Climate

Changes quite quickly. In general, it's rather rainy, especially in the south. Bring along some good sweaters and a rain slicker. The wind is always present and sometimes blows up quite a tempest. But this shouldn't prevent you from going. That would really be a shame. Don't visit Iceland on foot, by bike, or hitching after August 15 when the weather is really lousy.

Be Truly Ecologically Conscious

Respect the laws protecting nature. Don't go off the roads with your car: two trails of tires can prevent the grass from growing for two years. Don't gather flowers and stones. Icelanders have a hard enough time growing the least little thing. The flora takes a long time to grow back. They already worry enough about the ravaging by tourists.

Equipment

If you go to Iceland, you must walk a bit. Otherwise, stay in Mykonos. Pack woolens, rain slicker, boots, and a down bag, all truly essential. It's not a bad idea to bring along a bathing suit for the numerous warm water springs and outdoor swimming pools. High boots are necessary, for you must ford many a river, and they're more useful than hiking boots unless you are really trekking.

Topographical Maps

You can obtain a good map at Icelandair for a small sum. Survey maps are indispensable for hiking.

Lodging

—*Youth hostels:* You can get a list from the Icelandic Youth Hostel Association: 41 Laufasvegur, Reykjavik. They are expensive (less expensive with a card).

—You can sleep in farmers' barns, but that doesn't always work.

—*Camping:* You can camp in the wilderness when the terrain allows for it, which is not always the case. Camping is sometimes the only method outside of cities. All the pay campgrounds cost the same and are well organized. For cooking, avoid the camping stoves that burn oil or alcohol; it's very difficult to obtain the fuel. It's better to bring along disposable gas refills. The ½ liter size is almost impossible to find, except in cities where you can find stores that have the guide *Around Iceland*, but it's expensive. Humidity is the number one enemy of the camper. Experience proves that large plastic garbage bags (yes, solid and watertight) are very, very precious—to wrap up in at night, and to use for baggage on buses.

—Numerous shelters all over. Those marked with black triangles are shelters open to everybody. Those marked in red are for emergency use only—particularly *Langafall,* which stands by a pool of naturally hot water. The shelters marked in black are not too bad, but be careful of the camp stoves which often don't work and are even dangerous.

—*EDDA Hotels:* Schools converted into summer hotels; therefore, reasonable.

Means of Transportation

—*Hitchhiking:* Walk around the capital a bit. Difficult! Sometimes you can wait for 2 hours before seeing a car. Place yourself at gas pumps and approach the cars that stop. One trick: Hitch in front of rivers that must be forded (inland, the melting glaciers cover the roads). Drivers stop more readily.

We don't know how to stress enough that you must carry supplies.... In addition, tour the island clockwise; there are more cars this way. The first villages from Seydisfjordur are closer, so it's less depressing to stay by the roadside.

—*Air:* Don't hesitate to do part of the way by plane (not so expensive) if the weather is clear. Try to fly over the glacier regions. Fantastic! There's a 25 percent discount for couples (50 percent on one of the 2 tickets) on round trips. Go as a couple even if not married. It works sometimes.

—*Bus:* Throughout the country. Get schedules at the Tourist Office in Reykjavik (6 Reykjanesbraut) or in other cities (rather rare). It's a decent system but expensive. The driver stops when you ask him. There are 2 deals:

• *Omnibus Passport:* Allows you to go anywhere. It's a very flexible deal because you can even retrace your steps. It costs over $100 for 2 weeks.

• *Full Circle Passport:* Allows you to tour the island according to a very precise route with no time limit. Valid for one month. You cannot retrace your steps.

On some lines there are only 2 or 3 buses a week, so we strongly suggest that you get *Leidabok,* a small yellow book containing all the schedules. It's on sale at the bus station in Reykjavik (about $1.50).

Be aware that by the end of August there are even fewer buses, so visits to many tourist spots are no longer possible. By mid-September there are no buses between Höfn and Myvatn.

—*Cars:* You can rent a Land Rover for up to 5 or 6 people. It allows you to travel to places that would otherwise be too difficult to get to. Rentals are very expensive, and so is gas (diesel is the obvious choice).

State of the Roads

The cities have blacktop roads, but outside the cities the roads are rocky and sometimes in bad condition (potholes, ruts). You'll come across quite a few waterholes to ford. Pay careful attention to sheep, especially if they're on both sides of the road. Slamming on the brakes does not work too well on these rocky roads. The small bridges spanning the river are very narrow. Cross them with caution. The speed limit is 45 km/h (28 mph) in the cities and 70 km/h (44 mph) on the open road.

Interior Boat Line

—*Skipautgerd Rikisins:* Hafnarhusid, Reykjavik.

Food

Warning: NEVER EAT WHALES! Or shame on you! They are nearly extinct. So we say it and repeat it. Thanks. Fortunately, the whaling port will close in 1986. You can eat canned sardines in tomatoes, or other canned food made in Iceland, with *skyr*, a kind of farmer's cheese. Mix with cream and add sugar. This will take care of the heartiest of appetites. Sometimes it's flavored with blueberries. There are numerous cheeses, like *Laughing Cow,* with shrimp, mushrooms, and so forth.

White or rye bread porridge (the large packets are more economical): Boil the milk, add the porridge until it forms a type of gruel, and then add some powdered chocolate or sugar. You can buy eggs and milk from farms. You can also buy fresh fish at reasonable prices at the port canneries. Frozen fish fillets, frozen lamb chops, and chopped lamb burgers are not too expensive.

—Food is very expensive except for fish and lamb.
—Stores are closed on the weekend. Fill your baskets. You can buy food in some gas stations.
—Fresh fruits and vegetables are particularly expensive.
—*Mills Caviar* is "caviar" in a tube. Excellent and a good deal.
—Buffet breakfast in hotels: count on 100–150 Kr.
—*Hangikjot:* smoked "ham" of the famous lamb.
—*Surmjolk:* delicious yogurt with brown sugar. In short, great!
—Icelandic pastries with very good flat cakes. Taste the black spice bread, which has a faint taste of licorice; it's filling and keeps a long time.
—*Svid:* head of lamb.

Beverages

Icelanders customarily drink a lot on Friday and Saturday nights. Not to worry. *Au contraire,* get yourself invited (don't forget to buy a round). You'll make fast friends. Drink a good glassful of alcohol before going out for the evening, and then abstain at the bar. Exorbitant prices. But try 2 local specialties: the brandy and *brennivin.*

Brennivin is a brew they offer you in the street to be hospitable. The label resembles that of a bottle of poison; some flasks have a skull and crossbones.

Think about bringing some booze with you, for this stuff is really the pits.

The coffee and tea are like dishwater. They may appear expensive, but for the price of one cup you can have seconds.

Cigarettes

Generally very expensive. American tobacco is quite costly.

Film

Film is very expensive. Bring your own.

Purchases

Icelandic sweaters, of course. Hurry up because they are constantly going up in price. Try to buy them on farms. If you can't find them, meeting the people will be worth it. If you do find them, they will be of better quality and less expensive. Check if the sleeves are sewn well to the body. The sweaters sold at the Lofteleider terminal at the airport are more expensive than in the city.

Store Hours

Stores are open until 6 P.M. You can stock up on weekends at some kiosks and gas stations (limited selection of course). Banks are open until 4 P.M. and are closed on weekends.

Commercial Holidays

Stores are closed the first weekend in August. People dance and drink, and it is surely one of the best opportunities to meet people. Note: The people in Reykjavik tend to head for the country, so the city is deserted. In addition, the Monday following this weekend is also a holiday. Therefore, before noon on Saturday, stock up for a few days if you don't want to live on soda, hotdogs, and other junk foods.

Employment

Work on fishing boats is rather difficult to get because they take very few novices. There are some openings in September when the students return to school.

Know-How in One Easy Lesson

Avoid soaping up, shampooing, and washing clothes in any of the hot water sources, no matter how tempting. Icelanders are particu-

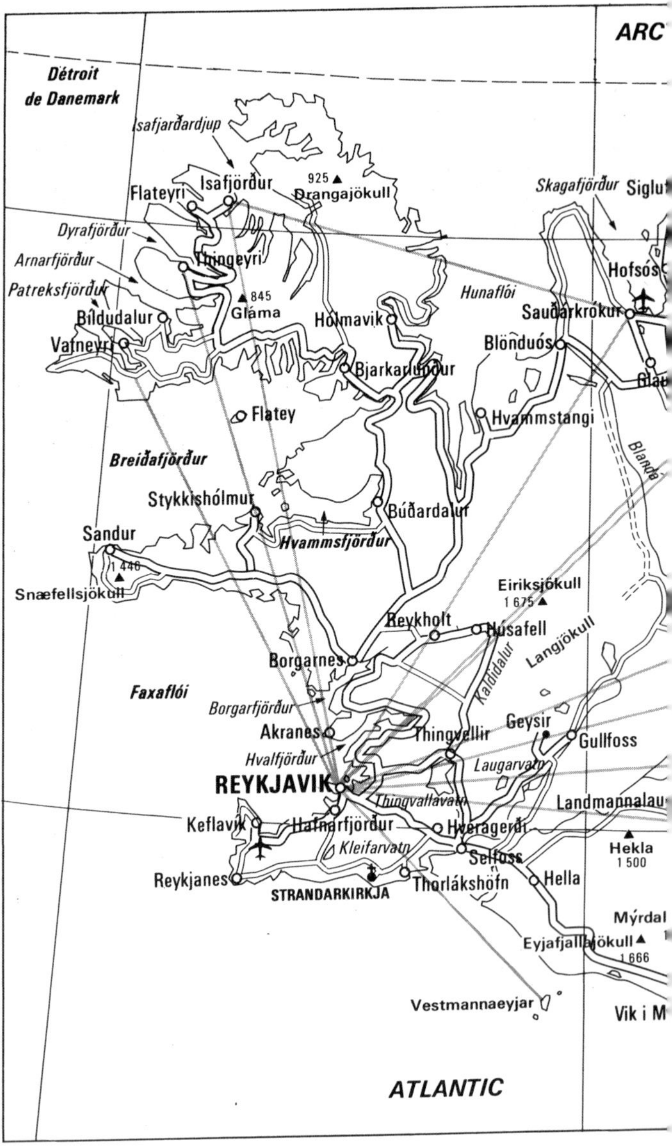
ARC
Détroit
de Danemark
Isafjarðardjup
Isafjörður
925
Drangajökull
Flateyri
Dyrafjörður
Thingeyri
Arnarfjörður
Patreksfjörður
845
Gláma
Bíldudalur
Hólmavik
Vatneyri
Bjarkarlundur
Skagafjörður
Siglu
Hofsós
Hunaflói
Sauðárkrókur
Blönduós
Hvammstangi
Flatey
Breiðafjörður
Stykkishólmur
Búðardalur
Hvammsfjörður
Sandur
1 446
Snæfellsjökull
Blanda
Eiriksjökull
1 675
Reykholt
Húsafell
Langjökull
Kaldidalur
Borgarnes
Faxaflói
Borgarfjörður
Akranes
Geysir
Gullfoss
Thingvellir
Hvalfjörður
Laugarvatn
REYKJAVIK
Thingvallavatn
Landmannalau
Keflavik
Hafnarfjörður
Hveragerði
Hekla
1 500
Kleifarvatn
Selfoss
Reykjanes
STRANDARKIRKJA
Thorlákshöfn
Hella
Mýrdal
Eyjafjallajökull
1 666
Vestmannaeyjar
Vik i M
ATLANTIC

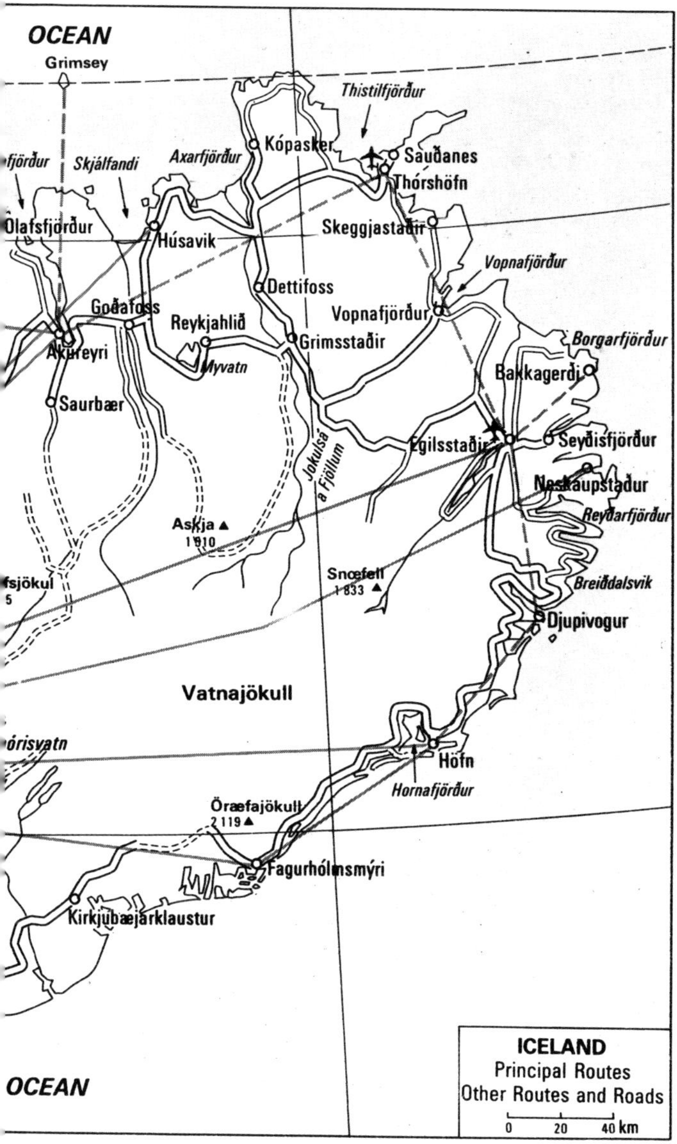
OCEAN
Grimsey
Thistilfjörður
Kópasker
Sauðanes
Þórshöfn
fjörður
Skjálfandi
Axarfjörður
Ólafsfjörður
Húsavik
Skeggjastaðir
Vopnafjörður
Dettifoss
Goðafoss
Vopnafjörður
Reykjahlið
Akureyri
Grimsstaðir
Myvatn
Borgarfjörður
Bakkagerði
Saurbær
Egilsstaðir
Seyðisfjörður
Jokulsá a Fjöllum
Neskaupstaður
Reyðarfjörður
Askja
1 910
Snæfell
1 833
Breiðdalsvik
fsjökul
5
Djupivogur
Vatnajökull
órisvatn
Höfn
Hornafjörður
Öræfajökull
2 119
Fagurhólmsmýri
Kirkjubæjarklaustur
OCEAN
ICELAND
Principal Routes
Other Routes and Roads
0 20 40 km

larly sensitive to pollution and don't appreciate any trace of suds or empty detergent containers in the middle of nature.

REYKJAVIK

The capital of Iceland has about 100,000 inhabitants (half the population of Iceland). You can obtain a free copy of *Around Iceland,* a brochure in English that isn't enthralling but tells about things to see.

Arrival at the Airport

Keflavik, Iceland's international airport, is about 28 miles from the city. The duty-free shop is open for arrivals and departures. In addition to alcohol and tobacco, a large selection of food products are sold. Buy alcohol for your future friends, which will really make them happy. And get some supplies for your journey since the cost of living is high. Change your money quickly and go to the bus for Reykjavik which fills up very rapidly. If you miss it, you'll have to wait a good hour.

Useful Addresses

—*U.S. Embassy:* 19 Laufasvegur, Reykjavik. Telephone 29-100.

—*Bus Terminal* (B.S.I.): Hringbraut. Telephone 22-300. Practical because it's only a few steps from the airport and has a bank where you can exchange money. You can obtain information on buses and tourism. Also has a cafeteria and a kiosk, where you can buy the *Leidabok* (bus schedule).

—*Main Post Office:* 5 Posthusstraeti (perpendicular to the pedestrian street). Free *Post Restante.* Open from 9 A.M. to 5 P.M.

—*Tourist Office:* At the Loftleidir Hotel, where the bus stops on its way from the airport.

Where to Sleep

—*Youth Hostel:* 41 Laufasvegur. Telephone 24-950. Take advantage of the shower (you often have to pay for them at other places). You can cook.

—*Campground:* Sundlaugavegur. Take bus #5. Warm water pool near the campground. Pleasant. Behind here, good breads and cakes. Supermarket nearby, toward the city, first road on the right.

—*Salvation Army:* 2 Kirkjustraeti. Telephone 13-203. Less expensive than the youth hostel, but the accommodations are less pleasant.

Nice Cafeterias

—*Nordic House* has a cafeteria frequented by students during the day. Exhibits Icelandic paintings downstairs.

—*Studentakjallarin:* Hotel Gaulli Gardur in Hringbraut. University cafeteria open all summer. Many people, particularly young people who want to meet other young people. Free admission. You choose your dishes, which are relatively expensive but less than elsewhere. Also, groups often play music in the evening on the ground floor. It's more relaxing in the basement, but it closes at 11 P.M. (1:30 A.M. on the ground floor). A student card is not required.

—*Svarta Sannan:* At the corner of Tryggvagata and Hofnarstraeti (near Austurstraeti). Cafeteria-style restaurant. It's not expensive and closes late.

—Cafeteria-style restaurants where you can eat cheap french fries while seated at a table:

• *Fjarkinn:* 4 Austurstraeti. Note: It closes at 7 P.M.
• *Hressingarskalinn:* 22 Austurstraeti. Somewhat expensive.

The big problem upon arrival in Iceland on Saturday afternoon is the question of food. Nearly everything is closed except for a small supermarket that is open until 4 P.M. (it's on the extreme western part of the peninsula of Reykjavik), and a small grocery store, *Vergamot,* located on Nesvegur.

To See

There are many museums. Ask for the brochures at the *Tourist Office.*

—*Municipal Art Gallery:* On Milatún. Open every day from 2 to 10 P.M. In particular, see the works of the best Icelandic painters, including Johannes Kjarval, and temporary exhibits. There are many beautiful landscapes.

—*National Museum:* Hringbraut. Great and free.

—*Nordic House:* Contains records, magazines, and truly instructive books on Nordic culture.

—*Folk Museum of Arbaer:* In the suburbs. See houses from the beginning of the eighteenth century through the beginning of the twentieth century, with their interiors. A small guide is available in English. Bus #10.

—*Old City:* Between the lake and the port. You'll find many wooden and corrugated iron homes painted in all sorts of colors. The neighborhood was saved by the residents, faithful lovers of the charms of the past.

Hitching North

Take bus #10 and ask the driver where to get off.

Purchases

—*Alafoss Factory:* Near Reykjavik. From Reykjavik, take route 1 north, then the first right after 431 (Reykir).

KRISUVIK

Krisuvik is a place south of Reyjavik with hot springs. No inhabitants. All along the road are lava fields to the horizon. There's a trail for cars. From the road, you can see the geyser. Explore on foot. From the hill there's a very lovely view of Kleifarvatn Lake when the weather is clear. If you want to return to Selfoss, the trail is difficult until Hveragerdi, and then the road is paved until Reykjavik.

VESTMAN ISLANDS

There are 2 ways to get to the Vestman Islands from Reykjavik:
—*By plane:* Consult Icelandair, Laekjargata. Telephone 16-600.
—*By boat:* Take the regular bus from Reykjavik to Thorlakshofn. Get the schedule from the Tourist Office. It's about a 3½-hour trip. The boat is about half the price of the plane. You can sleep at the youth hostel *(Hofdaveg),* which is very pleasant, or at the campground near a swimming pool.

To See

Visit the volcano at the top of the crater with a guide. It's dangerous to go down inside because rock slides and falling debris are frequent. It is still smoking at its age. See the puffin colonies living on the rocks overlooking the port, which can be reached by ropes and ladders. It's rather dangerous, so we don't recommend it to everyone. If you want to see the puffins up close, there's an easier way: Climb the grassy slope overlooking the campground. You arrive at a western crest by an easy path, and you're near thousands of them. In the evening young puffins, attracted by the lights, stroll through the streets of the city by the dozens, even by the hundreds. You can also see seals. There's a saltwater swimming pool and sauna. Visit the aquarium, containing over 200 species of fish as well as all the species of birds on the island (stuffed).

LAUGARVATN

A campground. You can stock up. Rather touristy.

GEYSIR

The big geyser hasn't gushed by itself for 5 years. However, when the local scientists think that the water level is high enough, they toss some cakes of soap and air bubbles into the crater. This seems to imprison the gas, and when there's a sufficient quantity, the geyser gushes for half an hour just as in the good old days. This little celebration takes place every summer generally on Sunday afternoon, between 3 and 5 o'clock.

All in all, it's rather disappointing: The sulphur field is covered with pipes, and the gas station sells overpriced food.

The *Strokur* geyser, smaller but quite impressive, is in good working order. It's surprising the first time, with its natural hot water basins of a stunning blue.

Free camping near the EDDA Hotel. The very nice small sites are alongside a stream that you'll spot easily on the left at the very beginning of the road to Gullfoss.

GULLFOSS

A superb 105-foot waterfall that plunges into a canyon. Very wild and not at all commercialized, it's the natural "monument" of Iceland.

Truly very pretty. Camp at the edge of the canyon that follows the waterfall. Grand. Bring a good rain slicker or poncho and go to the bottom of the waterfall, which you can approach up to 6 or 9 ft. Be careful, though—as a sign warns in all languages.

SELFOSS

Very pleasant camping area, with a kitchen and a common room. Swimming in baths of different temperatures. Supplies. Bank. Bus to Gullfoss, the Geysir, and the south.

THÓRSMÖRK

A superb (and that's not too strong a word) site about 95 miles southeast of the capital, at the foot of the Myrdals Jökull glacier. Two associations in Reykjavik organize weekend expeditions here during the summer. Ask for their addresses at the Tourist Office. You pay for transportation and lodging. Bring your food and sleeping bag. Of course you could go alone. Get info at the bus station (B.S.I.), in principle there are 2 buses a week. It's impossible to get here by car (except perhaps a Land Rover) because you must cross rivers. The trip itself is an adventure.

Once you're here, you can stay in wooden barracks or go camping. There are few tourists, only Icelanders. A great hike to the foot of the glacier takes 10 hours for a round trip. Magnificent landscapes.

SKOGAR

—*Popular Museum:* Very interesting. Old tools, fishing skiffs, reconstructions of interiors of traditional homes. The great guy who founded it explains everything in English. He is simply unforgettable. Before July he has more time to explain things.

—*Skogafoss:* A 228-foot waterfall near the village. The road is marked. A Land Rover can make it. You can camp near the falls. Stock up ahead of time because there are no stores. Try to buy milk and eggs from a farmer. Gourmets can save up to buy a great breakfast at the EDDA Hotel (copious and unlimited).

VIK

Don't think it's a port. There's nothing to see and nothing to do except stock up at the cooperative. On the other hand, Vik has a pretty black sandy beach. If you want to see puffins up close, you can scamper up the rocks (on the right side of the beach) at low tide. You can approach them with no problem as long as you are silent and motionless.

From Vik, ask the bus to stop at Dirholaey, a big rock used as a natural preserve for seabirds, although you can't see them very well. Camping is forbidden.

HVERAGERDI

This is a small, very interesting city between Selfoss and Reykjavik. It's full of hot springs and greenhouses where they grow bananas, tomatoes, roses, and cacti. The Eden of Austurmork is a bar inside a greenhouse full of flowers.

KIRKJUBAERJARKLAUSTER

If you're hitching, don't try to pronounce it, you'll get lost. Show it on a map. You'll find a rather interesting volcanic desert. There's a campground 20 minutes from the EDDA Hotel. Take the road toward Höfn and turn left at the gas station. You can camp on the open land behind the hotel and use its facilities. A pretty waterfall, plus a bank, grocery store, and post office. You can rent fishing gear for the lake.

FROM KIRKJUBAERJARKLAUSTUR TO SELFOSS OR REYKJAVIK

Since the summer of 1980 the bus passes Eldgja, the Landmannalaugar, and in front of the Hekla twice a week. The trip is called Behind the Mountain Road, and you must pay about $10 more if you have a bus pass because the road is really rough. Hold on to your seat, don't be afraid of being jostled, and don't get car sick. Strong sensations are guaranteed. When the weather is good, it's very pretty. The most interesting part lies between Kirkjubaerjarklaustur and the Landmannalaugar, and there's a very pretty waterfall at Oefarufoss—a cascade with a suspended basaltic arch. You can stay in the shelter at Landmannalaugar for 50 Kr or camp in front and wait for the next bus in 2 days. Hiking in the area reveals fields, lava, lakes, mountains of 100 different colors, volcanic smoke, and on and on. Natural hot spring at 104° F and mud baths are 50 yards from the shelter.

A Great Hike!

About 4 days of hiking toward the south, from Landmannalaugar to Thórsmörk (which we just discussed). A magnificent and varied region. Bring food. There are 3 cabanas on the way where you can sleep. You must request the keys at one of the cabanas in Landmannalaugar or Thórsmörk. The way is marked, but you are still advised to bring more detailed maps (obtainable from bookstores in Reykjavik). Count on five hours of hiking each day. You take the trail in Landmannalaugar going toward Thórsmörk, since it descends a bit that way. You'd be wise to carry along 2 extra days of food in case you are trapped in fog anywhere.

SKAFTAFELL

At the foot of the glacier, this is a very pretty natural park. Trails are marked on the glaciers, and there's a superb view of the sands of Skeidärsandur and the peak of Iceland.

The campground has a supermarket that is open from June to

August, from 9 A.M. to 10 P.M. It's all very well arranged, with impeccable sanitary facilities and pay showers. Some rooms are available for rent. The numerous hikes in the area are well marked; be delighted by snow-covered mountains, glacial strips, small rivers, a pretty cascade in Svartifos . . . Ask for the map of hiking trails at the camp.

Between Skaftafell and Höfn you'll find Lake Jökvlálóm filled with icebergs and rather vindictive birds.

JÖKULSÁRLÓN

Lies between Skaftafell and Höfn. A mandatory stop because it's truly wonderful. At the foot of multiple strips of the Vatnajokull (the largest European glacier) you can see a lake full of icebergs (in fact, huge chunks of ice broken off from glaciers).

Nearby, the sea is full of birds and seals. Thre's no campground, but you can camp by the lake. Shelter is available 2½ miles further, toward Skaftafell (useful in strong winds).

HÖFN

A small fishing port with a view of the glacier at Vatnajokull (weather permitting). Smelly cannery!

—*Campground* with sink and toilet; located quite off to the side. Less humid than in the center of town. Has a rather spongey terrain. Expensive for what it is.

—*Youth Hostel* (Alangarey).

—If you find the youth hostel too primitive and you have a car, drive toward Reykjavik. In about 3 or 4 miles you'll find the nice and inexpensive Hotel EDDA: Nesgaskoli. Telephone 97-84-70.

HÖFN–EGILSSTADIR

A very pretty mountain road with a view of the fjords. You cross a small forest. There's 1 bus a day between Höfn and Egilsstadir except for Sundays in July and August. From June to September 15, there are 3 buses a week. Berunes has a nice youth hostel.

EGILSSTADIR

Nothing to see in town, but the outskirts are interesting. You can exchange money and shop.

Note: Across from the pool there's a free campground and an inn where they serve good hot soup. You can always warm up there and use their tables to eat your food.

Stroll around the lake and see the small forest (a nursery) and the waterfall (Hengifoss).

You can sleep 12 miles from there, in Harlomstadir, along the lake, in the forest. Toilets and showers. Note: There are only three buses a week between Egilsstadir and Reykjahlid (Lake Myvatn).

SEYDISFJÖDUR

This small city at the end of a fjord is a fishing port (a good place for chatting with fishermen). You have to pay for camping. There's a youth hostel (Hafaldam).

EGILSSTADIR–GRIMSSTADIR

This is a very pretty road in the middle of a desert when leaving Mödrudalur. You can buy sweaters in Grimsstadir.

NJARDVIK

A small village at the end of a fjord. On the coast road toward Borgafjördur. Upon returning to Egilsstadir, stop and walk on the black sand beach (Heradsfloi); at sunrise and sunset it's a veritable lunar landscape. Perhaps you will see some wild geese and seals.

DETTIFOSS

You'll see the largest waterfall in Iceland and a grand canyon, which is very beautiful as night falls.

ASBYRGI

This is a horseshoe-shaped valley. Free camping.

HÚSAVÍK

This pretty little fishing port ñas snow-covered mountains in the background.

REYKJAHLID (LAKE MYVATN)

Wilderness camping is forbidden here because it's a natural park. There is, however, a pay campground. This area has incessant volcanic activity. You can tour on foot, by bike (rentals at Reynihild Hotel, near the campground), on horseback, or by boat (rental), hitching, in a car, or on a bus (organized tours).

There's an Exchange at the hotel. The owner of the hotel rents a few rooms at moderate prices above the service station's "Coca-Cola" store. (You're welcome in bad weather).

The most interesting area is between Reykjahlid and Skutustadir (many small craters). Different types of birds can be seen on the lake, including the famous harlequin duck, especially in the north. Reykjahlid has a post office and a grocery store and is the departure point of several trips (some of which begin in July) toward:

—Dettifoss, Asbyrgi, Húsavík.

—Inland toward Herdubreid and Askja, a volcanic lake with fields of superb desert lava. You can camp at the foot of Herdubreid and shelter in the area of Askja (an excursion bus passes by every 2 days).

Askja is a most interesting volcano. It reminds one of a lunar landscape, and American astronauts even trained here to go to the moon. Departures for Myvatn are on Monday, Wednesday, and Friday (July and August). The trip takes 16 hours. These vast desert regions are wild and desolate, resembling the earth as it may have looked millennia ago. Next to the largest crater lake (Viti Crater) is a small hot water lake in which you can swim. Going down into the crater is a bit delicate but a wonderful sensation. The hot bath is 104° F. milky, sulfuric, with snow and glaciers all around.

If the weather is really bad, you can go to the school or to the *Skutustadir Campground,* south of the lake. The school is a meeting ground for all nationalities; the classrooms serve as dormitories.

Get used to the gnats that buzz around and have a fondness for ears and nostrils. They disappear in a big wind or rain. The grottos with hot springs at Reykjahlid, right near the crossroads of Egilsstadir-Skutustadir, have become dangerous because of landslides. The baths are risky since the water goes up to 140° F. To balance out, right next to the food store there's a fault with more pleasant water. Make a tour of the Hverfjall volcano, then return to the grottos at Grjótagjà. Their hot water is very pleasant after a 3½-hour hike, but they'll knock you out.

Warning: It is dangerous to swim when the water temperature reaches 154° F.

You must visit the Krafla volcano. Recent lava flows. A geologist's heaven, ask around; it's about 5 miles north-northwest of the generating plant. To get there, follow the road to the ancient crater (lake) and stop at the first parking lot on the left. Then take the walking path; the smoke and vapor will guide you.

The interesting region of Dimmuborgir is south of the lake. It's easy to get lost in this astonishing lava formation. Note: Be wary in the desert between Myvatn and Egilsstadir. You could go roaming in the middle of it, so it's a good idea to have a little food and drink with you.

GODAFOSS

These waterfalls are less impressive after Gulfoss. (Jaded already!) But we should not be unfair, for they are pretty even if they aren't as high. More wilderness.

AKUREYRI

A large city that allows you to plunge back into a town-dwelling civilization.

—*Museum of Natural History:* Small but interesting, with Icelandic plants, bugs, and rocks.

—*Museum of Local History:* 58 Adalstraeti, toward the southern edge of Hafnarstraeti. Very nice crafts, costumes, and household objects. Open from 1:30 to 4 P.M. Old houses nearby.

—*Botanical Garden:* In Eyrarlandsvegver, behind the church.

—Overpopulated campground; instead, go above the city and the fjord toward the northwest.
—Youth hostel at Storholt.
—A great swimming pool.

GRIMSEY

A small island on the Polar Circle. You can reach it by boat or plane. The boat from Akureyri is less expensive, and the fjord of Akureyri is magnificent. You'll spend 6 hours in a nice old tub on a sea that is often rough after you leave the fjord. Avoid during the period of the midnight sun—too many tourists. Great at the end of July (calm, birds . . .). You might see the aurora borealis at the end of August.

THE NORTHWEST

The roads are passable for sturdy vehicles. On the coast, regular cars can go as far as Isafjördur. The fjords on this coast are simply magnificent. Don't miss the cliffs of Latrabjorg, some of which reach 1,300 feet. To get there, it's a 4-mile hike from the last village.

ISAFJÖRDUR

A pretty city built on a strip of sand, nearly at the end of a fjord. A ferry brings you here.

On the Road from Reykjavik

After Akureyri, about 220 miles from Reykjavik, stop at Varmahlid. After 8 miles there's the *Folklore Museum of Glaumbaer* (old converted farms). After another 2 miles you'll see the very old church in Viimyri. About 95 miles from Reykjavik an interesting stop is the Bilfrost farm. There's a very old volcanic region around Lake Hreavatn. No campground but you can see a waterfall with salmon going back up.

HUSAFELL

To get here, about 100 miles from the capital, to the northeast, take the coast road from Reykjavik toward Borganes. At the 85-mile mark, turn to the right toward Husafell. You pass several fjords and varied landscapes. You'll find blacktop roads in the beginning, but from the sea to Husafell it's a very bad road. Don't expect to go more than 15 mph. Make sure you're tanked up. Husafell is the final destination, with a campground, shower, and kitchen. You can rent heated mini-bungalows in the form of a tent, at moderate prices. There's a natural outdoor hot spring pool. Husafell is a favorite resort of Icelanders, and it has very few tourists. You're at the foot of the Langjökull glacier (the long glacier). Available to you are great hikes, lava fields, climbing, limitless horizons. To get back to Reykjavik, you can drive on the road alongside glaciers. Get info on road and weather conditions before leaving, and go only if the sky is clear. The landscapes are splendid, and you pass over gorges. This route is open only in July and August, and leads to the site of Iceland's ancient parliament in Thingvellir and across a natural park. Camping is possible.

AKRANES

The city holds no interest, but the ferry going to Reykjavik saves a lot of time.

MIDSANDUR

About 50 miles north of Reykjavik, in the Hvalfjördus (fjord of whales), this is the only whaling port in Iceland. The village thrives only in the summer during fishing season. The whaling is supposed to stop by 1986.

THINGVELLIR

A very pretty region about 30 miles from Reykjavik, by a lake. Immense volcanic faults crisscross the earth. Site of the oldest parliament in the world (created in A.D. 930), the heart of the Icelandic nation. A rather busy place.

FAERØE ISLANDS

You pass them on the boat coming from Scotland. You can camp nearby or sleep on any patch of grass, but avoid the *Torshavn* campground, which is ugly and expensive. Anyhow, you can use the showers on the boat and those of the youth hostel.